Fulm

The Making of a Hero.

Fulminia

The Making of a Hero.

Ben Kilgallon

ISBN 13: 978-1-7394866-0-0

Special Mentions

This novel is dedicated to my grandma and grandad, both of whom sadly passed away before they could have the chance to read it.

I would like to give special thanks to both my mother and my father. Without their boundless patience, support and enthusiasm, this book may very well have never been finished.

Table of Contents

MYSTERIOUS
ISLAND
PLA-KINGUS
TAN'GRAN'NE'SE
THE
KINGS' UNION
SATIA
ADARIA
ARISTINIA
JALDANA
ISTARIA
AERBONITAS
ASUN
THE
TENASIAN EMPI
YOXHARIA
TRIA
N
E
W
S

STRAEUM
WALL OF STRAEUM
THE SNAKE SEA
CALLIGII
THE
CALLIGIAN EMPIRE

Prologue

When *Duella* created the world of Fulminia, the divine realm was plagued with evil and war. Demons and Angelic Knights vied for control over all worlds, using their magics of *Purity* and *Corruption* to aid in their respective crusades.

Duella is the mother-goddess, and since this immortal age of battle still plagues the universe, she watches over her children with sadness, harnessing her gentle nature magic into the seeds and rivers of the mortal worlds in a hope to protect her lands from the ever-present threat of destruction that awaits them.

At the heart of this plague of war lies *Odall*. He is the very pinnacle of despicable wickedness, and his form is unfortunately the most powerful. Although the mortal worlds are made by goodness and life, the plane on which these worlds reside is dark. Odall has no true form but the eternal blackness of the universe, and this blackness has a magical strength which is not to be underestimated.

Violet clouds of evil drift through the voids of this plane, and often, if Odall wills it, these magical clouds of *corruption* remain, ever tormenting mortal worlds with their passing whispers and necromancy.

From the presence of these magics, mortal worlds often develop allegiances to the gods that channel them. Magic, in this universe, is not merely the ability to perform miracles or do the seemingly impossible, but it is a tool. The divine realm speaks to mortals through magic, and it is for this reason that (at least in the mortal worlds where Odall, Duella and Tiius have cast their clouds) there is little debate as to which gods are real and which are not.

Tiius is the god-form of purity. He is the eldest son of Duella, and he sees her vulnerability. As he has grown older, he has developed an aura of his own, golden in colour, and he is utterly devoted to helping his mother preserve mortal lives. Inside the divine soul of Tiius, there lies a fire that burns deeply inside of him; a relentless vigour, urging him forward to fight the violet clouds of Odall's corruption, and it is with his vigorous light, combined with the gentle soothing of his mother, that the two have been able to protect only a select few mortal worlds, though unfortunately, several of these mortal worlds were destroyed by their inhabitants, far before they could come to appreciate how lucky (and rare) they actually were.

Fulminia was such a world. Millions of years ago, mortals lived here, but they, like many others, tore the world around them to shreds, and it is only thanks to the interventions of Tiius and Duella, that life here has returned.

Chapter 1 Part 1 – The Troubling Message.

Royal Sparring Grounds, City of Pla-Kingus, Capital of the Kings' Union.

*

The clatter of wooden swords echoed around the training hall, and although the day was young, the smell of sweat was already stronger than that of a chopped onion.

Most of the combatants, who were fighting in pairs within the large stone walls of the Training Hall, appeared to be evenly matched in size and weight. Many of the younger boys had a pampered, well-fed look about them, and they were sweating profusely from their exertions as they clumsily whacked away at each other with more enthusiasm than skill, whilst the older boys had acquired a more polished style, and their healthy young bodies were clearly showing the effects of hard training, in trim, well-muscled physiques... but the pair sparring in the middle of the sand-covered floor made a very unlikely looking couple. The youngest was slim and frail looking with long blonde hair and was clearly a complete novice, whilst his sparring partner was a young, black-haired man in peak physical condition, who moved with the grace and speed of a leopard.

Despite their obvious physical differences, the family resemblance between them was strong. In fact they were brothers.

Panthalassa, youngest son of King Xanstus Lordborn, had been overjoyed when his famous older brother had turned up unexpectedly at his training session that morning. The ten-year-old boy idolised his older brother, who at the age of nineteen, had already earned a fearsome reputation as a warrior. Panth longed with all his heart that one day he too would become as strong, and more importantly as brave, as his brother. Since the small boy had started his formal training a few weeks ago, he had quickly begun to suspect in fact, that he, Panthalassa Lordborn, was a coward.

Although he was the king's son, he was granted no special treatment by the royal knights and guard-officers who taught at the academy, and many of the older boys who were his training partners (themselves the sons of noblemen or wealthy citizens), took great delight in dealing the son of the king painful blows and jeering when he cried out or showed pain or fear. Panthalassa had begun to dread the daily training sessions, and he had even made excuses to miss sessions, feigning sickness and injury.

Although he tried to act bravely in front of his brother, he actually hated conflict. In reality, anything violent which could involve him often made him wish he was back in the safe arms of his mother, or in the royal gardens helping the servants tend the crops.

Now sparring with his adored older brother, Panthalassa suddenly realised with surprise that he was actually enjoying himself for the first time since he had begun his military training. He had always loved play-fighting with Celdon since he was old enough to toddle, which was, of course, because Celdon had never once hurt him...

Being able to fully trust that Celdon wouldn't hurt him gave him back some of the confidence that had been knocked out of him over the last few months, and as such, he was slashing and parrying with as much devilish glee as he had done many years before...

Seeing the respect and awe his fellow classmates showed his older brother, Panthalassa now dared, if only for a moment, to hope that some of his courage would rub off on him, and he tried his very best to make a good impression on his older brother...

"When will I be old enough to fight with you and Father?" panted Panthalassa, swinging his training sword wildly at Celdon's head.

"When you're eighteen, but you have a *long* way to go yet!" laughed Celdon, quickly knocking his training weapon from his hands and moving in on him to fake a blow to the neck...

Panthalassa's face went a bright red and he threw his shield to the ground in a tantrum. He could hear the other boys jeering at him for losing his first duel of the day, but what hurt much more, was that his brother had laughed first...

"Something funny?" snapped Celdon, glaring around. His tone was assertive and protective of his younger brother.

He eyeballed one young lout who had been particularly loud... "You there, yes you! Do you think that you would have done any better against me?"

The squire shook his head submissively. He wasn't about to argue with the king's eldest son. He told himself that was the reason, but then he remembered Celdon's fearsome reputation...

Noticing the great scar across the prince's neck, the squire suddenly realised he was terrified of him...

"No, your highness," he quickly said, gulping down his pride at the sight of Celdon's muscular, towering presence...

'I was right to come here today...' Celdon thought grimly. *'These cowardly rats have ganged up against the young lion out of jealousy... no wonder my brother has been cutting classes! Well, I will soon put a stop to that!'*

Before Celdon could continue his train of thought, the oaken doors of the training hall suddenly burst open, slamming against the stone walls.

The intruder was clad in shimmering bronze chainmail, and his red tabard clearly identified him as a royal messenger, and so the initial outburst of surprise by the class subsided, as they realised he was there by the king's own order...

The boys in the sparring grounds quickly turned towards him, wondering what message could hold such importance. The messenger scanned the faces surrounding him, clearly looking for someone. He was still panting from his exertions, visibly trembling and clearly struggling to maintain his composure.

Suddenly, Celdon's gaze caught the messenger's eyes, and a wordless spark of communication seemed to take place between them...

'Marcus isn't himself... Whatever Mother or Father has given him to report must be urgent...' Celdon worried.

"Come with me, little brother..." Celdon murmured to Panthalassa. He moved quickly yet still at walking pace toward the messenger.

'How does he manage to walk faster than most can run, yet still maintain elegance and not draw attention?' thought Panthalassa.

The messenger opened his mouth to speak but was silenced by a barely perceptible shake of Celdon's head... "Speak to me in the armoury," he murmured.

'What's so secret?' Panthalassa wondered...

The messenger nodded his head in agreement and followed Celdon and his younger brother into the armoury, closing the heavy oaken doors behind them with a thud.

Looking around the room, Celdon thought back to when he was as young as Panthalassa, and he remembered the giant blacksmith, Bulvon, who at this time would usually have been hammering steel at the anvil, merrily telling the boys tales from when he had served the king in the Istarian wars...

'Usually this room is overflowing with new weapons and gear...' Celdon thought to himself, his eyes wandering around the nearly empty room, suspiciously.

'Bulvon will come to refill the armoury soon enough...' he reassured himself.

Panthalassa looked around curiously. This was his first time in the royal armoury...

"Go and explore the walls, Panth," Celdon said, giving him a dismissive nod, at which point he turned to the messenger.

"What is it then, Marcus?" he sighed.

*

Panthalassa watched from the battlements as a battalion of royal cavaliers thundered down Pla-Kingus's unique, red-bricked pathways towards the barracks on the city's outskirts.

"So much activity is going on today..." he said to himself.

'Maybe it's a special day... yes, and Mother and Father have called Celdon and I away to be with them at the keep, and they need the extra soldiers to guard our guests!' thought Panthalassa.

Suddenly, the boy noticed the messenger push open the gateway below him once more, this time to leave, and as Panthalassa watched from above on the walls, the messenger mounted atop a common brown mare without armour or cloth and galloped as fast as his horse could manage down the same pathway travelled by the cavaliers.

He turned around on the wall to face his father's keep which towered in the distance, its stone walls shining brightly in the sun... “But the keep is in the other direction...” he murmured.

The armoury door in the corridor creaked open, and echoing footsteps followed.

"It's urgent, little brother. Come with me now!" demanded Celdon from below the stairwell.

Panthalassa ran down the stairs back into the corridor.

"What is it?" he asked.

"We have to get to the royal barracks." Celdon said to him from the bottom of the stone stairs. His expression seemed impatient.

"Why?" Panthalassa asked.

"There's not enough time to explain, brother!"

Celdon walked quickly through the armoury and then through the gateway of the sparring grounds, still somehow managing to leave the other boys undisturbed as they sparred with one another on the large sand-scattered grounds.

The sun shone brightly between the gaps in the innumerable clouds which drifted over the forested mountains in the distance. Outside the gates of the sparring grounds, Celdon's jet black stallion, which had been cropping the grass beneath the shade of an old oak tree, lifted his head as he recognised his owner and whinnied a greeting. With one swift movement Celdon was astride the magnificent beast and held his hand out to Panthalassa. "Jump on!" he demanded.

"What's happening at the barracks?" Panthalassa asked, as he was effortlessly heaved into the saddle behind his brother...

"You'll find out," Celdon replied.

With his arms wrapped tightly around Celdon's waist, Panthalassa could feel his older brother's unusual tension...

'What is wrong with him? Usually he's so confident and light-hearted...' Panthalassa thought, beginning to feel worried himself.

"Ha!" Celdon lightly dug his heels into the stallion's sides to encourage his mount from a canter into a gallop, when as they were moving along the main street, he caught sight of a dim golden glow down a narrow passageway to his left.

Although Prince Celdon had only seen it a few times in his life, the magical glow that accompanied the *Pure Magic of Tiius* was unmistakable, and he reined in his mount to investigate the source of the golden light.

At the end of the dimly lit side street, he was startled to see a column of paladins, marching along on the street that ran parallel. Even more disturbed was he, as he realised that the glow at the front of the column of finely armoured men came from no less a source than the war hammer of Sir Ardwyn Keyscarre, one of the few high paladins in the *Order of Tiius*.

He halted his horse abruptly, watching as Sir Ardwyn's paladins crossed the gap in the houses and marched out of view down the adjacent street.

A carriage filled with weapons and armour thundered past Celdon's horse, escorted by a small division of swordsmen.

'Perhaps even I underestimated the matter... surely this can't be serious enough for the Order of Tiius to be involved?' thought Celdon.

"Brother why have we stopped?" asked Panthalassa, peering up at him innocently.

"I didn't expect the Order of Tiius to send one of their officers to help us..." Celdon replied. He nudged his horse lightly and carried on riding along the pathway.

"Well... don't they have to?" Panthalassa asked further.

"I wish the grand paladin and his Order was bound to our nation, brother... Indeed, it would make matters much easier," Celdon replied.

"Brother, if their allegiance doesn't lie with us, who does it lie with? With our enemies?"

"Their allegiance lies with Tiius alone, brother. They bear allegiance to no nation and are bound by no king," Celdon replied.

"Then why are they allowed here if they aren't bound by our father's laws?"

Celdon sighed. "Brother, the world is much less simple than you understand. If our father banished everyone who didn't always agree with him, he'd have no-one left to manage his kingdom."

In Panthalassa's head lay more questions than answers. "But you're glad they are helping us?" he asked.

"Hmfh... Yes." Celdon nodded his head gently.

Passing through the city's first layer of two huge stone walls, Celdon and his younger brother immediately noticed the buzz of activity around the barracks.

Rushing in the summer sun, men-at-arms frantically carried provisions and supplies to and fro.

Battalions from across the city marched in full force, high ranking officers bellowing commands, passing through the thick barracks doors which were flung wide open, revealing a huge open field filled with cavalry formations and common soldiers of all kinds, all scurrying around in a kind of organised chaos.

Such a powerful show of force reminded Celdon of his father's victory parade returning as a conqueror from the kingdom of Istaria... who, like the many lands before them in history, had now become a semi-independent state of the Kings' Union, ruled by one of the King's loyal lords.

"Brother, are you going on another of your skirmishes?" Panthalassa asked.

"Yes unfortunately - this one seems like it's going to be rather big," Celdon sighed.

"Why are you so tense? You're usually a lot more cheerful before a battle."

Celdon looked at Panthalassa for a moment, feigned a hearty smile and replied "Nonsense dear brother. Father and I will soon teach those scoundrels a lesson!"

Suddenly, Celdon heard the bellow of a familiar and well-loved voice. He turned around and saw the unmistakable figure of Bulvon the blacksmith, now for some reason at the centre of the field commanding a battalion of two hundred royal knights! The giant blacksmith seemed, as far as he could tell, to be the only man amongst the crowds with a skip in his step and a genuine look of joy painted across his face. Indeed, the blacksmith seemed positively gleeful as he roared his orders out to his men.

Celdon urged on his horse using slight pressure from his knees and cantered across the field towards him. There the middle-aged blacksmith stood wearing a cowhide tunic, his long ginger hair flowing freely in the light breeze, and a large double-bladed axe, which he had forged himself, balanced steadily on his shoulder.

"My word lad, it's you!" cheered Bulvon as he caught sight of Celdon. "Well, it looks like we are in for a real bit of action now, eh my boy?" Bulvon was one of the few commoners who could dare to speak to the young prince with such informality. Although not one to boast, Bulvon had been a legendary warrior in his youth, fighting alongside the boys' father in the First and Second Istarian wars that had brought such an enduring peace to the land for the last decade. The king considered him a close friend and had rewarded Bulvon's loyalty and valour in the peace that followed with a well-paid position as master of arms at the royal training grounds. As such, the blacksmith had known Celdon ever since he was old enough to hold a sword.

"But what are you doing... here... Bulvon?" asked Celdon, gesturing with his arm to encompass the battalion still standing to attention behind the blacksmith.

"Your father just made me the knight-centurion of my old battalion! That is what I am doing here!" Bulvon said, with an air of enormous satisfaction. "I can hardly blame him though. The Aristinians are rumoured to have around thirty-thousand strong horses on the march! Clearly your father has realised this is a job for men with a bit of experience!" Bulvon's barrel chest swelled with pride, but the words spoken by the newly promoted knight-centurion sent Prince Celdon into a spiral of despair.

"Thirty thousand?" Celdon gasped in disbelief. "We're completely unprepared..." he sighed.

Panthalassa went pale when he saw his brother's own fear, for it was something he had never seen before...

"Oh I don't know about that your Lordship, but we'll definitely have enough weapons. Your father has had me and the lads hammering steel around the clock all year!" Bulvon stated.

"Has he indeed?" said Celdon, thoughtfully. "Well, I had better get to my father right away... by the way Bulvon, one of my soldiers was injured the other day, James Ashenworn... I don't know if you remember the man? Do you know if my father sent him back to his family to nurse the wound?"

The knight-centurion chuckled heartily and shook his head. "That crazy bastard's been waiting around all day!" Bulvon said. "He's hoping for a chance to convince your father to let him come to war with us!"

He looked to his left towards the king's quarters, pointing towards the door of the waiting room. "If you're after him though, you'd better try looking in there. But I'll warn you, he'll be begging you too!"

Celdon suddenly smiled back. "Knight-Centurion Bulvon, thank you! Your high spirits are contagious!" he said.

He nudged his horse and tugged at the reigns slightly, encouraging the stallion to canter towards the waiting room.

"Brother, I thought Bulvon was a blacksmith... How did he become a knight-centurion so quickly?" Panthalassa asked, running his hand through his long blonde hair in confusion.

"He's always been a blacksmith at heart, young brother... But he was once one of our nation's finest warriors. There was a time before you were born, when songs were sung in honour of his bravery in Istaria, when he and his battalion single-handedly held off against a horde of three thousand foes," Celdon said.

"How is such a thing possible with only two hundred men?" Panthalassa asked.

"Geography, strategy and cunning. Other than that, I have no idea. But Father holds him in such high regard, the stories must be true. Father doesn't even make him wear a regular uniform, and instead he allows him to choose his own weapons and armour as though he were nobility!"

"I suppose," Panthalassa muttered, not entirely convinced.

'Yes,' Celdon reminded himself. *'Tales of old are always somewhat comforting, I'll have to remind myself of those songs if the Aristinian emperor truly does have thirty thousand men behind him!'*

At the door of the king's chambers, Celdon leaped from his steed, holding his hand out to Panthalassa, who took the hand and was helped to the ground.

As the two royal guards standing on either side of the large oak door snapped to attention, Celdon handed the reins of his horse to a passing stable boy. "See to my horse if you will good fellow!" he instructed.

"Yes, Your Highness!" the stable boy said, taking hold of the reins and leading Celdon's horse away to the stables.

As Celdon walked through the door of the waiting room, the first thing to catch his eye was the figure of an old soldier sat slumped on the first bench beside the door to the king's inner chambers. The inner door was guarded by two royal knights clad in finely polished steel armour. The two guards snapped to attention at the sight of the royal visitors, looking the very picture of military alertness and smartness. In contrast with them, the man sitting alongside them with his longsword balanced carelessly against an oaken table seemed a very poor excuse for a soldier, but Celdon knew that in this case at least, appearances could be deceptive. "James Ashenworn! Well met my friend! How is your arm? That was quite a tumble you took!"

"Celdon... it's an honour," said James, jumping to his feet. "I'm fine really. Perhaps you can convince your father that I'm ready for battle?" he asked hopefully.

"You don't look ready," Celdon sighed, looking at James's heavily bandaged arm, still stained with fresh blood.

Earlier that week, James had been injured in a minor skirmish against one of the many bandit gangs that still made travel dangerous in some of the more remote regions in the kingdom. Although the wound had weakened him considerably, it had not stopped him from showing his support for the king.

"I am ready! I've had worse wounds, friend!" James stated, with a note almost of desperation in his voice.

Panthalassa was intrigued by this man's raw energy - he had never known someone so old as him with so much remaining passion...

"Give me a moment, James. I need to speak with my father - wait outside." Celdon took Panthalassa into the king's quarters, where his father sat at his desk, already fully adorned in his polished kenthril plate armour; a gold-coloured metal, prized for its rare qualities of both lightness and a strength twice greater than steel. His armour was decorated with fine silver and rare jewels, and his greatsword was balanced against the stone wall.

"Ah my boys! I am glad to see you!" King Xanstus boomed, and his voice was as hearty as ever, but Panthalassa, always quick to sense people’s inner emotions, thought his father seemed strained and tired - and there was something else in his father’s manner that troubled the small boy...

Impulsively, Panthalassa ran to his father and hugged him tightly. "Celdon says the battle will be large this time! Will you be back in time for Winter's Hope?" he asked, his voice muffled and small, his cheek still pressed against his father's breastplate, which was warm from the fire beside his oak wood desk.

"Ah, the big winter feast, the promise of better times!" Xanstus said with a fond tone. "I'm afraid we might be longer this time my son, but Mother will still be there with you to make the celebrations joyous."

"Will you let her teach me the *green magic* while you're away?" Panthalassa asked.

Xanstus stood up abruptly, his expressions turning grim and cold. "No, I've told you a thousand times, green magic is only for women and poor farmers!"

Celdon shook his head at Xanstus with a subtle disappointment. *'I wish Father would stop crushing the boy's spirit...'* Celdon thought.

He cleared his throat.

"Father... I've grown concerned that Panth is being bullied by the other boys in the sparring grounds... with me away, it's sure to carry on, and the boy may lose his confidence. I have considered allowing James Ashenworn to take my place while we're away." Celdon held his breath waiting for his father's reply. Xanstus raised his bushy eyebrows and chuckled. "Hahaha! James will soon teach the boy how to best deal with his foes! What an excellent idea!" he exclaimed. "Plus, it will give me an excuse to send the champion home. He's been pestering me all day to let him come to war, even despite his injuries!"

Celdon smiled at King Xanstus and then hugged his younger brother. "I'm sure we will be back for Winter's Hope, Panth," he said, kneeling. "You keep Mother safe like the lion you are. We'll be back before you know it!"

Xanstus sighed lightly, placing his right hand upon the butt of his greatsword. "Tell your mother I love her very much, and I love you very much too, and I am proud of you - even if I don't always tell you that," he said gruffly.

The light of a burning torch on the stone wall glimmered through a tear rolling down Panthalassa's cheek. "Yes, Father."

"Hrrumppft!" the king snorted noisily, embarrassed by his own sudden rush of emotion. "Celdon, tell James young Panth is his responsibility now, and after you have seen the pair of them off, come back at once. We have a lot of work to do."

Panthalassa lowered his head at his father's sudden return to the bitter realities of life.

"I'll notify James of our decision, Father," Celdon said to King Xanstus. He put his arm over the shoulder of his younger brother as he led him out of the room, closing the thick oak door behind him.

"I heard every word, friend," James sighed. "I guess I'm not fit for battle with this arm after all..."

"I've watched you training young warriors before, James. I know you have what it takes to do great things," Celdon sighed. "Take care of him as though he were your own son," he said.

"Aye, friend," James nodded slowly. "That I will. After all, I owe you my life after all the times you've saved mine."

"Goodbye." Celdon widened his arms and hugged the old champion firmly. Both of them had a face bleaker than winter for the war that was to come.

Celdon knelt down and placed his strong callused hand upon his younger brother's shoulder. "Goodbye little brother. You can be sure I'll miss you." He waited for a moment, kissed Panthalassa's forehead and watched as he rode with James into the distance.

'If only Winter's Hope was here, brother... if only,' Celdon thought.

*

Much to the dismay of Prince Celdon, the king had decided to leave almost all his cavalry behind to guard the capital. They argued fiercely about it, but the king, as was his right, had had the last word. "Our cavalry are no match for the Aristinians. Their mounted knights are the envy of the known world - they can break whole armies in a single frontal charge!" he stated. "More than that," he continued, "our horses are like donkeys compared with those pedigree Aristinian Greys! We will take enough to scout ahead and carry messages back and forth, but we are not going to fight the war Emperor Celsidas wants!"

The following morning, King Xanstus roused his army to commence the long, hard march towards the enemy. With this, war had begun.

Chapter 1 Part 2 – Queen Dranah.

Four days later, Castle Lordborn Herb Gardens.

*

The sun was setting, turning the edge of the skies to orange flame as Panthalassa returned home from one of his daily training sessions.

Since the king had left, he had made a point of trying to spend this part of the day with his mother, to try and lighten her mood.

Panthalassa was tender hearted, and it had really upset him to see how troubled his mother had become since his father went to war. Even though initially, Panthalassa had only started joining in in his mother's daily *Duellan* practices to cheer her up, he had come to treasure these moments in his day, as he suspected he would. Panthalassa had started to recognise that the Duellan Magic, in its deep love of nature and all living things, spoke to something deep inside of him, that in fact had always been a part of his personal nature.

His father would always mock him unmercifully for taking an interest in 'Peasant's Magic,' so he had always tried to do this at times when his father wasn't around, to avoid the stress of confrontation.

In reality, his father knew all too well that this was happening, but as far as the king was concerned, Duellan Magic was only practised by superstitious women, farmers and children, and as such, he contented himself to believe that his son was merely going through a phase, that he hoped, at least, would end soon.

After coming home, Panthalassa got changed into the long brown druidic garments that he wore when helping his mother in the gardens, where the queen found it relaxing, after a long day of royal business, to help the servants and the druids do their work. As always, the soft smell of herbs and flowers filled the boy's nostrils as he came into the gardens of the castle.

'At last, the day's training is over,' thought Panthalassa, letting out a sigh of relief as

he absorbed the immense beauty of the gardens. *'I wonder what Mother will teach me today...'*

At that moment he saw his mother dressed in druidic garments of her own, stood at the other side of the royal gardens. "Mother!" he called, running towards her with a joyful heart.

Queen Dranah looked up to her son. "Panth!" They approached each other and embraced. His eyes were already basking in the beauty of the gardens. He watched the servants as they managed the plants, and the druids as they gently harnessed the warming green Duellan Magic from their palms onto the plants less suited to the climate, which seemed to aid their growth, just as the same magic had also done all the way through the winter. He could already feel the calming influence of the garden working on him.

"How has your day been?" the queen asked in a determinedly cheerful voice. "You seem much more jolly and less battered than usual after your training!"

"I am, Mother!" Panthalassa replied, sowing a handful of seeds into the soil as he spoke. "James has been training me in a way that is far different from how the academy officers do things. He makes the larger boys' weight seem like a weakness! I wish I could be as skilled as him…"

"Have there been any complaints?" the queen asked.

"Well yes, at least at first." Panthalassa replied. "A couple of days ago, the master swordsman challenged James to show his skill. Since his arm had not yet fully recovered, he spurned the shield and instead fought with one arm behind his back. I thought he was mad!"

"And did he win?" his mother pressed.

"All in about one minute!" the boy answered. "If I can learn how to fight like that, I won't need to worry about the tougher kids anymore!"

"Very good," the queen smiled. "Well then I hope he keeps up the good work!"

Dranah and her son spent the last hours of their day planting seeds and relaxing in the castle gardens. As the sun began to set, Panthalassa finally raised a question that had been troubling him for the last few days.

"Why didn't you come to see Father and Celdon off?" he asked hesitantly.

"I always get far too emotional, and that embarrasses your father," she replied. Then she smiled, even though Panthalassa could see that her eyes were misted with unshed tears. "Besides," she continued softly, "your father is afraid that he might cry too in front of the troops, and that would never do!

"Your father always tries to act sternly in front of the men. I think he believes they wouldn't respect him if they knew what a tender heart he has! I think they know how much he cares for them all though, anyway. That's why they love him so much!"

Chapter 2 Part 1 – Approaching Destruction.

One week later, Town of Gralmeny.

*

The king's spy sat astride a wide branch, high in the crown of a leafy old sycamore tree, watching the flat grassy plains below him. The small copse of trees he was in stood at the top of a small hill overlooking the market town of Gralmeny. The town was so close that he could still faintly hear the sounds of the marketplace.

From his vantage point, the spy could see the road to Aristinia on his right, stretching away across the open plains as far as the eye could see. To his left, the road out of town, leading further into the kingdom, meandered through gentle rolling hills.

Earlier that morning, the man had enjoyed a hearty breakfast in the town square at an open-air table, whilst watching the townspeople setting up their stalls of food. He had savoured all the rich aromas of the cooking and had listened to the cheerful banter of the townspeople and market traders with a quiet enjoyment as they prepared for their busy Annual Fair. He had listened quietly, but with mounting dismay, as an exhausted man had stumbled into the town, gasping out a horrible tale of an invading army coming this way. The Watcher had then left a few coins on the table, and just as quietly, he had slipped away from the town to find a vantage point from which he could survey the terrain, unseen.

As the sun rose higher in the sky, The Watcher revisited in his mind the scene when the first man had staggered into town. A crowd of stallholders and townsfolk had gathered around him as he shouted in a hoarse strained voice, warning them of a terrible army approaching them. The crowd had been sympathetic at first, for the man was clearly at the end of his endurance and seemed almost half dead. But after forcing a foaming mug of ale into his hands, and listening to his tale, the stallholders had gone back about their business. It was the day of the Annual Fair, and there was too much to do to waste time listening to the ravings of a madman waving his arms wildly. The exhausted man had tried to convey to them the sheer size of the approaching army, and The Watcher recalled the look of despair on his face when he realised no-one was taking him seriously.

A middle-aged baker woman had tried to calm him. "Don't be silly, it will take more than a few bandits to stop the Gralmeny Annual Fair!"

At that comment, the newcomer had thrown up his hands in resignation and slunk away from the crowds that had gathered around him to hear his tale. Shortly after, he had been seen galloping out of town in the opposite direction to which he had arrived, on a stolen horse. After a brief flurry of shouting and activity from the horse's owner, the rest of the onlookers had gone about their normal activities as though nothing had changed.

Since then, as the morning wore on and the sun rose higher in the sky, The Watcher in the tree saw a few more exhausted people stagger into town, clearly telling the same tale. Even from a distance, the leather-jacketed watcher could see the faces of the townsfolk grow worried, and some of them were stood around in groups discussing what should be done.

For several hours he waited, and the only thing which seemed to change was the growing sense of unease in the town, as a growing number of refugees stumbled into Gralmeny, their shoulders slumped in dismay. Most stayed only long enough to take food and drink before scurrying away over the western hills.

By now, the day had reached half past four in the afternoon, and The Watcher had seen no more refugees for a good while. *'Perhaps that's all of them...'* he thought... *'or perhaps there were more, but their struggle to escape was less fruitful...'*

A rumble like thunder echoed faintly in the distance off to the east. It was barely audible at first. The Watcher strained his ears to try and pinpoint the noise against the hubbub of the merchants and farmers, trying to sell the last of their goods. Each fellow was bellowing louder than the other in an attempt to advertise their wares. Then he heard it again from over the eastern hillside... drums! He fixed his vision, watching the hill in silent anticipation as the drums gradually grew louder, seeming to coincide with a slightly quieter, but still very present rumbling noise... *'Cavalry,'* he thought. *'Drums and cavalry... Formations?'*

He then felt a wave of helplessness, tinged with guilt, wash over him as the rumbling and the pounding of drums grew louder. He shook his head in sorrow. *'If only I could save the townsfolk from their fate...'* The Watcher thought. *'But they'd never listen, in their blissful ignorance!'*

'How I envy those refugees. They can simply pass through the town and flee on! They don't have the same duty to the king as I do...' he thought. His duty was to send secret word to the king of any new information from the border. His orders had stressed the high priority on any reports which might come from Aristinia or indeed their emperor.

Over recent years, many reports from a wide range of sources had reached the king's ears about the mighty army Emperor Celsidas was building. Now at last that army was on the move. It had already begun putting the insignificant border towns and villages to the sword, often even going so far as to burn them down, despite the lack of resistance.

Hundreds of years ago, Aristinia had ruled over a vast empire stretching half the width of the entire continent. Over time, this empire collapsed through a mixture of civil unrest and growing corruption. Although by now the justification for the Aristinians calling themselves an 'Empire' had truly gone, the Aristinian nobility, still in denial of their lost ancient glory, carried on the old ways of emperors and attempted territorial expansion. They were so far set in their ancient ways as to refuse their heavy cavalry the right to wear steel or iron rather than bronze. This made their armies particularly noticeable for the fact that they were the only fighting force in the known world still using full suits of bronze plates into battle, and it was a lucky thing that the mountains surrounding their nation were packed full with tin and copper ores.

The Aristinian knights' skill, however, was unmatched throughout all the continent, and a sense of fanaticism existed within them - their raw, unmatched loyalty to the old line of emperors, and their philosophy that skill through training often beats the materials used to fight with.

These were horsemen who had beaten their every opponent in previous wars. Even recently against other knights wearing steel or iron, their skills with lance and horse had beaten foes against all the odds, both in jousts and battles alike. This was what Aristinia had been sighted bringing into the lands of the king, and from what The Watcher could now hear from the drums' rhythm, it certainly sounded like what had been described to him in the past.

'Aristinians, it has to be! That's all we've been hearing about for the past three days!' The Watcher thought.

All of a sudden, as The Watcher watched the grassy eastern hilltop, he noticed the glimmering lance tips of the Aristinian knights appearing over the hillside for almost a quarter of a mile, with dull brown banners with the central symbol of a bull flying high in the air behind them.

Lance tips and weaponry were the exception to the ancient gleam of bronze in Aristinian armies. It doesn't take a genius to know that bronze doesn't pierce steel.

The Watcher waited for the knights to fully appear over the hilltop then widened his eyes in shock once they were in full sight.

They were hulking giants of men, holding their heavy weapons in one hand, clad in their full-plated bronze armour. The rumours of their ferocity were surely true.

After observing the column of knights for several further minutes, he caught sight of Emperor Celsidas himself, who, unlike the others, wore shimmering plates made of kenthril - a metal looking almost identical to gold, though both stronger and lighter than steel. His breastplate was lined with silver and his golden crown was fixed firmly upon his helmet. His face looked as hawkish as ever. Beside him rode another important looking man. The spy instantly recognised Imperial Guardian Kalsos from his bullish and terribly scarred face, and his finely polished and knuckle-spiked kenthril gauntlets.

He waited with great despair as the huge army advanced towards the town of Gralmeny, noticing that behind the Aristinian Knightly Order marched a further force of regular soldiering cavaliers, who each carried a long wooden lance, wearing coats of steel chainmail and steel helmets.

The regular cavaliers were a much larger force, having around three times the breadth of the emperor's bronze-wearing Knightly Order, then behind the cavaliers were three distinct squadrons, the spearmen and the swordsmen, who seemed much less professional than any of the regular cavaliers, or definitely any of the Aristinian knights, and then finally the archers. To the spy's expert eye, they looked much more like hunters, trained perhaps in precise shot. They certainly lacked the immense muscularity of the king's military archers anyway, who were trained to lay down a blizzard of arrows in rapid fire.

The Watcher had no stomach to witness the slaughter he knew was about to occur. '*I must inform the king of what has happened,*' he thought.

As he climbed from his tree in silence, the smell of smoke gradually filled his nostrils, coinciding with the harsh sound of screaming, which broke his heart, sending shivers up his spine as he vanished into the shadows of the forest.

*

Down in Gralmeny, the emperor's troops were already reducing many of the cottages to rubble, and all that would later remain of the small market town would be smashed windows, burning buildings and whatever little plunder the town had to offer, and marching through such a small town made next to no impact on the army's speed due to its sheer size and weight.

Celsidas reined in his horse. "Burn the houses! Slaughter them all!" he commanded, giving his men an arrogant and determined glare.

Though screams of horror echoed against the rocky cliff-side and the townsfolk had attempted to flee their homes in fear of the huge army, most of the townspeople had been slain in cold blood within only a few minutes, as the flat grassy plains which the town was built on ensured light work for the Aristinian cavalry, who took great pleasure in chasing down the fleeing civilians and impaling them with their sharpened wooden lance tips. Such work was found sadistically enjoyable, as Emperor Celsidas had promised them (and the rest of his men) the spoils of war.

From the corner of Celsidas's eyes he spotted two townsfolk running with all the speed they could muster, panting heavily as they ran from a burning granary.

A band of cavaliers adjusted their lances, grinned and charged towards them, only to be halted by the emperor. "Stay your lances, soldiers, let them escape! All we need now is a few more of these raids and we'll have angered the king into a frenzy of rage, and with any luck his anger will drive him forward onto the plains, where he will die!"

The cavaliers turned their horses around, reluctantly sparing the civilians by the emperor's will. "Yes, my liege," they saluted him, joining their comrades in the marketplace where the town stalls were being plundered.

"Gah! There's nothing in these towns and villages but more cheap food and ale!" called a swordsman to one of his comrades, biting into a large chicken leg plundered from a cooking stall, holding his ash-covered golden helmet filled with red wine in his arm.

"Tell me 'bout it!" agreed the other, his voice raw with drunkenness and war fever. "Can't wait until we get to Dessii though, I bet it's full to the brim with riches... and more juicy women!"

"If only we could get there sooner, eh? Hahaha!" the other replied with feverish glee.

Celsidas listened to his footsoldiers' comments with growing impatience. *'They're a bunch of swine...'* he thought, while still allowing himself a slight cackle of pleasure at their eagerness. *'These low-borns will believe any promises I give them of riches and wealth, but they're already growing tired of these plains... I'd better get my army moving.'*

"Give the signal to move out!" commanded the emperor, and his trumpeter placed a brass trumpet to his mouth and blew a long-sustained note.

The highly trained and disciplined Aristinian Knightly Order instantly re-formed into orderly columns and swept onward, the newly recruited footsoldiers however seemed reluctant to leave the town, especially now that several barrels of wine had been opened, and many of the soldiers were slow to obey the order to move out.

"Get a move on, or I will have your worthless skins flogged from your backs!" Celsidas roared. "There will be time enough for drinking, yes, and wenching too, after we put Dessii to the sword!"

Hearing the emperor's threat, the soldiers quickly rushed into formation and resumed marching along the grassy plains, for they knew their emperor's Knightly Order would ruthlessly enforce his punishments regardless of the barbarity.

Celsidas smirked with joy now that his troops were assembled and on the move once again. *'Soon I'll have him...'* he thought. *'All we need is one big battle here on the plains where we can win, and then the rest of the Kings' Union will be ours for the taking!'*

After that short siege of Gralmeny, the emperor swept through the plains even further, consuming the land like a blade through ripe corn as village after village fell to his might.

Three days turned to six, every day's march taking them deeper into the kingdom. They torched villages as they went but as they reached the end of the plains, the king was still nowhere to be seen.

The emperor was growing impatient, and even more noticeably so was his army.

"Hrmgggh..." Celsidas growled with deep dissatisfaction. "My plans aren't working, Kalsos. It looks like we're going to have to plough through the *Tan'gran'ne'se* after all."

Imperial Guardian Kalsos raised an eyebrow at him. Here was an old soldier. His hair was short and white, with many scars of battle tearing through his facial skin in their old glory. He commanded a large portion of the Aristinian Knightly Order, and his advice was usually sound. "Your Majesty, shouldn't we wait a while longer? Our scouts aren't coming back, and I fear something could go terribly wrong if we go too much further north..."

Celsidas shook his head at the very thought of holding his army back any longer. "I can advance as far as I like, Kalsos!" he snapped. His voice was like the flame, consuming all it touched with vigour and power. He had no time for any more waiting. "We've been putting these mediocre towns and farming villages to the sword for too long, and the king is yet to show his banners, and besides, look at the size of our army! Is it any wonder he's scared?!"

"All I'm saying is to exercise caution, my Imperial Lord. I have a terrible feeling that we are being drawn into a battle which won't be to our liking. The terrain ahead is far different from what our cavalry are used to."

Celsidas's white, armoured stallion whinnied slightly, swishing his tail.

"What could you mean by that?" the emperor laughed menacingly.

"The trees, Your Majesty - the county up ahead is heavily forested and there are steep hills and ravines. The scouts have already reported being ambushed by bowmen firing from the treeline," Kalsos went on.

"A few bandits picking off our scouts as they ride by isn't enough to imply anything of value," Celsidas assured him. "Are you really suggesting that a few measly tribesmen with hunting bows will be enough to stop our advance?"

"Perhaps you're right, sir," Kalsos sighed.

Several hours of marching proceeded after that conversation. The emperor's army grew in confidence with every mile, chanting "Dessii! Dessii!" into the midday sun as their marching tune.

During the morning's march the countryside around them rose steadily until by noon it levelled off into a grassy plateau. About a mile in front of them the army could see another small village, and in the distance, they could see glimpses of the road, as it wound through steep hillsides into a forest. The tops of the hills were currently shrouded in heavy cloud.

As the army approached the village a large band of unkempt warriors, perhaps two thousand in number, came out and drew up in a ragged clump. It was in fact the first time during the emperor's campaign so far that he had been met with any armed resistance.

Celsidas reined in his armoured stallion with a mischievous grin. He raised his hand in gesture to his trumpeter. "Soldiers, make formations and halt!"

He took a moment to observe the disorganised clump of barbarians rallied before him as his elite heavy cavalry formed their rows of bronze behind him and the Imperial Guardian.

The villagers paled in comparison to them. Their warriors held large round wooden shields decorated in several dark-themed red or green colours, brandishing a variety of weapons such as axes, leaf-bladed swords and flails, and the cottages this time, rather than being made of stone and thatched straw, appeared to be crafted from the earth itself, raising from the ground with smoke bellowing from their primitive chimneys, surrounding one central mound far bigger than all the rest, which was presumably where their warlord lived.

By the looks of things, the warlord's warriors were mainly the elders. The youngest ones, the emperor assumed, had retreated the rest of their people further north-west into Tan'gran'ne'se to relocate in the woods, and it was here on the plains that the elders would make their final stand to buy their people some time.

"Ah yes, Kalsos," the emperor sighed. "It appears you were right, we are truly no match for these savages."

The knights chuckled in mocking enjoyment of the emperor's sarcasm.

Kalsos looked to one side to hide the anger in his eyes.

"No, I mean it Kalsos! I mean just look at their immaculate discipline! We are going to be slaughtered!"

The laughing increased.

"Oh well," Celsidas went on. "I'm afraid we must press on all the same, even despite our - and I cannot stress this enough - even despite our simply terrifying opposition! I give you my men this final order!"

He raised his hand in gesture to the squire behind him, who placed the royal lance firmly in the emperor's hand. He lowered the lance slowly and roared. "Charge!"

The tribesmen then tore across the open field after sounding their own horn, flailing their weapons wildly in the air and screeching with all the breath remaining in their lungs. They knew they were certain to lose this time, but it was for the sake of their people.

Carnage followed. If ever there was a perfect example of overpowering force, this was it. Within a few minutes, the band of tribesmen had been utterly massacred by the emperor's charging wall of steel blades. The Aristinian Knightly Order had thundered forward towards them, kicking up a cloud of dust behind them and trampling the grass itself into soggy heaps of dirt.

Corpses lay scattered all along the field with blood spewing and splintered lance-tips firmly embedded in their flesh. As the emperor looked down at the immeasurably few faces that could be recognised amongst the hundreds of others, their faces and bodies laying as one with the ground trampled deep into the sludge by the weight of the armoured horses that had thundered past, it confirmed his suspicions. Not a single young warrior could be seen. This village had clearly valued its young and its women more than their elders.

"Pick out their warlord's corpse from the dead, Kalsos," the emperor commanded. "We'll make camp inside their measly village tonight, but tomorrow we will be on the march again, and I'm sure that his head will make a fine gift to the king."

Chapter 2 Part 2 - Preparations.

Three miles beyond Dessii, deep into the south-eastern woods of Tan'gran'ne'se.

*

On a remote dirt pathway half covered by thick silver-barked ivy, an old farmer was herding a flock of sheep with his trusty working dog. Normally in summer he would have left his sheep to graze untended on the high pastures above the treeline in the foothills of the great Tan'gran'ne'sian mountain range, fattening themselves on the wild salty moorland grasses.

The last few days, however, had been unseasonably cold for summer, and the old man knew from his experience of living in this land that it was only a matter of hours before a storm broke, and so he had worked from sunrise to sunset to round up his flock and herd them down through the forest to the sheltered pastures surrounding his farm. The night air was damp and cold now, and he wore a thick grey woollen jacket to shield himself from the chill. Tendrils of misty air were rolling down from the mountains, which even in the height of summer, never lost their mantle of snow.

As he finished his day's work, he began hearing tiny, almost inaudible sounds that he was not familiar with, which even after his many years of living in these lands, uneased him.

The night crept on and the winds from the mountains fell upon his farm, and after a hard day of working in those hills, he was eating by the window on his old oaken table while his sheepdog slept beside the crackling log fire behind him. The blinds were open, and he thought the stars looked especially beautiful tonight.

But the winds were howling through the glass panes now, and a few moments later, they had become stronger. A gust of wind then came, stronger than all the rest, and in the night sky he noticed the eerie blueish mist clouds roll back for a few seconds as he caught a glimpse of what appeared to be an entire army making its way across the mountain moorland. Through the rolling mists, silhouetted against the night sky, they seemed more like an army of long-fallen ghosts than living men.

Dead silence followed. It chilled him to the bone, and as he rushed to the mantle above the fireplace in a superstitious dread, clutching his holy talisman with both hands, he said a heart-felt prayer to Tiius in a pleading call, to shield him from *Odall* and his many cursed works.

*

The king's army had been marching for five nights now. The soldiers had become footsore and weary.

"Father..." murmured Celdon.

"Yes my son?" Xanstus whispered back, frowning. He had insisted on complete silence for this part of their march and was annoyed that his own son was breaking the silence. It set a bad example to the men.

"Surely we would make better time if we marched in daylight along the main roads? That way we could recruit more men as we marched through the towns?" the prince suggested, hesitant to question his father's years of fighting experience any further since he had already argued with him before.

"No, son," Xanstus replied to his heir. "I know what I'm doing. We'll face the emperor's army in due time, but for now you must march with me along the hills."

His forbidding expression left Prince Celdon in no doubt that further discussion would be futile. Celdon inwardly seethed with frustration as the army continued its stealthy march along the desolate moorland. *'Surely he understands the implications of moving in such a secretive manner... even the men who march behind us must think us afraid of battle!'* Celdon thought, his expression as grim as blood.

Since setting out from Pla-Kingus five days ago, the king had avoided all towns and even villages, and instead he insisted on night travel and silence. He had marched the whole army over trackless moors and deep forests, avoiding even sheep trails, and after marching almost all night through thick fog and harsh wind, Prince Celdon himself now had no idea where exactly they were, and he was beginning to suspect that his father was in fact lost.

As the army marched up a steep hillside, the fog gradually cleared, and Celdon suddenly realised he was now marching along a trail he knew all too well. *'We are almost at our secret training valley where we bring our new recruits for the Tribal Games!'* he thought, *'Surely Father doesn't intend for us to come here? We have a city to defend!'*

For several centuries, all of the tribes and small kingdoms which together made up the Kings' Union had a duty to provide trained soldiers for the king's army, but after ten years of peace, this obligation had quietly faded into disuse.

When Celdon had just turned twelve years old, his father, King Xanstus, had begun enforcing this law again.

Although some of the tribal chieftains came close to rebellion at being forced to pay for training and equipping their young men with valuable steel, everyone knew that the countries around them were becoming more warlike, and Xanstus, by a mixture of bullying and persuasion, had forced his way.

Each people under the Kings' Union then once again agreed to train and equip all their young men from the age of twelve, in all the skills of war. To keep them to their word, the king cunningly suggested they should send the best of their young men to a summer training camp for a few weeks each year, to test their skills against each other. This event had become known as the Tribal Games, and now for some reason, it seemed the king was heading towards this huge outdoor training area again, rather than heading towards the emperor's invading army!

Whilst Celdon was still trying to come to terms with this new information, a band of warriors suddenly appeared from the shadows of the forest.

The king's chest swelled with joy. "Do not worry, men!" he bellowed. "These are our friends. They have come to join forces with us!"

As the two forces grew closer, the paint on the warriors' faces became clear, arrayed in blue, black and burgundy. Most of the warriors wore chainmail or wolf-skin, and every last one of them had long flowing hair. This was the Kad'aeri tribe, one of the many tribes of Tan'gran'ne'se, who in peace times specialised in the ways of mining and stonemasonry. These people were also feared berserkers of the woods, famed throughout the land far before the Calligian Empire's civil war, which saw the empire's rebels travel overseas in search of a new home, bringing them here.

As King Xanstus led his army further down the hills deeper into the woods, the moonlight was almost blocked out by the leaves above their heads. The air around suddenly came alight with a fuzzy green glow, coming from a spell cast by one of the druids as a blessing for the warriors.

Then, as the marching proceeded, the sound of rushing water came to the soldiers' ears. Shortly after, the army came to a river at the foot of a steep ravine.

King Xanstus urged his horse over a huge, fallen yew tree, which formed a natural bridge over the ravine, but the horses of the men following behind reared up, their eyes rolling in fright and refused to set foot on the bridge. Sir Ardwyn Keyscarre, High Paladin in the Order of Tiius, calmly followed the king across the bridge and upon his crossing, the night sky above the tree was filled with a bright golden aura, which flowed from his war hammer, illuminating the fine kenthril plate armour worn by all of the elite paladins under his influence. After that, the horses and the rest of the men crossed without further fears.

Once the king's men had crossed over the fallen tree, another band of tribal warriors became visible to the front ranks, appearing out of the forest as silently as wraiths.

Wielding leaf-bladed swords, the warriors at the front effortlessly slashed through some thick brambles which impeded their progress. The Danz'kanari tribe all carried finely carved bows made of bone upon their backs, with quivers that could hold up to a hundred arrows at a time. Their warlord was a tall, old but intelligent looking man with long silvery-grey hair. A warm smile immediately crossed his face upon seeing King Xanstus and his son.

Hundreds of years ago, the Danz'kanari were once the dominant tribe of Tan'gran'ne'se. Allied with the Kad'aeri, their combined bows and berserkers once made for almost an equal force to that of the Calligian rebels who, having been forced out of their own homelands, were fighting to carve out a new nation for themselves in these lands. The Danz'kanari had fought the newcomers in a bitter fifty-year war, but after the Danz'kanari (and all the other tribes) had been defeated, the rebels had generously allowed each of them to keep their own lands, and even their independence.

Over time, the Calligian rebels had earned the respect of their neighbours, and one by one, all of the tribes and small Kingdoms in Tan'gran'ne'se soon became a part of what would later become known as the Kings' Union.

"Warlord Airen, it's good to be fighting alongside you and your hunters once more!" said King Xanstus.

Airen smiled with a thousand silent words. Unlike many of the other chieftains, he had fought by the king's side before in Istaria, and although the Danz'kanari were primarily a hunter-gatherer people, they were not unaccustomed to fighting, and very much understood the importance of his cause.

"It is an honour to fight alongside you too, Xanstus!" Airen replied in his deep gravelly voice. "I can only pray that this war is shorter than our last."

Airen's hunters joined the marching army.

As Celdon and Xanstus led the slowly growing force through the fuzzy green glowing woods, many more tribal warriors joined forces with the Unionites, each being granted the druidic blessing of their ancestors whose sacred whispers filled the darkened leafy skies above them.

'The main road isn't even within sight... we're nearly at our yearly training camp! Surely Father must know this!' Celdon worried, but despite his concerns, he felt his hopes rise and his mind become more peaceful as he allowed his gaze to wander around the woodland, absorbing the view of magnificent green-glowing rivers and ancient forests, the likes of which had been allowed to grow and flourish for many thousands of years.

They marched on, and a new way became clear between a tall snowy mountain on the left, and the forest, which ran steeply down a slope to their right.

Far below, the wide (yet winding) main pathway leading out of Dessii was hidden behind the vast sea of leaves and old tree branches.

"Father, our training camp is just to our left around this mountain... why have you brought us here? By now we could have met the emperor in battle!" Celdon asked. His tone was hot with confusion.

King Xanstus chuckled, seeming oddly calm. "Have a little faith in me, boy!" he said. "I know what I'm doing. Why else would I have spent the last ten years unifying the tribes and training them with you in this very place?"

"That's all very good Father, but..." Celdon was interrupted by his father.

"I'll not be talked back to, thank you very much, young prince, you're not king yet!"

Xanstus had a short fuse. He had a plan and was not soon going to be interrupted by his son's misunderstandings.

'I wish he would listen, damn it! The kingdom's safety hangs in the balance!' thought Celdon, sighing heavily. His expression was cold as stone, and at this very moment, he despised his own inferiority in title, his inability to overrule his father's seemingly unnecessary caution. "Very well, Father. I apologise," he said. The words squeezed from his mouth like puss from a wound. It was painful.

Knight-Centurion Bulvon sighed too. In a quiet part of his mind, he sympathised with the young prince's eagerness for battle but dared not speak up, fearing he would only make matters worse. *'Aah... you can surely tell those two are father and son. My word, if I had a son, I wouldn't let him talk to me like that!'* he thought.

Before Xanstus had fully left the main pathway, the giant blacksmith had assumed that the king would make for the city of Dessii with full speed. That city's huge walls and fortifications might have given them some chance of fighting off the Aristinian army, which if the reports were true, vastly outnumbered them. If they had travelled along the main highways, they could have been there days before and also had time to strengthen their defences in the meanwhile.

Dawn broke, the tired soldiers had almost reached the secret training camp. For most of the soldiers in the king's regular army, this was their first time they had been here. But the youngest amongst them, the tribal warriors who had been here before for their training, had whispered their news to their comrades, and now there was a murmur of excitement throughout the army even despite their exhaustion through continued marching.

The last few hundred feet of the march was up a hill so steep the men had to scramble, and those very few who were still on horseback had to dismount and lead their horses by foot. At the top of the heavily wooded slope, a huge cliff of volcanic rock soared above them, seeming to form an insurmountable barrier. But Xanstus and Celdon led their horses through the narrowest of gaps formed by a huge crack that ran from the top to the bottom of the cliffs, and within minutes, the whole army was standing on the other side of the cliffs, looking down into a large valley. The men who were seeing this sight for the first time gasped in amazement.

At the bottom of the large valley was a lake surrounded by magnificent mature trees, some hundreds of feet tall, and between the trees' foliage, they could see hundreds of huts that had clearly been built since the last games.

'I see now, Father must have been planning this all along... since I was here last he must have got the local tribesmen to construct more and more huts, even after we thought there were more than enough of them. But how can he be so sure the emperor's army will ever even come this way?' Celdon wondered.

The army entered the camp, and at the sight of the central training circle the army was in awe. The circle was hundreds of feet wide; a variety of wooden weapons hung inside well-made sheds along with spare armour, real weapons and even siege equipment. The circle was surrounded by well-made (but small) stone walls, the only structures of stone in the whole encampment, and around the stone walls the sheds of various equipment allowed for easy access to real weapons, and also those used for training. Above the rocky pathways, rope bridges were strung, high up between the trees. The whole camp was linked together by this aerial pathway which spanned out from the centre like a kind of spider web.

"Alright, men!" bellowed King Xanstus "You should find more than enough huts in this encampment to house yourselves. Get yourselves settled in and then get some rest!" King Xanstus paused at the doorway of his hut which unlike the others was painted in vibrant red and yellow. "Meanwhile, I am calling a brief Council of War!" The king turned and led his son, the senior officers and tribal chieftains through the wide oaken doors of his long-hut. As he was entering, he noticed his standard bearer had already fixed the scarlet banner of the Kings' Union on its long ash wood pole onto brackets built into the side of the hut, and as Sir Ardwyn Keyscarre, High Paladin in the Order of Tiius, approached to enter, he gestured to his own standard bearer to fix their Order's white banner up alongside it, and both banners held in the centre a golden symbol of *Tiius's Glimmering Sceptre of Justice*, which with three simplistic lines bore resemblance to both the sceptre, and the letter "Y."

The king felt a surge of gratitude and relief at the high paladin's gesture of support to his cause.

It wasn't the first time, but King Xanstus was struck by the resemblance the Kings'

Union's flag bore to that of the Order of Tiius - both with Tiius's sacred golden sceptre in the centre.

He remembered something from his childhood history lessons. Xanstus thought back to the origins of the two flags' similarities. The long-dead ancestors of Xanstus, the old kings, were once themselves refugees, simply fleeing from the tyrannical rule of the Calligian Empire.

With the help of the Order, the Calligian rebels had managed to escape from their old imperial overlords in a fleet of stolen ships. They finally found shelter far to the west in the wildlands of Tan'gran'ne'se, to whose shores the Calligian rebels had fled. With the help of the Order of Tiius and its paladins, the former Calligian rebels had managed to subdue the many warring tribes in their new land - and more than that, with the Order's wise counsel, the early kings had established such a just rule that they had forged the tribes into a powerful union. In gratitude, The Kings' Union (as the new kingdom became known) had made their banner as one with the Order of Tiius, in all but background colour.

Although the Order of Tiius to this day has never sworn allegiance to any of the kings, they were an important part of *Unionite* history, and because they are a Holy Order dedicated to fighting injustice and evil, Xanstus hoped their support would help to persuade the tribal leaders to continue to support him.

As the tribal chiefs and his own army's commanders filed into the long hut and took seats around the large central table, the king took a moment to gather his thoughts and calm his emotions. He could count on his own commanders' loyalty to him, but he needed the full support of all the tribes if his plan was to work, and he sensed that this meeting would be a stormy one.

"Now, I have gathered you in here to discuss the plan," the king began. "Reports have been coming in about the size of the Aristinian army, and not only that, but also the types of soldier they have brought with them. As you all know, the Aristinians have been rumoured to have around thirty thousand men. I can confirm those rumours for you. You should know, their army consists primarily of heavy cavalry."

Gasps of dread broke out at this announcement, and the king paused for a moment to allow that news to sink in, and for the noise around the table to subside.

"Now, some of you might have been wondering why we have not spent the last few days rushing to meet Celsidas's army. Here is your answer. We have no heavy cavalry. The horses we have left are barely enough to form even one full unit, and so if we were to meet the invading army on the open plains, they would cut us all down like a field of ripe corn." Angry murmurs greeted this comment, but the king glared around, daring any of the tribal leaders to meet his eyes in open challenge.

The king glanced at Bulvon. "Now, some of you might be wondering, in that case, why we did not rush to Dessii instead and shelter behind its massive walls, but once encircled by the emperor's cavalry, we would be caught like rats in a trap."

"Better that, than scurrying through the forest like scared rabbits!" clamoured one red-faced tribal chieftain. "My warriors aren't afraid tae' fight!"

"Even now, after taking time to gather all the tribes together, our army numbers only around fifteen thousand, and with all respect to the courage of your warriors, they are more hunters than soldiers," replied the king, "and it is your skills as hunters that is going to allow us to defeat this much larger army of Aristinian knights!" An excited murmur ran around the room at that bold statement.

King Xanstus shuffled the papers on the table, unrolling a scroll which contained the map of the area around them. "Now here is my plan..."

The tribal chiefs gathered around the map as the king pointed out their current location. The king's meaty finger outlined all of the curves in the pathway below the steep forested slope. He pointed to the precise location of Dessii compared to where they were, and he gestured to a point at the edge of the map. "This is where Celsidas's army is right now - currently on the plains of Gralmeny, in the territory of the *Varnixye* tribe." Finally his thick finger jabbed at a point along the pathway towards Dessii, where the road was sandwiched between two steep forested slopes. "And this," he said with a tone of utter certainty, "this is where we are going to ambush our foe."

Bulvon shook his head. "We will still be outnumbered just as heavily," he rumbled.

"Yes," said the king, "but the cavalry will be at a massive disadvantage in the place I have chosen to do battle." Xanstus squeezed the bear-like knight-centurion's shoulder in a comradely hug. "Just wait until the morning, when you see the hidden fortifications along the treeline," he chuckled.

'How does Father know so much about the emperor's forces before they are even within sight?' wondered Celdon.

"Your job then, Bulvon, will be to hide your battalion of royal knights along the treeline. You, and only you, may peer above the defences. This is because unlike the others in your battalion who wear the regular uniform of glimmering steel and golden decorations, you wear cowhide, and if you allow the Kad'aeri berserkers to cover you in green warpaint, you may even be indistinguishable from the trees. When the time is right and the Aristinians are within around a hundred feet, you will blow a ram's horn and issue your seasoned heavy infantry into the fray."

Celdon suddenly interrupted his father, luckily after he had finished speaking to

Bulvon. "Father, how do you know the emperor will come this way... doesn't it all seem a little optimistic?"

"Spare me the questions until *after* I have explained the plan, will you my son?" Xanstus snapped.

"I hate to question you my lord," said Bulvon, "and I apologise too, but the prince may be correct. Wouldn't Celsidas choose a path more suited to his cavalry?"

"I have eyes everywhere, Bulvon. Believe me, from the string of towns and villages he has plundered, he'll be here in a matter of days, probably tomorrow. He has left himself little alternative unless he has found a way of flying over the mountains," Xanstus said firmly.

The King fixed his gaze at the other knight-centurions. Unlike Bulvon, they all wore the regular royal officer's uniform. "You will command your battalions forward at the sound of Bulvon's horn, and as one you shall emerge from the tree-line fortifications at either side of the valley and crash into the enemy lines.

"What of my Paladins, good King?" questioned High Paladin Ardwyn Keyscarre.

Xanstus looked at Sir Ardwyn with a look of appreciation. "I am honoured to have your Order stand beside us in this fight, for it is well known that your Holy Order gives its allegiance to no king and only fights in the cause of justice and to combat evil. When Knight-Centurion Bulvon sounds the ram's horn, I will trust you and your paladins to contribute to the battle as you see fit. We have all heard of your Order's skills in battle and in magic, and so I trust you to enter the fray at the decisive moment." Xanstus smiled warmly at Ardwyn. "The Order of Tiius is also famous for its healing spells," the king said. "After the battle, we may have much need of those skills."

Ardwyn nodded his wise old head signifying his agreement with the king's comment, and he bowed slightly, acknowledging the high compliment the king had paid him by giving his paladins a free hand to do battle as they thought best.

Xanstus peered at Celdon with a slight smile. "As for us, my son, we will be at the side of Bulvon hiding behind the treeline. Bulvon will keep me informed by silent gesture, telling me of any enemy movement - yet the screams of dying foes should be more than enough to keep me informed, as Warlord Airen of the Danz'kanari assures me that his bowmen have been hard at work these past few months, making their tree platforms along the sides of the road where the hillside is steepest. His men will be thinning the emperor's army with every step he takes."

Celdon nodded at Xanstus, not entirely convinced by the plan.

"Any questions?" the king asked.

Bulvon looked at him. "I'm sure we all have plenty of questions, Your Lordship! One that I have is this: apart from thinning the emperor's numbers from the trees, what role do the tribesmen play in this battle?" he asked.

"I'm glad you asked, my friend. The Kad'aeri berserkers and the other smaller tribes who have followed their example will serve our lines as invisible eyes, hiding behind the trees in their camouflaged fur-coated chainmail armour. Each tribe has their own highly specialised fighting style. I can safely say that we have quite a few surprises in store for the emperor."

At this moment Celdon finally felt a glimmer of excitement. '*If the emperor really does come this way, we are ready for him...*' After all, he thought, he and his father had been training in this very camp for seven years now, and had not only mastered their own fighting style, but along with every young tribal warrior who had now joined their army, they had in fact mastered each of the best fighting styles in the whole of Tan'gran'ne'se.

Suddenly, the door of the royal long-hut creaked open, shedding a flash of afternoon light. A messenger entered the room. He wore shimmering bronze chainmail and a bright red tabard with the symbol of Tiius's Sceptre of Justice in the centre. "My King," spoke the messenger, bowing low his head, "We have visitors from the southeast."

Xanstus looked at the intruder. "Ah! Well, I shall forgive your intrusion this once. Come, my son! we must greet our guests!" He walked around the table and patted Celdon on the back, then turned around. "Thank you for your time, gentlemen. May I suggest you see to it that your troops spend the rest of their day getting fed and rested?"

Upon leaving the long-hut, Xanstus and his son were immediately greeted by a large group of young warriors. A man watching from a tower on the palisade wall could clearly see there were anywhere between two or three thousand strong, bringing with them women and children, but almost none of the elders seemed present.

Immediately, as Xanstus observed their hair tied back with springy willow sticks, he was sure of who they must be. *'The Varnixye have finally arrived!'* he thought.

Hundreds of years ago when the Calligian rebels landed in the dense forests of Tan'gran'ne'se, they conquered Pla-Kingus after a bitter three-week long siege. Pla-Kingus was already a sprawling capital of the Varnixye people, but over time, the Varnixye migrated south eastward following the loss of their city. They too were granted protection after the hostilities ceased, and their warlords through each generation had always been surprisingly close to the Calligian-blooded Unionite Royal Family. Their immense respect for each other stemmed from their recognition of fellow warriors of bravery and valour. These were the core values of both their fierce warrior-cultures.

"Where is my good friend, Falxyr, young warrior? Surely he must be honoured for allowing so many fighters to aid me in the coming battle!" cheered Xanstus, unaware of their many unarmed refugees still outside of the palisade walls beyond his sight.

"He and the oldest warriors stayed behind to fight Emperor Celsidas, my Lord. By now, I am certain they are all dead," he said sadly. "I, Zalxorr, Warlord Falxyr's only son, have been given his title..."

The king had scarcely time to react to this sad news before a roar of noise from the entrance to the valley attracted his attention. Looking up to see the cause of the commotion, the king made out a group of Varnixye warriors, dragging a prisoner towards him. "We have captured a spy my Lord! On the road to Dessii!" one of them shouted. "He claims he has a message for you from Emperor Celsidas himself!"

The Varnixye warriors dragged the captured messenger before the king. They had bound his hands behind his back and stuffed a leather gag in his mouth to prevent him crying out. "Untie him! And bring him water!" the king ordered. "Let us all hear what Celsidas has to say!"

The messenger gulped down the water thirstily... his mouth was dry not just from thirst, but with fear. He had no doubt what his fate would be once he had delivered his message. *'Well... we all owe the gods a death...'* the messenger thought to himself... *'I might as well die bravely without giving these scum the satisfaction of seeing me grovel in fear.'* The messenger set his shoulders straight and looked King Xanstus in the eye insolently.

"My Master, Emperor Celsidas, sent me out to find you, Lord Xanstus. He thought perhaps you had got lost," he said in a loud jeering voice. He took another long swig of water and then threw away the empty waterskin on the ground. "So my emperor sent me to tell you he is waiting for you on the plains of Gralmeny... He bade me to tell you, that while you are dragging your feet, in your fear of meeting him in battle, he is keeping himself and his armies amused... by raping your women... and killing your old friends!"

As the warriors around him roared their anger and surged towards him, the messenger reached into the leather satchel he had slung over his shoulder and pulled out its grisly contents. The crowd of Varnixye warriors drew back in horror as they saw what he had in his hands... brandishing the severed head of the old warlord above his like a trophy, the messenger snarled his defiance at them... "The emperor sends you this gift, King Xanstus!" he yelled, and flung Warlord Falxyr's head into the crowd.

Without a second thought the king gripped the messenger-boy by the neck, lifting him from the ground. In some narrow corner of his mind, Xanstus knew that the boy was not to blame for Falxyr's death, but the rage that had filled his mind had to go somewhere. "Do you think me a fool, boy?" bellowed the king, his eyes red with rage as the muscles tensed beneath his kenthril plates. "I will not fall into your emperor's trap and forsake the safety of my people! Do you hear me?!" he continued. In his flare of energy he had tightened his grip around the boy's neck so much that the boy now flopped lifeless in his hands.

He threw the young messenger's dead body to the ground and sighed grimly. "Give this one a decent burial. At least he died like a man."

Warlord Zalxorr set his shoulders straight to Xanstus with a seething rage. "Burial?! We should send this one's head on a bloody stick back to his leader!" he roared, unsheathing his sword. On his right-hand side, the king sensed Bulvon instantly reaching for his axe in response to this threat to the king. With his right hand, the king gestured Bulvon to lower his weapon. All the time, Xanstus never lost eye contact with the young man, meeting the young warrior's fierce glare with a look of gentle sorrow.

Xanstus placed a gentle hand on Zalxorr's shoulder before speaking. His tone had dropped to a compassionate whisper, but the words carried through to the warriors around them like soothing water. "Your father was one of my closest friends."

He spoke quietly, as if just to the boy, but his voice carried to all the soldiers encircling them. In the sudden hush, the drawing of weapons ceased.

"Now - do you want to live to help me avenge his death? Or do you simply want to share his fate?" he asked.

*

Night was falling now, and King Xanstus wanted his men well rested for the morning. He made his way to the training circle where he was sure to find Bulvon polishing his combat skills with one of his men. Sure enough, after opening the wooden gate of the small stone wall, there the giant ginger-haired knight centurion stood, swinging a double-handed training axe at one of his royal knights in fierce combat training.

Hesitant to interrupt the champion, Xanstus watched Bulvon for a moment as he effortlessly bested his first opponent and charged with immense speed towards his other.

In a flurry of well-crafted blows, Bulvon had both parried his second royal opponent's many strikes and reduced him to the ground just as quickly as he had the first. "Bulvon!" Xanstus then cheered his interruption, smiling warmly.

Bulvon turned around with haste, raising his training weapon with an eager but sweaty glare that portrayed the madness of war that seethed inside of him. He straightened his back when he regained his senses. "My Lord! It's you!" he clamoured with a cheery voice, lowering the axe to the ground and chuckling, his right hand sitting upon the butt of the weapon.

"It's been a long day, Bulvon. Call the trumpeter to blow the final horn." he instructed.

"Of course!" the blacksmith replied. "I'll take first watch!"

Chapter 2 Part 3 - The Plan Unfolds.

The morning after, Unionite Training Camp, One mile in front of Dessii.

*

A ram's horn sounded loudly from the watchtower on the palisade. The first rays of the morning sun were just starting to appear over the rim of the cliffs that sheltered the secret training camp, and the sky was cloudless. The breeze was gentle, and the soft, cheerful sound of chirping birds filled the air.

Knight Centurion Bulvon, with King Xanstus and Prince Celdon at his side, stood in front of a vast disciplined formation of royal knights. Their polished armour and spear tips glimmered wonderfully in the sun, and Bulvon's chest swelled with pride at the honour his king had shown him by putting his finest troops under his command once again. He cast an approving eye at Sir Ardwyn, who stood in front of his columns of kenthril-plated paladins, ready to move out at a moment's notice. He had never actually seen the Order's paladins in battle, but he could tell by the quality of their weapons and armour, and by their every gesture, that these were formidable warriors. *'I'm glad they are on our side!'* he thought.

The rest of the tribes, still rousing themselves from their slumbers, were gathering into untidy groups around their chieftains, stretching and yawning. *'They are laughing and joking with one another as though they're at the start of a day's hunting!'* Bulvon thought, scowling in disgust at their lack of discipline. In fact, as Bulvon inspected them more closely, it occurred to him that it actually looked more like each of the tribes had shown up to hunt different animals!

Many of the tribesmen from the mountainous forest regions to the north and the east brandished heavy iron wild boar spears, others from the central plains had bundles of throwing spears slung over their backs, and a couple of fishing tribes from along the coastline to the west had actually brought tridents and nets! Bulvon shook his head in disbelief. *'I don't know what the king thinks he can use this lot for!'* he thought grimly, but when he glanced across at Xanstus he saw that the king's face was calm and confident.

Last of all, the Kad'aeri berserkers appeared from their huts. Most of them had heavy two-handed axes slung over their shoulders, But to Bulvon's amazement, many of them were also carrying pickaxes, enormous crowbars, or even shovels, as if they were heading off for a day of work in the mines! Their warlord, Xoddayr, emerged last scratching his bum, and instead of joining Ardwyn and the king's formations, the Kad'aeri mustered themselves around a wide wooden structure near the base of the cliff. Without any command being given, the berserkers methodically dismantled the wooden structure revealing an underground tunnel. "Alright, warriors! This is what we've been training for! Come on!" commanded Xoddayr in a gritty, goat-like voice. He raised his heavy iron war axe into the air to salute his king then led the fur-coated berserkers into the tunnel.

King Xanstus Lordborn waited until the last of Xoddayr's men had disappeared from view, and then he turned to face the rest of his men. "As we speak, Celsidas and his generals are marching down the main road to Dessii, and in a few hours after we leave this valley, they will be in plain sight. Not far from here, the main road is sandwiched between a sheer cliff on one side, and a steep, heavily wooded hillside on the other! That is where we will trap our foe! When we leave this camp, we must return to a strict rule of silence. Your generals know this and understand why. Have faith in your knight centurions and obey their orders, and fight bravely, then we will each share a great victory! Move out!"

Xanstus's trumpeter sounded a broad, low-pitched note. The noise ricocheted against the cliff sides of the valley, keeping the sound contained in what would be the last noise coming from the Unionite force permitted by the king. Immediately, the whole army marched as one through the gates of the training camp, looking the very picture of finely sharpened discipline.

It had taken the king many long years of battle training to teach the men to march in step with one another without the aid of drums, but now that this was possible, it made their advantage of stealth all the better.

Xanstus, Celdon and Bulvon marched leading from the front of their columns of royal knights. High Paladin Ardwyn Keyscarre followed them closely with his paladins, and within an hour Xanstus had led his army within sight of the main road to Dessii. He made a silent gesture with his hand for his army to halt. From this vantage point they could catch a glimpse of the road below them through a clearing in the trees, and on the far side the road followed the contours of a steep cliff.

Among the various sounds of tweeting birds came a gentle whistle from atop one of the trees, and if not for their years of training together, Xanstus would never have noticed the Danz'kanari Warlord Airen's whistle and would instead have mistaken him for yet another chirping bird. He peered around the treetops looking for him, when all of a sudden a rustle of leaves caught his attention, and he realised it was Airen's well-camouflaged arm. Only King Xanstus and his son seemed to notice his gesture, but to them, Airen's hand gesture was unmistakable. *'The path is clear for now, come on.'*

At the king's command, the Danz'kanari tribesmen had quietly moved out of the camp before dawn to make sure they could reach their battle stations completely unseen. Although the king could not see them, he knew that high in the treetops overlooking the road, over two thousand highly trained Danz'kanari hunters were settled in their camouflaged fighting platforms.

Danz'kanari bows were made from horn, wood and sinew rather than the traditional yew wood hunting bows. These were deadly war bows that would pierce through the Aristinian knights' bronze cavalry armour with ease. Xanstus raised his greatsword into the air in mute gesture to move onward. "Garrison the treeline fortifications," he commanded in a whisper, and his order quickly made its way through the army.

Within minutes, the army had spread out along one side of the valley. For about three hundred yards, the valley rose so sharply that it provided a natural barrier. The steep hillside was bare of vegetation, apart from the gigantic elm or ash trees. The ground was strewn with rocks and prone to landslide. On foot a man could only scramble up it on all fours, clinging to the roots of the great trees that soared above. This was where the Danz'kanari tribesmen had built their treetop fighting platforms. Then for a few hundred feet, the valley sloped more gently, and the forest floor between the trees was thickly covered with brambles, ivy, wildflowers and small bushes. Here to their amazement, the king's soldiers found three rows of fortifications that had been prepared.

Ditches wound around the tall trees and followed the natural contours of the hillside. The bottoms of these ditches were filled with sharp wooden staves firmly planted in the soil beside the pathway. The earth from these trench works had been shovelled uphill to form a defensive barrier. In the time that had passed since they had been dug, the mounds of earth had become overgrown with brambles and ivy, hiding them from view of the main road. In fact they were all but invisible, even from close up. Each ditch was about fifty feet above the next one on the hillside. In some places where the ground began to level off, huge trees had been felled to create additional barriers, and behind one of these felled trees, King Xanstus, Bulvon and Prince Celdon had settled, in an ideal position to look straight down the valley towards the cobbled pathway, where it curved to their right.

While they settled in to wait for Aristinia's army to arrive, Bulvon had his face painted green by some of Zalxorr's Varnixye warriors, and with his leather tunic and wolfskin leggings, Bulvon now had more the appearance of a berserker than a knight centurion. His outfit allowed him to stand tall above the rest of the plated army. They had been ordered to remain behind cover, lest the light gleaming off their polished armour reveal them to the approaching army.

After the face-paint had been applied, slow movements from the clifftops overlooking the road in front of him caught his attention. To his amazement, it was the Kad'aeri, and Warlord Xoddayr made a silent gesture to the king to signal that the enemy had been sighted.

Bulvon looked at Xanstus and smiled, while the king received the warlord's gesture and waved his acknowledgment silently.

A sudden snapping of a twig behind the king caught his attention. The king turned around with lightning speed and readied a dagger instinctively. A young boy appeared from the woods. He was sweating profusely and panting. He looked at King Xanstus. "They're coming, my Lord... the emperor's army!" said the boy. "They'll be here in just a few minutes. The Watcher on the mountainside told me to be sure to tell you that Celsidas is marching at the front, with what looks to be the most of his personal Knightly Order, and a further host of three times as much regular cavalry, followed by three small columns of swordsmen, spearmen, and archers."

Xanstus sheathed his dagger and glared at the boy with eyes like razor blades. "My word!" he hissed. "When you go back to the cliffs, do be more quiet! You'll blow our cover thumping your feet like that!" Xanstus turned around again, peering over the fortified treeline rampart in an attempt to catch Warlord Airen's signal... he saw none for now, so he looked back to the messenger-boy. "Go back now. Tell The Watcher and his scouts to do absolutely nothing until you hear my signal, am I clear?"

The boy nodded his response and shuddered to think what his punishment would be if he blew the cover of the king's own army and consequently cost him the battle. "Yes, my liege.... at once," he murmured, his voice so inaudibly small and silent that Xanstus doubted that even his son, right behind him, would be able to hear his words at all.

The king smiled as the boy crept back off into the woods with as much speed he could manage while still being silent, and then upon returning to his hiding spot behind the fallen log, Xanstus peered over the fortifications waiting for Warlord Airen's signal.

Minutes passed them by, and the suspense was building, but when Xanstus stood up to see what was happening, he caught a glimpse of Airen's stern glare telling him that the emperor was approaching.

He tapped Celdon's arm, gesturing him to be silent and pass on the gesture. The army was already silent, but a gesture like this could only mean one thing. *'Breath gently now. If I even hear someone break wind, there will be trouble!'*

In fact, had Xanstus been stood up for even three more seconds, he would have single-handedly blown his own cover. In the valley below him the first column of the emperor's army came into sight, and the emperor's drumbeats were beginning to sound louder with each passing second.

"I don't believe it... they're really coming this way..." mumbled the prince to his father, who shot him a sharp glance as soon as the words left his mouth. "Yes...what a coincidence," Xanstus whispered with sarcastic urgency. "Be quiet now, will you? Complete silence!" he added.

The emperor's forces were growing closer. The king's men could just make out the Aristinian noblemens' pompous voices as they laughed with careless confidence. Their finely made bronze plate armour mirrored the green shimmer of the woods from the blinding sun above them.

Drums were pounding in the distance, now-- methodical and menacing, and trumpets followed them in a musical rhythm. Brown banners waved with flowing elegance in the gentle wind by either side of the emperor's cavalry, and in the middle of the banners was the rough depiction of a raging bull, coloured in a vibrant yellow.

Time seemed to slow. Seconds felt like minutes and minutes felt like hours, but within those minutes, Warlord Airen of the Danz'kanari could just make out the figure of the emperor himself at the head of a huge column of cavalry. Their armour gleamed in the sunlight and they looked invincible.

As the archers in the trees waited impatiently for the signal to attack, the minutes seemed to stretch into further hours. The emperor continued on along the road until he was out of Airen's sight, and Airen let out a sigh of frustration. All of the elite troops had gone past. The troops marching below him now were far less armoured than the other horsemen, and many were even dressed in leather. Airen began to wonder if the king had missed his moment...

For the king's troops who were hidden behind the treeline fortifications slightly further on, the suspense was becoming unbearable. Hardly daring to breath, they crouched behind their barricades seeing glimpses through the trees of the huge army coming towards them. They waited for the king's signal. The lead horsemen were so close now that the voices of the riders carried quite clearly to them, on the still morning air.

"My Lord, the forest is too silent, there is no birdsong. I fear an ambush!" the booming voice of Kalsos, the Imperial Guardian of Celsidas, carried clearly over the background sounds of horses' hooves, the jingling of harnesses and the steady pounding drumbeats.

Emperor Celsidas rolled his eyes, growing tired of the conversation. "For the mercy of *Duella*, Kalsos! First you annoy me with your paranoia of being attacked by bowmen, and now you are complaining about the silence? You're heading the right way for replacement, old man! Be silent!"

Kalsos felt a growing sense of resignation wash over him as a thought crossed his mind. *'One day, even if it is not today, the emperor will see the error of his ways...'*

Upon hearing the emperor's conversation, King Xanstus glanced at Bulvon, grinning like a snake. *'I'll make the emperor wish he hadn't said that...'* he thought, and Bulvon smiled back, sharing the joke.

At the treeline, Bulvon suddenly arose from the ground and pulled a long white ram's horn from his leather belt, blowing on it with a tremendous gasp of air from within his lungs.

"It's an ambush, my Emperor!" bellowed Kalsos, drawing his long silvery sabre from its sheath as their horses whinnied in shock.

"I won't let some small tribesmen deal blows to my grand army, Imperial Guardian! Knights of Aristinia, lances at the ready!" Celsidas roared. Cries of alarm and confusion came from the rear of the emperor's army, where the Danz'kanari archers were now shooting volley after volley of arrows into the tightly packed formations of foot-soldiers and light cavalry. The emperor twisted round in his saddle to try and see what was causing the commotion behind him. As his sharp eyes rapidly scanned the landscape, he spied a group of shaggy haired men, dressed in animal furs, high above on the clifftop overlooking the rear of his army. As the emperor watched them, he saw the tribesmen were in the process of levering two enormous boulders over the edge of the cliff top. He looked on with horror as the boulders rolled down the mountainside triggering an avalanche which crashed into the supply wagons and crushed the life from their drivers. The road behind was now almost completely blocked!

Kalsos, his Imperial Guardian, had taken in the situation at a glance. "We need to get out of here, Your Majesty!" he yelled.

"Now!" bellowed King Xanstus to a unit of Kad'aeri berserkers on the left side of the valley, who upon hearing the command immediately pulled a rope from three pre-chopped trees which then fell in plain sight of the emperor's formations, blocking their path to Dessii.

'I don't believe it, Kalsos was right all along! It's the king's army!' thought Emperor Celsidas of Aristinia.

"Infantry, climb those bloody trees!" Celsidas commanded. *'No matter, I'll deal with the king myself!'* he thought further. "Knights of Aristinia, charge!" he commanded.

As the Knightly Order's warhorses thundered forward, they attempted to create the same compact formations which on flat terrain had earned them their ferocious reputation in previous battles, but as they reached the first trench, the leading horses and riders collapsed into bramble-covered pits, filled with long, camouflaged wooden spikes.

The cavalry charge thundered on. Rather than halting, the Aristinian knights were blinded in the heat of the rush and simply galloped forward into the death pits. By the time some of the heavy cavalry finally managed to struggle over the ramparts, the trenches were filled with the bodies of dead and wounded men and horses. A mix of spearmen and boar hunters manned the first line of defence, and the boar hunters had set the butts of their spears in the ground, so when the thundering cavalry came over the defensive ramparts many were impaled by heavy boar-spears and forcibly halted at the crosspiece. This greatly slowed down the charge as they now had to carefully manoeuvre around the gaps formed by their own slain horses. Many of them dismounted and tried to face the king's men on foot.

Standing in the third line of defences, the king readied his greatsword as the Aristinian Knightly Order fought their way past the first trench. As soon as the first line of defences was breached, the King's crack infantry troops, clearly identifiable as royal knights by their red tabards, turned and ran. They made no attempt to stand and fight. Instead, following the king's orders given before the battle, they fled for the protection of the second barrier. “Look at the cowards!” gloated Emperor Celsidas. “They run like rabbits!” Just as the king had hoped, the Aristinian cavalry charged straight after them up the steep slope and was soon hopelessly entangled in the second line of defences.

Xanstus realised this was the precise moment to strike. “Charge their flanks!” he commanded with a deafening roar, knowing he had them encircled. The emperor's cavalry at the head of the formation were scattered across the wide dirt pathway in complete disarray, and many of them lay slain by the hail of iron-tipped arrows. Some of his cavalry who had had the sense to dismount from their horses had managed to scramble over the defensive ramparts and were fighting hand-to-hand with Warlord Xoddayr's Kad'aeri berserkers, as well as spearmen and boar hunters from other tribes. Even fewer of the Aristinian knights still remained on horseback, but the ones who were, remained by the side of Celsidas and the imperial guardian.

To the king's immense satisfaction, the Order of Tiius chose this moment to join the battle. Leaping from the deepest corners of the woods, their war-hammers pierced the Aristinian knights' armour with gruesome efficiency whilst their battle-priests rained holy fire upon them from the skies.

The emperor stared around wildly at the chaos of battle. Temporarily he had no idea what to do. "This is madness, Emperor! We have to get around the trenches or the king will rout our main army!" shouted Kalsos urgently.

"Cavaliers, take the flanks!" commanded Celsidas. Six quick, short brass trumpet notes echoed across the battlefield, and two squadrons of regular cavaliers charged away into the forests at either side of the clearing, meeting no resistance. Suddenly however, two huge nets more than 10 feet high and hundreds of feet long, rose up from the forest floor of tall grass and fallen oak leaves. The two columns of cavaliers galloping at full speed had not the slightest chance of avoiding the utterly unexpected obstacle. Cheering wildly, the tribesmen heaved on the long nets pulling them tight. The cavalry were caught like a shoal of herring!

As the emperor looked on in horrified disbelief, a shower of javelins and harpoons rained down upon them from the trees, sealing their fate in blood. In a matter of minutes, two squadrons of cavalry had been butchered effortlessly by tribesmen!

By now, those of the emperor's Knightly Order who had had the presence of mind to dismount, had managed by sheer weight of numbers to fight past the second line of defences, leaving the death pits filled with the trampled corpses of their comrades and fallen horses. Although by now the Aristinian Knightly Order was greatly weakened, they still outnumbered Bulvon, Celdon and the king's royal knights, but not by much, and their morale was quickly fading. As the tiring, heavily armoured knights slithered and scrambled over the third and final line of defensive earthworks, they faced the elite of the Kings' Union's troops.

"Come on then you bastards!" clamoured Bulvon, now surrounded by the emperor's dismounted knights, swinging his heavy iron battleaxe with the ferocity of a grizzly bear as he chopped through the heavy plate armour of one of the men surrounding him.

Xanstus and Celdon now fought side-by side with one another. "I see what you mean about Bulvon, Father! I can finally fully believe the tales of his exploits!" said Celdon, parrying the silvery steel blade of a knight's sabre and lunging forward with his longsword, which pierced cleanly through the bronze plate.

"Now is hardly the time for chit-chat my son!" the king panted. "Hold your ground, men! They're breaking!" commanded Xanstus.

To the rear of the emperor's army, a trumpeter sounded two low indistinct notes. The foot-soldiers at the back of Celsidas's army chose to interpret this as an order and began scurrying back towards the boulders blocking the road below. Atop the hills on either side of the valley, Xanstus's second force of archers nocked their arrows, firing mercilessly at them as they fled.

"Come back you cowards! I didn't order this retreat!" roared Emperor Celsidas, beside himself with fury. His men seemed unresponsive to his commands for once. Desperately, they ran towards the boulders blocking the road and attempted to climb them, although most of the Aristinian Knightly Order still fought on, sacrificing themselves in the heat of the battle, while the riderless horses, spooked by the carnage around them, fled the scene and darted off into the woods.

"Emperor!" called Imperial Guardian Kalsos urgently. Celsidas ignored him at first. Beside himself with fury, Celsidas was hurling curses and threats at his rapidly retreating infantry.

"Come back you cowards! One more step away from me and I'll have you all flayed alive!" the emperor screamed. Kalsos yelled at him again and grabbed him by the arm. "Emperor!"

"Yes! What do you want now?!" Celsidas shouted.

"The battle is lost, my Imperial Lord!" Another volley of arrows whistled from the trees and showered the pathway once more, piercing through even some of the emperor's personal bodyguards' armour and toppling them to the ground.

"Order the retreat, we must wait for them on the open plains!" Kalsos entreated.

All at once the fury in the emperor’s face seemed to drain away. As the reality of the situation finally hit him, the emperor’s shoulders slumped in defeat. "I'll order the retreat. See to it that I am escorted to safety!" Celsidas raised his blade into the air and gestured behind him. The trumpeter blew a long-sustained note which echoed across the battlefield.

Immediately, many Aristinian knights turned to the sound in realisation and fled towards the boulders to escort their emperor away. Bulvon cheered. "Hahaa! We've got them now, sire!" He raised his battle-axe and leaped over the fortifications with a single bound. "Charge! Hunt them down, men!" he roared with enormous enthusiasm.

"No! We must stick to the plan! you fool!" yelled Xanstus, but it was too late. Warlord Zalxorr and the rest of the young Varnixye warriors were already pouring over the side of the defences mad with the desire for vengeance. Bulvon's two-hundred strong battalion of royal knights followed only a moment later, despite the king's furious commands for them to hold their position. The men idolised the giant Bulvon. There was no way they would leave him to fight alone. Running in tight battle formation they crashed into the backs of the fleeing Aristinian troops, cutting them down as they attempted to run.

"He's right, Father! Come on, they're fleeing!" called Celdon, who followed the same action as Bulvon. "No!" roared Xanstus. He knew at this stage that all he had to do was stay behind the defences. The archers in the trees could slaughter the emperor's fleeing men at their leisure and the battle would be his! Now these hot-headed young fools were ruining his plans!

He shook his head in disgust. Then casting aside all of his remaining hesitation, he roared the command to charge. The remaining Unionite forces poured over the ramparts eagerly. Cheering and roaring their battle cries, they ran through the woods and then all clashed with the emperor and his fleeing army.

Xanstus was now berserk with rage. He could not catch up to Bulvon or Celdon, but one thing was for sure, all enemies in front of him now fell before his greatsword as he whirled it through the air, cleaving through both bronze and flesh.

In the king's red mist of battle-fury, desperately trying to reach his son, he had temporarily lost all sense of reason and strategy. Still way behind Bulvon and his son, he had allowed himself to become dangerously isolated far ahead of his own troops.

Celsidas felt his heart leap with a sudden surge of hope when he caught sight of Xanstus. There was an element of dread too, for in his sheer ferocity the king was cutting down men like a farmer's scythe to tall grass, but the emperor knew that the king couldn't last long on these fields to where he had now advanced. *'The sentimental fool!'* he thought, contemptuously. *'He has abandoned his own tactical strength just to save a few men!'*

"On me men!" the emperor roared. "Charge!" As one man, the emperor's personal bodyguards wheeled around to follow him. His mind was racing with an eagerness to at last salvage some dignity from the jaws of this defeat. Even if he wasn't going to win this battle, his twenty household bodyguards could at least take the king down with them.

The king's troops were now running with all their might to protect the king but none of Xanstus's men had horses now, and Celsidas and his bodyguards were galloping towards him at tragic speed. Bulvon and the king's heir looked on in horror, realising they could not hope to intercept the emperor in time.

When Xanstus saw Celsidas and his elite bodyguards thundering towards him, it was too late. Their twenty lances were tipped towards him, and now that his greatsword had clove through the remaining troops that fled, he was in the emperor's direct line of sight.

Menacing laughter echoed fiercely as the emperor's lance collided with the king's helmet. Piercing through the gaps in his visor, the lance blow struck the king with such a ferocity that the weapon itself splintered, a shard of the metal making its dreadful path from the king's right eye to his chin. The impact of the emperor's charger flung the king to the ground as nineteen more stallions galloped ferociously over his kenthril-plated body. Then the men around Celsidas roared with triumph. They were sure that victory was theirs.

The emperor suddenly came to his senses as the king's troops surged around him. The emperor's bodyguards formed a defensive square around him and galloped into a hasty retreat. By the time they had escaped the furious arms of the Unionites, all that remained of his twenty household knights were himself and the imperial guardian, the rest had been ripped from their horses and torn limb from limb in a savage frenzy.

Celsidas and what was left of his army now fled in complete disarray to escape the fury of the king's soldiers. Neither the emperor or his bodyguards reined in their horses until they had put several miles between them and the battlefield. Whilst the emperor and his cavalry waited for the rest of his army to regroup, he took time to evaluate his situation. The battle was now truly concluded, but even if they had managed to kill the king, their campaign would surely have to wait now that the supplies and wagons had been crushed beneath impossible amounts of ancient stone.

Not only this, but many of his soldiers, the emperor noticed, were no longer on horseback. Many of his troops limped in on foot. Some had even discarded their armour and weapons to decrease the weight they were carrying, in their desperation to escape the battlefield. Their battle fatigue was visible as they panted heavily, sweating through their cloth garments. This army would not be taking to the field again this year.

*

Bulvon and Prince Celdon gathered their troops around the king's fallen body.

The pungent scent of death filled the air as they tripped over mounds of dead and wounded men. The Danz'kanari made their way from the treetops to mourn the losses of war... so many families had lost loved ones this day.

"Is he dead?" Celdon murmured. He could barely contain his emotions as the Order of Tiius's battle-priests carried the king's body away into the distance. He sobbed fearfully, even after telling himself that he would have to be strong if King Xanstus, his own proud father, was truly dead...

"I hope not," sighed Bulvon, who with a large heart, swelling with the painful thought of losing his closest friend, was in floods of tears, even despite his physical strength. "At least if there's any chance of him getting better, he's in very capable hands..." though he said this to himself, more than saying it to Prince Celdon - a form of gentle reassurance, you could say. At this, the battle was over.

Chapter 3 Part 1 - The Broken Figure.

Earlier that day, Castle Lordborn, City of Pla-Kingus.

*

A bright summer sun shone through the glass panes onto the stone walls of Castle Lordborn, casting gentle rays of morning light onto the bright red banners at either side of the fireplace.

Prince Panthalassa Lordborn, who had recently eaten a lavish morning feast, was playing soldiers by the fire as his mother, Queen Dranah, watched him somewhat irritably from the other end of the room. She was sat next to her husband's chair, which was, given the circumstances, empty.

"Prepare our prisoners for their doom, you idiots!" shouted Panthalassa, eagerly impersonating Emperor Celsidas as best as he could with his miniature ivory knight figures. He was playing out a battle scene from his mind, of which many followed these recurring themes: his father's and his brother's assured easy victories, the emperor's ever-failing evil schemes, and last but not least, the emperor's ultimately cowardly motives.

Although his play-battles were far removed from the bitter realities of warfare, to his young mind they were as good as the real thing, and often he would play out scenes like this as a sort of daily ritual, to mitigate the very real fear he felt for his close family.

Panthalassa selected his father's and brother's figures and moved them to the top of a hill, which in this case was represented by a hand-sized pine log, which was cut in half. "There they are Father! Let us fight them!" said Prince Celdon, his older brother.

"Yes!" replied King Xanstus, his father. "Charge!" he ordered. But Panthalassa didn't want him to charge just yet, the emperor and his evil soldiers had to make clear their plans first!

"No!" replied Celsidas. "You have come too soon!" The boy moved the emperor's figure towards one of his soldiers. "Take the prisoners and throw them into the river!" he commanded.

"Yes, my Lord!" replied the soldier, running across the carpet towards the flimsy wooden boxes, which in this case, were supposed to represent prisons, and Panthalassa moved the boxes off from the carpet onto the solid wooden floor, which in this scenario, of course, was the river.

Then, signalling a change in terrain, Panthalassa pulled the half pine log from underneath his father's and brother's figures, and threw it into the fire, which mentally he did to show that his father had led the army away from the hill.

Panthalassa grasped his brother's figure and moved it to the front of the army. "You will pay for your crimes, Emperor!" he roared, showing how he saw his brother; someone who fought for the right side, someone who could stop any injustice at the snap of his finger!

He moved his father's figure forward. "Charge!"

Panthalassa fully extended his arm across the carpet, putting it behind his family's representing army, and with one lazy, yet swift movement, brushed the entire force forward towards the emperor and his men.

This was usually the most expensive part of his battles. Over the past week, countless ivory figures had been replaced because of this pinnacle moment, and as he brought his large heap of soldiers towards the centre of the carpet, his mother suddenly put down her cutlery.

Earlier that morning, she had watched as the *Royal Life-Weavers* soothed the plants and flowers in the castle gardens, caressing them with a gentle flow of *Duellan Magic* after the servants had finished watering them. Usually, the presence of this green magic would encourage a heightened sense of optimism in her throughout the day, yet this time she felt worried, for unlike the other times, today the magical soothing had no effect on her whatsoever.

Panthalassa went on battling with his ivory figures, mimicking the sounds of sword fighting and death with a naive innocence that belied the true horrors of war, when at the last moment, noticing a breakage on one of his figures, he stopped the battle short.

“I thought that figure would never break...” he sighed, his shoulders slumping as he held the figure in his hands. “I've put this one at the front of the army in every single battle! Why did he have to break now?”

The queen threw a glance of fear through the window. Her chest heaved with a dark suspicion that her husband was in danger... “Which one broke?” she asked.

"Father..." her son replied. As he turned around, Panthalassa saw her expression. Still holding the broken figure in his hands, he made his small, humble approach towards her, with his elbows packed tensely at his sides...

"I'm sorry," he murmured. "I didn't mean to break it!"

His mother took a deep breath and tried to compose herself. *'He mustn't know how I feel...'* she thought. *'At least I'm glad he's misunderstood my expression as anger...'*

"That's fine, I suppose," the queen replied to her youngest son. "I just wish you'd stop being so careless with your figures."

Chapter 3 Part 2 – Troubling Revelations.

Castle Lordborn, one week later.

*

The wind rattled the glass panes in the queen's bedroom. Her silk blinds were swaying gently from the impact, and the room was lit up only by the faint light of the moon.

The queen lay sleeping in her bed, even in slumber looking the very image of decency and womanhood.

All of a sudden however, a slow triple knock on her door shook her awake, and she lit a candle beside her bed to illuminate the darkness. "Who is it?" she groaned, her voice drowsy with sleep...

"Marcus, your Highness," the messenger's voice echoed. "There's a paladin who has come to see you. He says it's about the King!"

Queen Dranah widened her eyes in alarm and whispered a short prayer to Tiius.

"Fetch me water!" she demanded. "Tell the paladin I will see him after I am dressed."

"Yes, my Queen," Marcus replied.

Moments later there was another knock at her door. It was more gentle this time, and as she recognised the knock instinctively, she allowed entry.

Two servant girls hurriedly entered the room and helped the queen don her regal silken dress, which was alive with vibrant shades of purple and gold. She brushed her teeth with rough cloth and salt, then rinsed her mouth with cold water, and after having her long blonde hair combed into a grand shine, she put on her crown and made her way downstairs to meet her holy guest.

Sir Ardwyn Keyscarre was stood to attention in the almost empty throne room.

Accompanied only by the four royal knights who were standing guard over the double throne on the elevated stone platform, the *High Paladin* was dressed in his finest suit of armour.

His kenthril plates had been polished to a fine gleam, and they reflected the sunlight beaming down from the windows like a diamond trapped above a candle. His arm rested naturally on the hilt of his sword, and in the other arm he carried his helmet, and when the queen caught his eyes, she noticed a certain sadness trapped inside them.

She feared the worst.

"High Paladin Ardwyn Keyscarre," she greeted him with a controlled tone.

"Your Highness," Ardwyn replied, acknowledging her presence with a bow. "May I have a moment of your time in privacy?" he entreated with a solemn expression.

At the high paladin's request for more privacy, the queen's face turned a deathly pale. Struggling to maintain her composure, she knew that something serious had happened. "You may, Ardwyn," came her reply. She dismissed the castle guards with a brief gesture. “So, what is your message?" she inquired.

At this question, Sir Ardwyn told the queen of her husband's heroic victory over the emperor, but leaving the worst till last, he drew a deep breath...

"The king was charged down by the emperor's own men, your Highness," Ardwyn admitted.

A small gasp of dismay escaped from the queen's lips, but she listened bravely to the rest of Ardwyn's message, until he finally fell silent.

"I shall have to send Panthalassa away for the summer,” she finally said, and her voice sounded unnaturally calm. “He could not be expected to keep a secret of this magnitude from the other boys.”

Ardwyn agreed.

It was at this point that the queen noticed how travel weary Sir Ardwyn was. “Thank you for delivering this message to me,” she said gently. “I have had the servants prepare a room and some refreshments for you. Please get some rest.”

Chapter 3 Part 3 - New Experiences.

The Following Morning

*

It was mid-morning. James Ashenworn, his instructor, had come to collect Panthalassa for his daily training. He had got into the habit of meeting him in the castle and walking to the training grounds by his side.

As Panthalassa made his way through the oaken doors, he walked sluggishly towards the drawbridge, and James could tell that he wasn't feeling up to the task.

James however, had some news to tell him, and made his way towards the young prince with a twinkle of joy in his eyes.

With a firm pat on Panthalassa's shoulder, James made his announcement. "I've decided that from now on, we will no longer be training in the royal sparring grounds," he said.

Panthalassa's expressions grew even more dissatisfied. He pulled his shoulder back to avert James's grip and sighed quietly. "You think I'm scared, don't you?" he asked. "Do you have any idea how angry my father would be?"

James chuckled light-heartedly. "Your father won't be angry at all, Panthalassa. He and Celdon have seen me train countless warriors before you. And remember, courage does not lie in never being afraid, but in knowing how to control your fears."

"So. Where will we train now then?" Panthalassa inquired.

"On my farm!" James replied. "My son is both your size, and your age. He will make an ideal sparring partner for you. I think you will get on much easier with one another in your training sessions and will have much less distractions too!" he stated. "I have spoken with your mother. She has agreed to let you spend the rest of summer training at my farm, so you have no need to worry."

As the young prince started to realise that James was being serious, a delighted grin spread across his face. “You really mean it? My mother has said that I can go?” Panthalassa asked.

James nodded. “She has. In fact we're leaving today!” he replied. “And since I have no stables at my place, we'll be going there on foot. You'd better wear some stout boots.”

After rushing back to his room, Panthalassa quickly changed into some clothes more suitable for travelling. He threw a few of the things he thought he might need into a rucksack and declared himself ready. “I must say goodbye to my mother!” he exclaimed.

He found the queen in her private chambers, deep in conversation with Sir Ardwyn. He thought she looked tired and distressed. '*She must be sad at the thought of losing me for the summer...*' he thought.

When the queen saw him, she broke off her conversation and rushed to give Panthalassa a huge hug. “I will miss you, but it's for the best.” she sighed. “I will see you back here for the Harvest Festival. I am sure you will have a lovely summer.”

*

As the day wore on, they reached the outskirts of the capital. The prince had never visited such a dilapidated part of the city before. Some of the houses seemed to have been abandoned, in fact some of them were so old that they looked as if they hadn't been changed since the ancient times. Many of them even had letters carved into their walls, in an ancient dialect so long dead that the words had become meaningless.

The forest was slowly reclaiming the city here. Most of the roofs on the houses had completely fallen in, and some of the houses even had trees soaring high into the sky, growing straight through the gaping holes in the buildings that had once been their ceilings.

About five miles out of the city, they left the main road leading to the neighbouring town of Aerinven. From this point on, they were following rough tracks that seemed to lead ever upwards. “How much further?” gasped Panthalassa, his legs sore from the day's exertions. His voice was hoarse with fatigue, and his feet weighed him down like lead.

“Not long now Panth. We'll be able to see the farm from the top of this hill,” he added. Panthalassa heaved a sigh of relief.

At the summit of the hill, a spectacular view stretched before them. An endless expanse of farmland, forests and lakes. “You see that river down there, shaped like a snake?” James asked, pointing his finger at a small ribbon of blue, barely visible in the distance. “There's my farm!” he chuckled. Panthalassa shot him an evil look, which only made James laugh harder. “Remember, a soldier has to get used to marching!” James chided.

It was near dusk when James opened the wooden gate at the end of a dirt pathway, announcing that they had arrived. Atop a branch high in a distant tree, an owl hooted ominously, gazing with wise eyes at the pair.

The young prince looked around curiously. "Where will I sleep then?" he asked, ignoring the roundhouse in front of him, which he had wrongly assumed to be a cowshed. "I can't see anywhere to sleep, please say we're almost there!"

James raised an eyebrow at the prince's statement. "Can't see anywhere to sleep?" he asked in a puzzled tone. "But my home is right in front of you!"

"You sleep in there?!" the prince asked, the pitch of his voice raised to imply a certain element of shock.

"Aye, lad. I do," James replied." I'm glad I've had the chance to show you this while you're still young," he added. "Many aristocrats and noblemen like yourself grow old never realising the privilege they truly enjoy."

It was at this point that James's son suddenly materialised, appearing as if by magic out of the corn field in front of Panthalassa. The prince leaped backwards in fear when he saw the boy, for in his hand he carried a six-foot-long iron scythe, which to Panthalassa's mind, untrained in the ways of agriculture, looked indistinguishable from a weapon of war.

Clutching his chest with laughter at Panthalassa's reaction, James patted the prince on the back with a firm hand. "Don't worry, this is Foxeny, my son! He has not come to kill you with his farming scythe!"

Foxeny laughed along with his father's joke.

"A scythe?" the prince asked to cover his embarrassment. “What is it used for?"

"Harvesting crops, like corn!" James replied. "And you will be shown how to use one in the morning!"

"Aren't we supposed to be training?" Panthalassa went on, furrowing his brow into a puzzled expression.

"Yes, and train we will," James replied cryptically.

“So,” said James's son, folding his arms over the pole of his scythe to rest his tired muscles. “I assume you're the king's son?” he asked.

Panthalassa smiled at the boy, who had finally attempted to greet him. “I am... I assume you'll know my name?”

Foxeny nodded. “I do,” he replied. “I'm pleased to meet you."

Looking at the two, James was struck by the resemblance to one another the two boys had. Both of them had the same shade of blonde hair. They were of almost equal size, and although their facial features were completely different, he observed that from a distance, if not for their clothes, he would scarcely be able to tell the two apart from each other.

After shaking hands, James ushered the two boys inside the roundhouse to end their day with a warm meal. Foxeny balanced his scythe against the door frame, while Panthalassa, who was used to the more decorative walls of his great stone castle, eyed the compacted dirt walls of the roundhouse with silent distaste.

With a fire crackling in the hearth, the little house seemed at least slightly better than Panthalassa had originally feared. Raindrops from a brief summer shower pattered soothingly on the thatched roof, and as Panthalassa rested his head on the unfamiliar and scratchy sheep's wool bed, within seconds he was fast asleep.

Chapter 3 Part 4 - Finding Nature.

The Next Morning.

*

The sound of a rooster crowing loudly shook Panthalassa awake, and instinctively, he shot forward into a sitting position. In the process however, he bumped his head against a wooden beam, and for a moment, looked around in complete bewilderment at his unfamiliar surroundings.

The events of the previous day suddenly came flooding back to him.

He had spent the night sleeping on a raised platform above the main room of the roundhouse, and next to his sheepskin mattress, there were two other mattresses, but of the companions who had shared the night with him, there was no sign. 'Where have those two gone?' he wondered. 'Surely they can't be working already!'

Now that the sun was rising, he could hear the birds tweeting eagerly in their nests. On the fields around James's house, mother birds plucked worms or slugs from the rain-soaked soil, bringing them back to their chicks. Panthalassa took a moment to absorb this comforting sound.

With the bright morning sunlight streaming into the roundhouse through little windows, and through the open door, he could see the room clearly for the first time. It had a well-built wood stove that also served as an oven, and around the walls, he saw gleaming copper pans and kettles, earthenware pottery, and drying herbs, hung in aromatic bunches. It was, in fact, very clean and homely - even cosy looking!

After he had finished inspecting his surroundings, Panthalassa eventually decided that this place was nowhere near as bad as the gloomy first impressions he had gathered from the night before.

As he lay on his side, he yawned sleepily, eyeing the white ashes at the foot of the wood stove, which had been a roaring fire just the night before. *'I dread to think how I'll cope with the training session today,'* he thought, for although he had slept well, his muscles were still aching.

No sooner had he had that thought when James appeared in the doorway, his slim body silhouetted in the sunlight. “Rise and shine, Panth!” he called cheerfully. “We've got work to do!” Before Panthalassa had time to reply, James had disappeared from sight.

The young prince reluctantly emerged, blinking his eyes against the brilliant morning sun. Foxeny appeared and grabbed the scythe he had balanced against the door frame the night before, and then he set off purposely towards an outbuilding. Panthalassa stumbled after him, still half asleep.

James creaked open the old wooden door. “Ignore the cobwebs in the corner of the room if you can,” James urged. “You should find everything you need in here.”

Panthalassa peered around the dark room curiously. “I don't see any swords or shields,” he mumbled.

“You're not training with weapons today, Panthalassa,” James replied. “The way I train my students differs from the traditional methods. For now, your focus should be on developing your muscles and learning to live off the land.”

Panthalassa grabbed one of the scythes balanced against the old stone wall, visibly confused. “So you are suggesting that I'll learn how to fight a war by... farming?”

James smiled at Panthalassa's curiosity and held the door open for him, leaving the shed. “Yes,” he replied simply. He led him towards a barn. “But first, we have a cow to milk.”

James came into the barn and squatted on a tiny three-legged stool, next to a fierce looking brown cow. Panth watched in horrified fascination as James's strong hands squeezed the cow's udders, squirting milk into a wooden pail. He had never actually seen a cow being milked before, and he thought the whole business seemed very unhygienic.

James dipped a beaker in the pail and drank thirstily. He finally lowered the empty mug, then grinned, showing a white milk moustache round his lips. “You can't beat the taste of fresh milk, can you?” he chuckled, offering Panthalassa a fresh mug.

Panthalassa took it reluctantly, not wanting to appear impolite, and eventually forced himself to swallow some. To his surprise, however, it actually tasted very warm and sweet! Within a few seconds, he had drained the mug dry. “That was delicious!” he said.

“Hah! It's your first time I see!” James smiled. “Now then lads, let's get cracking. That meadow isn't going to mow itself!”

Foxeny got straight to work. Panthalassa watched with awe as he effortlessly swung the iron scythe from right to left, cutting a huge crescent of tall grass with each swing. "You see my son, Panthalassa?" James asked, beaming a smile of pride warmer than the summer heat itself. "He is only ten years old. The same age as you in fact, and I have already taught him how to feed himself from these fields, and these woods and streams," he said. "One day, Foxeny will likely be drafted into the army, to fight in another of your father's wars, but when *he* goes, *he* will survive, and not merely because he knows how to fight with sword and shield, but because he knows how to forage. This, Panthalassa, is one of the most valuable skills you will learn here."

"But James, I'm a prince!" Panthalassa said. "I can just get other people to forage *for me!*"

"You could, yes," James agreed. "But a good leader should have full knowledge of all the workings of his men, before he gives them orders."

James looked back towards his son, his smile returning. "And the best leaders of all, Panthalassa, do not merely order their men, but work by their side."

Patting Panthalassa on the back, James thrust him forward to work next to his son. "Now, young Prince," he said. "The first true training session begins!" With that, he grabbed a straw hat from the oaken table beside the tool shed and leaned against the wall, seeming the very picture of hypocrisy.

Panthalassa shot James an uneven look, his jagged brow hinting confusion. "So you're not going to help us?" he asked.

James met Panthalassa's eyes with an eager grin. "Before you command, Prince Panthalassa, you must learn to obey," he answered, folding his arms and legs to enjoy the full heat of the summer sun. "I've served my time under the king's banner. Now you must serve your time under mine."

*

After four hours of hard work, Panthalassa was hot, sweaty and thirsty. He was more tired than he had ever been in his young life, but Foxeny, working beside him, seemed to be totally relaxed. He had hardly even broken a sweat! The prince wondered what his secret was.

Pausing for a moment to catch his breath, Panthalassa wandered over to the nearby cornfield. *'I'll have to ask him about his technique later on!'* he thought.

Grabbing one of the sweet baby corn cobs to munch on, he noticed a caterpillar on one of the smaller cobs beside him and eyed it with a silent fascination.

In the back of his mind, Panthalassa secretly envied the smaller life forms like the caterpillar. How much more simple life must be for them, never having to worry about training or warfare, flitting from one meal to the next with no regard to human politics.

After eating the corn cob, he got back to work.

The boys laboured in the field as the sun rose higher, and it was getting even hotter. All morning as they worked their way across the seemingly endless meadow, Panth kept catching glimpses of James, out of the corner of his eye. He sat in the shade weaving something or other and occasionally pausing to smoke his pipe, or to take a sip of a cool drink. Finally, at noon, he called the boys over for a rest. “Drink some of this, boys.” he said, offering them a big jug.

“What is it?” asked Panthalassa, eyeing the murky, cloudy looking liquid suspiciously.

“Homemade ginger beer!” James replied. “Too much cold water on a hot day like this can give a working man a bad stomach-ache. The ginger warms the stomach,” he continued. He waited until the boys had finished their mugs. “Why don't you both go fishing for a while? It looks like you could do with cooling off.”

After a brief walk, they were soon swimming in the river. The cool water felt so good after the morning work. Foxeny showed Panthalassa how to creep upstream into the shallow water and find fat trout sheltering behind rocks in the stream, scooping them up with his bare hands. Within a short time, Foxeny had half a dozen fish, which were wriggling in one of the willow baskets James had weaved that morning. “Bah! I can't seem to catch any!” Panthalassa sighed, resolving to try again.

“You just need more practice,” Foxeny replied, quietly. “Try making less noise!”

After a few more minutes, James took off his shirt and joined them. As he was getting in the stream, Panthalassa looked up and saw the recently healed scar on James's arm. *'That's quite gruesome,'* he thought, suddenly feeling ashamed of himself. *'I shouldn't have acted so bitterly when he decided not to work with us. I'm glad he took the time to rest.'*

After splashing around for a while, James got out and gathered up some driftwood to make a small fire. They all tucked into grilled trout with enthusiasm, for the morning's work had given them an appetite. After the meal, James let them laze in the shade for a while to rest their food, and Panthalassa asked something that had been on his mind all morning. “How do you make the work seem so easy, Foxeny?” he asked.

The other boy looked baffled, until he figured out what Panthalassa meant, and after that, he explained what his father had taught him. “Relax your arm and let the rotation of your hips swing the scythe around. If you're using your arms to swing the tool, you're doing it wrong,” he replied.

James smiled warmly. *'That's my boy!'* he thought. The look of pride was beaming from his face like rays of sunshine. *'If the prince just practices that technique for a week, he might just start to make a bit of progress with his fighting,'* he thought to himself. *'Above anything else, it will teach him endurance.'*

'Today I have only learned one thing, which is to keep the blade of the scythe level with the ground, and to keep going, no matter how tired I am,' Panthalassa thought, when the long day was finally over and they were walking home.

The swishing sound of his iron blade biting through the tall grass still seemed to ring in his ears, and even though they were heading back to the roundhouse, the echo of the day's work still remained.

He felt a sense of fulfilment wash over him. He saw now that rather than spending a day learning how to kill his enemies, he had spent the day learning how to sustain his friends. Everyone, whether he is rich or poor, old or young, strong or weak, must eat. If an army knows not how to sustain itself from the land around it, it will fall prey to an enemy far worse than any emperor. It will fall to hunger itself.

Although physically, Panthalassa was more tired than he had felt in his whole life, mentally, he felt full of joy. His legs felt as though they trailed on behind him like the sodden wake of a snail, his shoulders sagged in a weary trance, and his breath heaved under the full weight of his aching body, but his expression bore a smile that stretched from ear to ear, a sense of peace that gave him so much more hope than the endless cycle of bullying and warfare training in the sparring grounds. He had found nature.

*

It took a week of hard work to gather in the hay to feed the cows and pigs for the winter. Then their daily routines got much less hectic. James explained that the next period of really hard work would come in autumn when all the crops needed to be harvested. For now, there were still the regular chores to be done; the cow to be milked, the chickens and pigs to be fed, but the boys had a lot more free time on their hands. James took both the boys hunting for deer. He taught Panthalassa how to make snares to catch the rabbits that were a perennial threat to their vegetable garden. James still drilled both boys in combat for at least two hours every day, and Foxeny was teaching Panthalassa how to wrestle, but most days still felt like a glorious holiday to the young prince.

The style of fighting Panthalassa had learned from the instructors at the royal training grounds was all about brute force and practising the same things over and over. But James's style was much more slippery, Panthalassa was discovering. It was all about dodging, disappearing, and not being where your opponent was striking.

James encouraged creativity and doing the unexpected. He always insisted, with a perfectly straight face, that the regular tasks Panthalassa was doing on the farm were really valuable lessons. He set the young prince the task of grabbing a young rooster to be killed for the pot. Panthalassa spent over an hour chasing the rooster around the farmyard till he finally managed to catch the thing. “Great footwork training, Panth!” James chuckled.

Another time, he had set Panth to catching a piglet, and Foxeny and James both roared encouragement and suggestions as Panthalassa chased the slippery animal around its muddy pen, finally emerging covered from head to foot in mud, and in some places, even worse than mud.

“That's the spirit Panth! Not all battles will take place on nice sanded floors!” James said. Panthalassa knew they were roasting him, but it was all meant in a spirit of fun, and he was beginning to appreciate their rough humour, seeing the real friendship underneath.

And so the days turned into weeks, and weeks into months. Panthalassa grew sturdier, and his skin turned a deep bronze tan from all the sun and exercise. He had never been happier in his life.

As summer turned into autumn, Panthalassa became increasingly homesick. He missed his mother, and he longed to see his father and brother again, to hear all their tales of battle. He began counting down the days until the Harvest Festival, which was the day his mother had set for his return.

Chapter 3 Part 5 - Celdon Takes Action.

Late afternoon, Shortly after the Battle for Dessii.

*

After King Xanstus had been struck down, Prince Celdon, Panthalassa's older brother, finally gained enough control of his emotions to realise that with his father out of action, he needed to take charge of the situation.

Though the battle was clearly won, he was still facing a scene of total confusion. Shortly after the emperor and his bodyguard had fled, the Kad'aeri tribesmen atop the cliffs had sent a final cascade of rocks down, completely blocking the road, and trapping thousands of the emperor's fleeing troops. These had now all surrendered, and Celdon realised his first order of business had to be preventing the vengeful Varnixye tribesmen, who had had their families killed and homes destroyed, from butchering the captive soldiers. He felt the need for vengeance himself for his father, but as the madness of battle faded, he was starting to realise that so many captive cavalrymen might actually become a massive asset in the future. He set Bulvon and his battalion to work rounding up and guarding the prisoners.

The Order of Tiius was already ministering to the wounded and dying among the king's men and the emperor's, and neither needed nor would welcome any orders from him, and so the next thing Celdon turned his attention to, was setting the tribesmen to work capturing the thousands of loose horses still milling around the battlefield.

Once again, Prince Celdon felt a little thrill of an opportunity to be grasped. The Aristinian cavalry were famous for a good reason, their war horses were the best in the known world. Some of the horses running around loose, the fabled Aristinian Greys, were worth a king's ransom! With this bloodstock of fertile mares and stallions, the Kings' Union could one day have cavalry to rival any kingdom in the known world!

Lastly, he set the captives, and all the common soldiers, to the grim task of digging graves for all the fallen.

*

The next morning, Celdon set his mind to doing all the things he knew his father would have done, if he were still there.

He gathered the tribesmen and thanked them for their valiant efforts. With the emperor's army so completely defeated, there was no need for them to remain, and he gave them his blessing to return to their tribal lands, to their farming, their hunting, and their fishing. He set his mind to helping the Varnixye tribe, who had lost so much when the emperor had invaded, and put all of the royal knights to work, helping to rebuild the towns and villages that had been destroyed by the emperor's armies.

As they rebuilt, he heard the same thing over and over. “What is the point of this, if the emperor can just come back and destroy it all again?” they would say.

Finally, Celdon realised he had to do something about this. He talked this over with Bulvon one night over a camp fire, and Bulvon just said “Well, your dad's defences seemed to work quite well!” and so, the prince set his men to digging ditches around every settlement they helped to rebuild.

They dug a six foot deep trench around the whole thing, throwing all the earth and clay inwards, so they ended up with a roughly twelve foot high defensive rampart, with sharpened stakes in the ditch. It seemed like a lot of work to the villagers, but they were motivated, and they had five thousand brawny helpers. Finally, Celdon helped to rebuild Gralmeny and constructed a huge defensive wall around the town.

Throughout the summer, many of his men had formed attachments to the women from the villages and towns, and Celdon decided to establish a permanent garrison of infantry and archers in Gralmeny, to guarantee the most vulnerable outpost of the Kings' Union some security from invasions. But as autumn's chill started to paint the countryside in red, yellow and gold, he turned his mind to home, and decided to bring the troops back for the Harvest Festival, in a triumphal parade. His countrymen had sacrificed much, and they deserved to have a celebration for their victory.

*

Meanwhile, Emperor Celsidas had limped home with his much-depleted army to lick his wounds. His pride had been dented, and he had not been able to keep the rumours of his defeat from spreading like wildfire throughout Aristinia.

Although he had suffered heavy losses, he still had a large army of cavalry in reserve; the regiments helping to guard the eastern border of his primary ally, the Kingdom of Straeum.

The emperor, alongside the rulers of Tenasia, Tria and Asun, all helped to guard this border. Two hundred years ago, the Kingdom of Straeum had forged them into a powerful alliance, to check the growing power of the Calligian Empire. Together they had pooled their resources and built a huge wall spanning the entire length of the border, from the foot of the mountains on the Tenasian side, to where the land itself ended, at the Snake Sea.

In the initial aftermath of the battle, Celsidas agonised over the decision of whether or not to withdraw those troops. It would be a humiliating admission to his allies of how complete his defeat had been - but would his remaining cavalry be enough to hold back the Kings' Union's army, if they decided to counterattack in revenge?

So much depended on whether he would be facing the young and inexperienced Prince Celdon, or the crafty old warrior king, Xanstus.

As the summer wore on, his spies assured him that King Xanstus was dead, and that his son, Prince Celdon, was intent on building a defensive wall.

The emperor finally made the decision to send letters assuring his allies he would be able to continue honouring his commitments.

He would keep the rest of his Knightly Order in Straeum, to help defend their borders against their powerful shared enemy, the Calligian Empire.

Chapter 4 Part 1 – A Grand Return.

Pla-Kingus, Late Autumn. On the eve of the Harvest Festival.

*

The capital city of the Kings' Union was a hive of activity. It would in any event have been busy on the eve of the Harvest Festival, but for weeks the rumour had spread that the victorious army would be returning on this day, and so the city's streets were thronged with crowds eager for a sight of their returning soldiers.

Another persistent rumour throughout the kingdom was that King Xanstus had fallen in battle, and that it was Prince Celdon who would be leading the victory parade. Many in the crowd had made the journey to the capital city for the express purpose of seeing for themselves if this was true.

The taverns were full to bursting and street vendors were doing a brisk trade keeping the crowds fed. The pastry cooks, pie makers and bakers had outdone themselves to create the finest delicacies to celebrate the Harvest Festival. The air was filled with the appetising aromas of roasting meats and baking bread and all manner of appetising smells. It had been a hot summer and a mild autumn, and the harvest had been bountiful. The capital was alive with the sounds of laughter and gaiety.

The parade ground in front of Castle Lordborn had been filled with well-wishers since the early morning. From time to time Queen Dranah and Prince Panthalassa would appear on a balcony overlooking the Square and wave to the crowds. Each time, the Queen was greeted with rapturous applause.

Suddenly the crowd fell silent as the sound of distant trumpets came to their ears. Then from the direction of the main city gates a huge roar went up, followed by what sounded like a hum of confused murmuring. The queen gripped Panthalassa's hand tightly. "They are here!" she said.

Soon they could see the troops approaching the castle. The victorious army made a magnificent spectacle, their banners proudly held aloft as they marched. A squadron of royal knights led the way mounted on splendid war horses. Regiment after regiment of men in gleaming armour followed along behind, their banners proudly held aloft. As the troops passed through each section of the crowds there would be another roar of applause followed by the same sound, like a collective indrawn breath of surprise, or shock.

As the leading column of horsemen drew up in parade formation in front of the castle, the queen realised the reason for the crowds' muted response. She could see her son Celdon, and the burly figure of Bulvon beside him, but the king was nowhere to be seen...

Besides the queen, young Panthalassa looked down in dismay, his face going white. The queen put her arm around him in compassion.

There was a hum of troubled conversation from the crowds in the square, as the absence of King Xanstus was noticed.

Suddenly to the east of the city, came the sound of another trumpet fanfare. This was followed shortly by the distant sound of a tremendous roar. The sound swelled and swelled and drew closer as another body of troops made its way through the city. Soon, the banners of the Order of Tiius, who had looked after the wounded king, became visible, followed by a deafening roar of exultation. The king was riding in front of them. Against all the odds, he had returned.

Chapter 4 part 2 – Reactions.

The Emperor's Castle, Aerbonitas, the Capital of Aristinia.

*

When news of King Xanstus's triumphant return reached the ears of Emperor Celsidas, he flew into a towering rage. The hapless messenger who had delivered the sealed letter containing the news cowered in terror, fearing for his life, as the emperor vented his fury at his assembled courtiers. Finally, bringing himself under control with some difficulty, Celsidas sent for the imperial guardian, General Kalsos, and ordered his courtiers and the trembling messenger to leave him.

"That cunning old fox must have planned this!" he raved at General Kalsos. "He allowed everyone in his kingdom to believe he was dead, just for the sole purpose of tricking me! He waited until I had committed myself to my allies before he showed himself. The man is as cunning as Odall! Now if I go back on my word and withdraw my troops from the Straeiian border, I will be a figure of ridicule to my allies!"

Kalsos pursed his lips thoughtfully and paused before speaking, to give himself time to think how to best phrase his response to the emperor. He knew Celsidas to be a vain and proud man, who seldom acknowledged his own flaws and errors of judgment... In the emperor's current uncertain temper, advice which appeared critical of his recent military campaign could prove to be fatal.

"Your Imperial Majesty, I believe you were utterly correct to reassure our allies of our continuing support," he finally responded. "However, if I understand your train of thought correctly, may I say I shared your concerns about spreading the armies too thin, and having to fight on two fronts at once?"

The imperial guardian took a sip of wine whilst glancing at the emperor, to try and gauge his reaction. Encouraged by what he saw, he continued.

"However, if we pause in our plans for expansion in the northwest for a year or two, we should have no difficulty in holding the territory we have won up to now, without reinforcements. The king's savages might have proved tiresome to us in their rocky mountain passes, but on the open plains, even a single regiment of our cavalry would be enough to rout whatever *disorganised peasant rabble* King Xanstus might be able to throw against us."

The emperor looked relieved, although he was clearly trying not to show it. His general's suggestion gave him a way out of an embarrassing situation, without losing face. "Perhaps you are right, Kalsos." he said. "We will leave Xanstus to lick his wounds for now. We can smoke him out of his lair by and by, when the time is right," he said airily.

"I am quite sure that is for the best, my liege," Kalsos replied, saying a silent prayer of thanks, that for once, the conceited young fool had listened to reason.

*

Back in Castle Lordborn, reactions to the king's return were mixed.

For Queen Dranah, who had known the true situation ever since the midnight visit of Sir Ardwyn Keyscarre, there was the relief that she no longer had to keep the secret to herself. She was just glad to have him home safely, and she had already given much thought to how she could aid his recovery using her druidic skills and a wife's loving care.

For Celdon and Bulvon, who had spent the last three months under a crushing burden of guilt, thinking themselves to blame for the king's death, his sudden re-appearance seemed almost miraculous. They had burst into tears of joy when the old king had taken off his helmet at the parade, and they realised he truly was still alive. Both planned to ask for his forgiveness for the part they had played in him receiving his injuries and made solemn vows to themselves never to disobey his battle orders again.

Panthalassa, thanks to his mother, had spent the last three months on James's farm. As such, he had been completely unaware that anything was even amiss and was overjoyed when he first caught sight of his father.

Standing on the castle battlements with his mother, he watched proudly as his father, far below him in the courtyard, waved at the cheering crowds. He put his hand in his pocket and felt the ivory figure he had broken all those months before. He had carefully repaired it and carried it as a talisman ever since, and now, thankfully, his father was home safe. He saw the king wave one last time to the crowds and start making his way into the castle, and both he and his mother rushed from the battlements to greet him.

Making his way down the final flight of stairs into the great hall, Panthalassa suddenly got his first real glimpse of his father, and froze in horror...

The king's face was scarred from the tip of his chin, to just above his right eye. In place of Xanstus's lost eye were stitches, and the skin from his eyelid had glued itself to the thread, with a hardened yellow puss. More terrifying, his nose was slanted, as though the lower half had been sliced clean off by the force of the metal shard trapped inside his helmet, and to accompany these main grievances, there were a great many more smaller scars around his face, adding to the many wrinkles and hard lines of an ageing man...

Panthalassa felt his legs grow weak in sorrow, and he slid into a sitting position on the last step on the staircase. He clutched his ivory figure with both hands and sobbed in clear despair, and upon catching sight of his ivory figure, he realised that it had been damaged in the exact same place as his father's real wound...

"This is my fault," he mumbled, tears sliding down his cheeks, as he dared not look at his father again. "I should have listened to you, Father... I need to stay away from magic I don't understand."

Queen Dranah walked towards her son, placing her hand on his shoulder as she sat with him. "This isn't your fault, son," she soothed. “Some things are meant as messages from the gods, this is *not* your fault."

"What is the meaning of this?!" Xanstus boomed, signalling the guards to close the doors of the keep. "'My fault,' he says? What nonsense have you been teaching him now!"

Prince Celdon sighed at his father's undiplomatic return, and walked towards the other staircase, opposite Panthalassa and his mother. He needed to rest and was in no mood for this discussion after his long campaign.

"I have taught him no 'nonsense' dear. Tiius himself sent us a sign through his ivory figures. You need to rest your wound."

The king took a controlled breath and barely kept his anger contained. "Tiius sent the sign, you say?" he replied with sarcasm in his tone, looking briefly at his youngest son's broken figure. "The breakage could just as well have been Celdon's! It could have just as easily been a common soldier behind our ranks! This 'breakage' did not affect the outcome of my battle in any way, and you should be ashamed of yourself for teaching the boy that a toy figure, made of ivory, can miraculously harm real people!"

“I'm sorry father,” mumbled Panthalassa, hugging Xanstus's arm for a moment before making his way up the stairs.

“He has nothing to be sorry for, Xanstus. I've already told him that,” Dranah said calmly, but a lump was stuck in her throat as her heart wept. Her fears had been correct all along...

"Well, if we agree on that, then I suppose I was wrong to shout at you," Xanstus sighed, listening to his son's weary footsteps vanish up the staircase. "But Panthalassa needs to toughen up! We are not at peace anymore."

He sighed heavily and then decided he had been too harsh on the boy. "I should go and comfort him."

Despite his grim exterior, he loved his family dearly, and he was dismayed that his homecoming was already marred by a quarrel.

The queen followed him up the stairs with an expression of disbelief. "You won the war! The emperor is beaten! How can you say peace has not returned? You have a son to raise and a kingdom to run!"

Xanstus kept his right hand on the wooden handrail as he turned to face his wife. "I won a battle, not a war, Dranah." he snapped. "The emperor is still alive, and the war can only end when he is dead!"

As the king went up the stairs to be with his son, he tried his best to shut out the seething hatred he harboured for Celsidas. *'That man has made me look like a cripple,* he thought. *'By the time I'm done with him, I'll have his head on a spike.'*

Chapter 4 Part 3 – Winter's Hope.

Castle Lordborn, nearing the end of winter.

*

As autumn turned to winter, the king's relationship with Queen Dranah took a turn for the better. Over the last couple of weeks that remained of autumn, the queen set aside her worries about Xanstus's eagerness for war, and she realised that the king needed peace and tranquillity if he was to fully recover from his injuries.

Xanstus had taken notice of Panthalassa's newfound enthusiasm for his training lessons and showered him with fatherly praise, telling him that one day, he may after all become as strong a warrior as his older brother.

The king observed that his son's stay on James's farm had clearly done him the world of good. His physique had filled out nicely, and the boy now moved with a new grace and confidence when sparring.

Xanstus rewarded James by granting him the well-paid position as his son's official training instructor. This pleased the old veteran enormously, for up until now, he had served the young prince as a mere replacement while his brother was away. During this time, he had grown fond of the boy.

Xanstus had listened with some amusement as Panthalassa explained some of James's unorthodox training methods, but there was no denying the results. He now gave James full permission to train the prince however and wherever he saw fit, so long as he kept him safe, and it helped him to develop as a young warrior. It would do the boy some good to see more of his kingdom.

From now on though, Panthalassa was to be guarded by a troop of royal knights wherever he went, whom he decided to put under James's command. The king made a mental note to have spies keep a close watch on his son from afar, to mask him even further from any real danger.

As the heavy snows of late winter fell like a white carpet across the nation, the king sent word to the leaders of all the tribes and small kingdoms in his land, inviting them to partake in the *Great Winter Feast* of *Winter's Hope*.

*

It was late afternoon. All day long, the servants of Castle Lordborn had been hurrying around in a frenzy of preparation, for not only was today Winter's Hope, but it was also Panthalassa Lordborn's eleventh birthday.

Exotic sticks of frankincense burned in every room of the castle. Candles burned next to them to illuminate the room, and the royal knights guarding the castle were dressed in their finest suits of ceremonial kenthril armour. The knights guarding the doorway of the banqueting hall were tapping their feet to the merry songs being played by the minstrels of the castle, who played their tunes on a variety of fiddles and flutes as they pranced about the hall.

The dining room smelled so strongly of incense smoke and seasoned meat that the mouths of each guest watered from the intense aromas.

The king was sat next to Queen Dranah at the end of the table. Present with them were their two sons, along with Bulvon Bravesoul, the three lords of Xanstus's subject states (those states being Adaria, Istaria and Satia), a varied host of several tribal chieftains, and last but not least, James Ashenworn and his son, who, in receiving the goodwill of King Xanstus for improving Panthalassa's spirits, were personally invited to Castle Lordborn to fill their bellies on the warm delicacies of royal feasts and strong ale.

"Well!" came the beginning of King Xanstus's speech, interrupting the vibrant multitude of conversations around his long rustic table in a loud voice. He keenly observed all of his guests and saw that they had all dressed in their finest clothes. Even Bulvon, who was well known for his bearskin, berserker-like appearance, was dressed in a smooth red vest of fine silk. In fact, his suit was so impressive that it almost made him look like an aristocrat.

"What a glorious year we have had!" the king remarked, although many in the room could have mistaken his tone as sarcasm... "Many of you will be relieved that the emperor was defeated soundly this summer, and others, I think, are still coming to terms with the magnitude of my victory."

The tribal chieftains who had followed the king into battle only a few months ago began whispering amongst themselves briefly. An air of excitement seemed to hover above them, but many of the chieftains could barely contain their feelings of resentment towards the emperor, for as they spoke amongst each other, they couldn't help but notice how horribly disfigured their king's face had become.

"A great victory, sire," muttered Warlord Zalxorr, the leader of the Varnixye tribe, who just this summer had seen his own father slain by the emperor's cavalry before razing his village to the ground.

Xanstus raised his hand a small few inches from the table, indicating that he was not finished talking.

"...And while this victory in the woods may have allowed us the *opportunity* for another peace," he continued, "I fear this peace would only be for a year, or possibly even less."

Panthalassa felt his heart sink as a thought crossed his mind. *'My father is about to say he's going to war again...'*

A sense of dread crept over him like a dark cloud of rain... *'If he does, I will have to try and stop him leaving...'*

"Therefore," King Xanstus went on, "we must all be prepared for war. If the emperor is allowed to regain his strength in supplies and manpower, he will only seek to strike at the core of our kingdoms and people again - and this, as a king, I cannot allow!"

The chieftains' faces brightened and gave way to smiles. Some of them even cheered for war! Yet Warlord Airen didn't seem too pleased...

"Lord King..." he mumbled, from the gruff of his ashen grey moustache...

Xanstus looked at him with a raised brow.

"If it were my place to offer advice, your Majesty, I would suggest allowing our people time to recover *our own* strength before rushing towards conquest."

The queen gave the warlord a faint smile. *'Hah. - he says that as though I haven't already tried to say the same thing to him,'* she thought, looking to one side in disappointment.

Xanstus narrowed his eye, considering briefly whether or not the Danz'kanari warlord had been told to give him that message on purpose.

"But it is -*not*- your place to advise me, Warlord Airen," the king reminded him. "And since you are under my command, your people will provide me with bowmen *when I* demand them."

"Yes, my king," Airen sighed.

Xanstus kept his expression neutral and scanned the room for further discontent. He knew that he could count on his wife to maintain her composure even despite how she loathed the idea of another war, and he knew that Celdon would remain silent out of sheer respect for him, but he was less sure of his subject kings. How did they feel about the war?

"Is there anyone else here who would like to voice their concern?" he asked, scrutinising the expressions on the faces of his lords. "Is there anyone else here who would suggest allowing the emperor time to muster his forces for even longer?"

Lord Aleric of Adaria shook his head passively.

"Ten years of peace, we enjoyed," Xanstus continued. "We had all of ten years to recover our strength, and yet even after this, the emperor thought we would be broken under his might like an old wooden tool!"

He took a sip of ale from his flagon.

"Not only does the emperor seethe in rage that I am alive, and not only does he plot to subjugate every last one of you, but the emperor actually spreads rumours amongst his troops, that we are allied with the *Calligians!*"

Outraged whispers circulated the table at this statement.

"And with the stench of such a foul rumour plaguing the nostrils of his followers, can we expect anything less than another war?" he asked.

"No!" came the response from a few tribal chieftains.

"So too does he spread this dark rumour amongst his allies in *Straeum*, who even now fight the Calligian scum on their borders," Xanstus intoned. "Those same Calligians who defile their own lands in their worship of Odall, and those same Calligians who allow necromancers and skeletons to walk in chorus with their own mortal armies."

"But the emperor does not realise that we too speak with Straeum; Straeum knows we are not Calligian puppets, and the Order of Tiius *themselves* have allied themselves with us, in order to repel this threat from the emperor!"

Bouts of cheering broke out around the table. Xanstus grinned with satisfaction as he saw their growing support, yet, in remembering it was Panthalassa's birthday, he immediately brought the speech to an end.

Standing up from his seat, King Xanstus raised his flagon high and said this: "So together, we will cripple the Aristinian efforts to conquer our lands. Together, we will win not only glory, but we will be remembered in history as the men who ended the tyrannical, ancient regime of the *Baeres Dynasty*! Emperor Celsidas will fall!"

Cheering erupted around the table from the lungs of the tribal chieftains and Bulvon. The king's subject lords were more reserved in their shows of support, yet even they couldn't help but give their loud applause, lest they be noticed by the king and his loyal supporters.

Taking an enormous swig of ale, Xanstus finally sat down again and raised his hands to gesture the beginning of the feast. "For the spring!" he bellowed, and since this was the traditional three-word announcement of the *Winter's Feast*, all his guests followed suit and then drank to their hearts' content.

Panthalassa had kept quiet. While chewing on a piece of lamb meat he peered off to his right, spying the expressions of James and Foxeny with a curiosity that stemmed from his months of training on their farm. *'James and Foxeny seem a lot less enthusiastic about the war than the king's nobles do,'* he thought, remembering what James had taught him as men quaffed ale and feasted all around him. *'Perhaps working so close to nature allows James to see things in a broader light...'*

Foxeny noticed Panthalassa staring at him and shot back a half-hearted smile. *'I wonder what he's thinking,'* he pondered, while his half-happy expressions belied a truer sense of fear for his own father. What would the king do this year? With James now more important to the king than he was before, would he too be drafted into service? What if he came back injured - what if he came back dead? Even more troublingly, what if he didn't come back at all?

Prince Celdon gently shook Panthalassa by the shoulder. "Everything alright, little brother?" he asked. "You seem put off by something."

Panthalassa turned back towards his plate, averting his brother's stare... "I'm just concerned," he sighed.

"About Father?" Celdon asked.

"About Father, yes, but I'm also worried about the soldiers," Panthalassa continued. "Where will you find more soldiers if the ones you currently have fall?"

Celdon prodded a strip of chicken with his knife and took a sip of ale. He raised an eyebrow at his younger brother with curiosity. "Has James got you thinking about strategy as well, brother?" he inquired, smiling at him in admiration. "Hah! If he has, then my word you'll be a general by the time you're fifteen!"

Panthalassa gulped down a mouthful of apple juice. He quietly felt annoyed that his father wouldn't let him drink ale yet. "That's not it, Celdon," he sighed. "I mean to ask - who will you recruit first?"

Celdon thought carefully about this question.

"Well," came his slow response, "naturally, we need the men in the city hammering steel for our troops, repairing our armour and so on..." he continued, "so first, we would have to levy the peasants, maybe even some of the retired veterans."

Panthalassa took a deep breath through his nose as he absorbed this answer. "So what about James?" he asked.

Celdon chuckled at Panthalassa in delight. "You're more thoughtful than I was at your age, I'll give you that much, brother," he stated. "You can rest assured that both James and Foxeny will have the privilege to choose whether or not they will fight; for even their presence in this very room has raised their social status quite considerably."

Panthalassa allowed himself to smile at last. "Thank you, brother."

Listening in on their conversation, Foxeny proudly straightened his back as he realised his new position of privilege. *'I wonder what my dad thinks!'* he thought, yet as he looked to his right, he noticed that his father's expression had barely changed as he sat quietly munching on his food. "H-have you heard what the prince said?" Foxeny whispered, gently pawing his father's arm to grab his attention.

James brushed off his son's grip and shot him a glare implying he should behave himself.

"Yes," he sighed quietly. "We can choose to refuse the levy to war if we so wish," yet the frown on his face was solid and unchanging as he lowered his tone to a barely audible mumble. "But who will run the farms if all the workers are levied off to war?" he asked rhetorically.

Bulvon slammed his flagon of ale down on the table. He had already gone through eight fills, and the side effects from his first, second and third fills were beginning to set in. "Another!" he called to a passing servant.

The king raised his eyebrow at him in admiration. "It's a wonder the plebs haven't invented a song for your drinking yet!" he joked, to which a few more drunken voices rose in laughter.

'A kingdom relies on its farmers...' James worried... *'And if the farmers' labourers are gone, then food must be imported from abroad...'*

'But if the land's wealth is spent on war, then the people will starve...'

Queen Dranah had grown tired of hiding her feelings from public view. She hated all this talk of war, even though she had long ago decided it would be fruitless to try and persuade her husband against it. She leaned in to whisper something in his ear. "Xanstus..." she mumbled, and her tone was soft and unassuming... "I'm tired now.... I think I should rest."

The king took a deep breath and sighed gently. He knew she loved peace over war and had blamed his talk of war on his wounded pride. In his heart, he knew she spoke the truth, yet even despite this, the king felt unable to see things her way. "Very well..." he said, holding her hand for a brief moment as she excused herself from the table."

*

The meal continued far into the night. Before too long, Panthalassa and James had both excused themselves as well, and yet the king still sat on his commanding chair at the end of the table carousing with his subject kings and chieftains.

Prince Celdon had asked for the king's permission to leave, but Xanstus, valuing his eldest son as a close tactical adviser, had flatly refused him.

Having by now pushed away his sadness relating to Queen Dranah, and having completely discarded the thought of properly celebrating Panthalassa's eleventh birthday, the king allowed his guests to speak more openly about the war to come, and with this being the case, it didn't take too long for the chieftains' thirst for vengeance to become clear.

Panthalassa, however, had not gone to bed. All the talk of war had sickened him, and he was afraid his face would betray his feelings to his father. He was now sat halfway up the spiralled stone staircase, so he could secretly listen to what they were saying, and his mind raced with the dreaded thought of saying his last goodbye to a wounded father.

"I think your war is justified, my King!" Shouted Warlord Zalxorr of the Varnixye, his voice raw with drunkenness. "We may have won one battle, but the emperor still lives! My people still cry out for vengeance! I lost my father to the emperor and his men, and all my tribe lost friends and family to them! I say we should attack them at first spring! Celsidas must die!"

Panthalassa listened on as the men in the dining hall cheered for war. He wondered whether his peaceful approach was truly the right way forward... *'Perhaps if I weren't so cowardly, I'd cheer for war too...'* he thought to himself scoldingly. Warlord Zalxorr's words had sparked something in his mind. *'I know that peace is preferable, but, well-- is it? If the war stopped now that would mean the emperor has gone unpunished for nearly killing my father.'*

Panthalassa then heard Bulvon's voice rise to speak, yet rather than speaking in anger, the legendary blacksmith's drunken state seemed to have faded into a more tearful tone, and this too made him think carefully. His father had always taught him that sadness leads to weakness, but Bulvon was the most ferocious man he knew, even stronger, he suspected, than his brother. He listened closely...

"How could I have let the emperor harm you, Xanstus," he sobbed, and Panthalassa heard Bulvon loudly slurp at what was probably his eleventh flagon of ale that night, before slamming it down on the table in front of him. "I feel as though I have failed you not only as a warrior, your Majesty, but as a friend," he continued, "and although peace would guarantee your safety, I cannot - *must not!* - allow the emperor to go unpunished for what he has done to you!"

Panthalassa widened his eyes in a realisation. *'Is Bulvon a psychic as well as a warrior?'* he wondered, *'He said that as though he could see straight into my mind!'*

The thought then increased in its intensity, and Panthalassa suddenly felt the urge to announce his presence... *'If I go back down there and reveal myself to them, then there's no telling how my father would react...'*

Time itself seemed to slow, and fear suddenly rushed through him like water from a burst dam, flooding him with dread at all the possible outcomes of his decision. *'He only praises me when I'm brave,'* he finally concluded. *'I have to stop my cowardly peace-making... The emperor must be punished.'*

And when Panthalassa steeled himself to announce his presence, Xanstus turned around and saw the expression on his son's face. "You look as pale as a ghost, my son. Go to bed!" he said.

Panthalassa turned around and almost gave in to his desire to run back up the stairs. Every inch of his body was tensed, and he clearly had something to say...

"Go on then, it is your birthday, " The king sighed. "Say what you must but make it quick!"

Panthalassa took a deep breath and faced his father once again. The expression on his face was forced and fear stricken. "I just came to say that..." he said slowly, "I know you are doing the right thing... and I support your war... even if... if... I am afraid you might die."

A tear trickled down his face as he contemplated his father's death... Xanstus felt a lump in his throat and instantly knelt down to hug his son. Panthalassa wept in his arms, and Celdon, his older brother, placed a hand on his shoulder and smiled painfully.

Moments later when Panthalassa had gone to bed, the talks continued. Without knowing it, Panthalassa, in one act of inner bravery, had inspired every soul in the room. This eleven-year-old prince, who had never held a real sword in his life, had touched the hearts of the king's men. In that moment, they would have followed their king to the ends of the earth to make his son proud.

Chapter 5 Part 1 – Preparations.

Castle Lordborn.

*

The morning after Winter's Hope, it began to snow heavily in the capital, and within a few hours, the snow was so deep that travel was all but impossible. For the first few days, the king took this enforced passivity with good spirit. Queen Dranah showered him with affection and delighted in cooking him his favourite dishes. He taught his youngest son how to play a strategy game with his toy soldiers, and he was delighted at how quickly the young boy picked up the intricacies of the game. For his part, Panthalassa was overjoyed to have his father's undivided attention for a change, and glowed with pride whenever Xanstus praised him for some particularly cunning tactic. "This is the real art of war, my son," he said. "You always need to out-think your opponent and plan several moves ahead."

The blizzard raged on for a week, and after a while, the endless moaning of the wind and the feeling of being cooped up began to grate on everyone's nerves. For the king, it was especially trying. He was not used to inactivity, and although he tried to hide it, his headaches were a constant strain on his patience.

The first clear day came as a relief to everyone in the castle, because despite his best efforts, the king had become short tempered and irritable. Over breakfast, with a low winter sun shining brightly through the windows, Xanstus proposed that he and his sons should try and venture out. His suggestion unsurprisingly was greeted with great enthusiasm.

They were soon saddled up and on their way. The servants had worked hard to clear pathways through the snow to all the outbuildings and stables around the castle's inner courtyard. Once outside the castle gate however, the snow was still waist high. In some places, the wind had scoured the snow away leaving bare frozen ground, whilst sweeping it into huge snowdrifts in other places. The king and Celdon, who were both mounted on splendidly muscular Aristinian greys, had no difficulty ploughing a path through the snow even when it came up to their horses' bellies. Panthalassa however, sitting astride a small shaggy-haired pony, was soon having difficulties.

The boy was close to tears anticipating being sent home, but his father quickly noticed his predicament. Reining his own horse in, the king waited until Panthalassa came up alongside him and then lifted his youngest son into the saddle behind him. After ordering a groom to take the boy's pony back to the stables, the king and his two sons resumed their jaunt.

It was a glorious frosty day. The horses' breath came snorting out of their nostrils in huge plumes of steam, making them look like mythical beasts. The sunlight glinted through the icicles, turning them into sparkling, rainbow-hued jewels. The blue sky and snowy landscape were breathtakingly beautiful and raised all of their spirits.

Celdon and his father soon fell into a discussion about the fine qualities of the many Aristinian horses they had captured, and the impact it would have on the battles to come. "It's all very well having first rate horses, Celdon, but we don't have first rate cavalrymen, and that is just the plain truth," said the king. "The Adarians are our best, but even if we mounted all of them on these splendid creatures, they would still be no match for the Aristinians. We beat them last time because we fought them from behind trenches and spikes, but on the open plains, we would be massacred."

"Well what about the Aristinians we captured?" Celdon asked. "Won't they be of any use to us?"

"The Aristinian cavalrymen who surrendered are fine horsemen, but can we really trust them in battle? We need to find another way to get across the plains safely," Xanstus sighed.

Panthalassa, sitting behind his father, was only listening with half an ear. He was just happy to be with them.

He had only the haziest idea of the tactics that had decided the outcome of the last battle, and he was reluctant to ask a question that might make him appear foolish. Finally though, in a momentary lull in the conversation, when the two men reined in their horses to allow them to rest, Panthalassa timidly asked his question. "I don't understand..." the young prince murmured. "Why can't you just take the trenches and spikes with you?"

The king and Celdon roared with laughter and Panthalassa's face burned with shame. He had clearly made a terrific blunder. He had no idea what a trench even was.

The laughter died away, and for a while there was a thoughtful silence. Then suddenly, Xanstus let out an enormous bellow. “By Tiius, I think the boy’s got it!”

*

The king never did explain to Panthalassa what it was that he had got, but whatever it was, it had put his father in an excellent mood.

Over the next few weeks, the king bustled about cheerfully, shouting orders and turning the castle into a hive of activity.

Since Panthalassa had failed to get an answer from his father or his older brother, the young prince sought out Bulvon, the giant blacksmith, and eventually found him at his forge, merrily hammering away.

Bulvon gave the young prince a warm smile when he saw him. He was always happy to gossip with one of the king's sons.

Panthalassa posed his questions.

“Well,” Bulvon said. “Me and my men are working around the clock to make spades and pickaxes, fifteen thousand of them, and any number of spearheads. Your father hasn’t taken me into his confidence yet as to his plans,” he told the boy. “But whatever they are, I am certain of one thing. Somewhere down the line, they involve a lot of digging!”

*

As winter turned to spring, James asked the king’s permission to return home for a few weeks to put his affairs in order. With him now committed to training the young prince full time, he would have no time to run the farm, he explained.

He hoped to find a tenant farmer who could manage the farm in his absence. Since that might take a while, he also asked for enough time to at least get the spring crops planted before returning to his duties.

In his current sunny mood, the king had no problem granting his request, and when Panthalassa begged to be allowed to accompany him, King Xanstus made no objection. He had been impressed with the improvement to his son's health and strength, following his last stay on the farm, and saw no reason to change a regime that was clearly working.

“The farming life seems to agree with the lad,” he told James. “So get your tenant farmer in to run the farm. Come and go as often as you like, to keep an eye on things. Just as long as it doesn’t interfere with the boy’s training,” he said. “Oh, and one more thing," the king continued. "If you are going to be on the farm for weeks on end, you will need to make some provision for your troops' accommodation, and you will need some stables," he insisted. "I want Panthalassa to become an expert horseman, and all his bodyguards will be mounted on Aristinian greys!" He threw a purse of gold coins for James to catch. "That should cover any expenses, but if you need more, just ask."

James breathed a sigh of relief. This was much more than he had ever dared to hope for.

"I'm not bothered if you house my royal knights in a barn," the king added, with a twinkle in his one eye. "But don't go cheap on those stables, alright? Those are valuable horses!"

*

Word of King Xanstus's drunken boasting about vengeance on Winter's Hope had quickly reached the ears of Emperor Celsidas, through his network of spies and informers. As soon as winter's snows had died, he deployed what remained of his cavalry and infantry to the outskirts of Dosonarmon. This city was the only strategic target of note, against which he could imagine the king being able to mount a credible attack, but it was one hundred or so miles inside his own borders. This had a dual benefit. He hoped to signal to the king that he stood ready to guard what was his, yet at the same time, by stationing his own troops so far away from their shared border, he wished to reassure the king that he had no desire to renew their conflict.

In any event, Emperor Celsidas took comfort from the fact that on a clear day, his lookouts could look right across the plains to the rising hills, which had always been considered the natural boundary between their two countries.

If Celsidas had failed to find a way of battering through the natural barriers of mountains and forests protecting the Kings' Union, he felt equally sure that the old king would find no easy way to surprise him on the open plains. Nor could he imagine any way the wily old king, for all his cunning, would be able to order his rag-tag rabble of barbarians to stand firm, against the mass onslaught of his Knightly Order, at full gallop, on level ground.

And as spring turned into summer, the reports from his spies added to his peace of mind. The king's eldest son, Celdon, was often sighted in the border towns and villages, but from the reports of the spies, it was hard to make much sense of what might be on the mind of the king.

The movements of Celdon's troops seemed to consist of forced marches, in a meaningless zigzag, around the contours of their shared border, followed by a frenzied digging of trenches and barriers around villages, many of which were so small and insignificant as to appear nameless...

From this analysis of the situation, Emperor Celsidas drew the following comforting conclusions: Xanstus had become either too feeble, or too damaged by his head wound, to maintain effective control of his kingdom, and secondly, along with this, that his eldest son had taken over as leader in all but name, and felt out of his depth in command, and was desperate to strengthen his defences.

Emboldened by this analysis of the situation, as midsummer drew near, the emperor left the task of guarding his western borders to Imperial Guardian Kalsos, and while his main advisor commanded the army, Celsidas, troubled that rumours of his unexpected defeat had seriously weakened his prestige, embarked on a diplomatic mission to the *Senate of Straeum*.

Chapter 5 Part 2 – Early Success.

Valley of the Tribal Games, less than ten miles away from last year's battlefield.

*

The Tribal Games went ahead as usual, with every chieftain sending his best trained soldiers to compete.

King Xanstus had sent word to all the other tribes, telling them that he would be attending in person, and he was pleased to find that every chieftain and warlord had agreed to come as well.

As the games progressed, he could tell by the military displays that all of the leaders had been hard at work giving their men fresh training.

Their secret valley, in truth, was a secret no more. A great victory had been won not ten miles from here, against an army feared throughout the known world. This enormous bowl protected by cliffs and mountains, with its lake in the centre, had become a part of the folklore of the Kings' Union. In some ways, it had even come to symbolise the very values they stood for.

On the clifftops surrounding the valley, vast crowds of onlookers watched each day's staged battle scenarios fought out below and wagered on the outcomes. The winding roads, the cliffs and forests of this landscape, had defeated an Empire.

For many of the crowds thronging the clifftops, this place represented the boundaries of their world, a place of safety, and so the crowds came. Some of the more enterprising citizens had brought sheep and goats, to slaughter and feed the masses, hoping that with any luck, they might be able to pocket a few pennies for when they finally returned home.

The king saw the boundary the majority of his subjects saw as their land, their security. He saw the anger, the fury of the Varnixye tribe, who had lost whole families and towns on the plains. He remembered how they had sacrificed everything to be the living wall against the invasion of the Aristinian horde, and how they clamoured eagerly to fight again.

When Xanstus mentioned there would be no war this summer, the king noticed how their faces darkened into rage, contained only by the memory of his fair rule.

Celdon, who had come to the tribal games as well, had spent the whole summer fortifying the outer boundary of the kingdom, but the citizens there had lost too much to care, even despite all the goodwill and bravado of the victory felt by the other tribes. They knew that nothing would bring them security, apart from expanding the kingdom. Failing that, they would have to give up their lands and retreat to the safety of the hills and mountains behind them. They were primed and ready, to be the spearhead for any future invasion.

As King Xanstus watched his son, Celdon demonstrated how his troops on the border could throw up a defensive wall against cavalry. He could hear the angry murmuring of the crowd. He knew they saw this emphasis on defence as a betrayal of the king's promise of revenge, and he hoped that amongst the watchers on the hilltops, there were spies who would share that information with the emperor. He wondered just how much the emperor might modify his plans based on that information.

It would have been almost impossible to stage a realistic cavalry battle. There was not enough space for one thing, and also, there was no safe way of enacting a massed cavalry charge against pikes. Too many men would die. More importantly, there was now a huge amphitheatre of citizens looking down upon the staged battles. They had to be pleased.

Everyone in the king's army had lost comrades and loved ones to the emperor's horsemen, some of which, after being defeated, had agreed to fight for the king instead, and it was for this reason that he had decided to leave the captured Aristinians in the capital city.

Sensing the mood of the crowd, he thanked all the gods he had made that decision.

The king glanced at the faces of the tribal leaders sat around him. He had purposely invited all of his subject lords too. The Varnixye were there, with their massed armies thirsting for vengeance, furious that Xanstus seemed to have abandoned his promise.

'If only I could share my plans with them more thoroughly...' the king thought. *'The scowling faces I can see around me would be wreathed in smiles...'* But for now, since it was likely that the emperor's spies were listening, their resentment was of more use to him.

The Danz'kanari put on the last competition of the games. Storming the castle was the theme.

Given the extreme dangers that falling from ladders presented, the Danz'kanari had suspended a rope bridge right across the middle of the lake. As a substitute for siege towers and ladders, they had fastened cargo nets to the guard rails of the bridge, anchored at the bottom by huge rocks at the edge of the lake. In this way, attackers repelled by the defenders on the bridge would either become entangled in the cargo nets or fall into the lake. There were no weapons, but the defenders on the bridge had vast stores of rotten fruit, with which to pelt the teams of attackers, as they swarmed up the cargo nets.

In the scorching sun, this proved to be a huge amount of fun for both the contestants and the spectators, and so the Tribal Games ended on a note of celebration and laughter.

*

The King found the job of keeping secret his plans tiring and vexatious, especially from people he loved and respected. He found some comfort in working with Bulvon and Celdon, because they tended to simply follow his orders without questioning his motivations or his purpose.

He got Bulvon to make some steel tubes, the thickness of a man's forearm and twice as long, with two holes at either end wide enough to accept the passage of a sturdy nut and bolt, about two hundred and eighty of them. Also, he told him to make a few hundred steel staples, shaped like the letter "U".

Celdon was given the task of training the infantry, doing twenty miles of forced marches and manoeuvres every day, and then digging fortified camps at the end. Celdon, as he liked to, threw himself into the ditches with his men, digging like the most common soldier among them, to show comradery and help in fortifying their camp.

Since that fateful day when they had both disobeyed him, leading to the king's terrible injuries, Bulvon and Celdon both felt not only guilt, but also a sense of shame that they had neither been smart enough to figure out the wisdom of his orders, or even the loyalty to simply obey them. Since that day, they had both taken a solemn vow to never forsake his words again.

*

Autumn was almost over. The harvests had been gathered in, and almost everyone assumed the king had abandoned his plans for war for that year.

Xanstus noticed cynically that some of the tribal leaders, like Warlord Airen of the Danz'kanari, who had now become publicly critical of his lack of action, had not seemed so keen on the idea of war back in spring. *'Well good!'* he thought. *'Soon I will give them a chance to show me their eagerness for battle.'*

The day after the Harvest Festival, the king sent out his most trusted messengers, ordering the tribal leaders to muster all their troops at the secret valley, in one week's time. Once they were gathered together, he outlined his plan to the other leaders. There were still some objections, but when he revealed some of the secret preparations he had been making, his arguments won the day.

The key to his plan was to use infantry in a new way. To neutralise the emperor's cavalry on the open plains. Once they were out in the open, the army marched in a huge square formation, with pikemen on the flanks, in ranks ten men deep. The baggage train and the archers marched on the inside of the square. That way, there was no way for them to be outflanked by cavalry. Whichever direction they were attacked from, the infantry could quickly present a bristling wall of ten-foot-long pikes, and at the end of each day's march, the infantry dug trenches around the camp, creating a secure stockade, to prevent them being ambushed in the night.

Throughout each day, the Unionite cavalry roamed the countryside in large squadrons. At every village and town along their route, they gave every fighting-age man the choice of massacre, or recruitment. By these measures, over the next few days, the king's army added an extra seven thousand or so men to their ranks.

On pain of death, Xanstus had ordered there to be no looting or raping in any of the towns they passed through. Whenever they came upon some of the emperor's tax collectors, these were promptly beheaded, and their heads were put on spikes by the roadside.

Whenever the army came across wagons laden with taxed grain, headed for the emperor's granaries in the city of Dosonarmon, they would give any accompanying guards the same choice. Death or recruitment? The soldiers would then tell the trembling cart drivers to carry on their way, and if there was more than one wagon, the king had instructed them to send one back to the town they had just left, as a gift.

These actions proved popular with the local population, because the emperor was feared, but not loved, and the ordinary people suffered under a heavy burden of taxation, having to give one sack of grain out of every three they harvested to the emperor.

The king continued to send scouting parties on ahead, mounted on the fastest horses. He also received messages from his many spies about the emperor's movements. At last, when they were within two days' march of Dosonarmon, the king received word that the emperor's army was finally on the move.

Xanstus decided to rest his army on a large flat plain and let the Aristinians come to *him*.

Whilst they waited, he called back all his cavalry inside their defensive stockade. While they waited, he got Celdon to put all the infantry through their drills, for if the troops stood around idly, it could quickly sap their morale.

The new recruits had all been given pikes, helmets, a good pair of boots, and warm sheepskin coats, as indeed had everyone else in the army. As they marched to and fro, the experienced knight centurions worked hard to try and drum, into their heads at the very least, how to march in formation. *'Oh well,"* the king thought, *'at least they look like soldiers!'*

Xanstus pondered his tactics. He had briefly toyed with the idea of just waiting behind the stockades, but he knew that General Kalsos would never be foolish enough to try such an assault, although when he thought about it, Emperor Celsidas might be. He recalled his spies telling him that the emperor had returned.

It would become a siege if he was trapped in the stockades. With so many untrained recruits in the ranks, leaving the walls once the emperor actually arrived might prove impossible to do in an orderly manner.

Finally, as night fell, he posted double sentries on all four watchtowers and ordered patrols to go out regularly throughout the night to scout for enemy movement.

At first light, the king made sure all his army had a good hot meal in them before they broke camp. In front of them, there was a wide highway leading to Dosonarmon, and so the baggage train made good progress, surrounded on all sides by a wall of pikemen. The men had come to call this formation: "The Hedgehog."

As his troops marched along at an easy pace, a huge war drum beat out a steady rhythm, and his soldiers sang rude songs at the top of their lungs. On either side of the road, the prairie was completely flat and bare. A low sun cast a golden glow over the landscape. Under the clear blue sky, the horizon seemed to stretch away to infinity.

His scouting parties started coming in, their horses lathered in sweat. Their reports indicated that if both armies continued their current speed, they would be within fighting distance by midday.

At present, the emperor's infantry was marching down the highway, rows of bowmen and skirmishers were followed by swordsmen, spearmen and men-at-arms. Scouts estimated that the emperor's army numbered perhaps thirteen thousand. These troops were flanked on either side by two full battalions of Emperor Celsidas's dreaded Knightly Order and eighteen further battalions of regular cavalry, so overall, the cavalry alone numbered perhaps four thousand.

Xanstus decided to stick with the deployment he had discussed the night before with his generals. He anticipated Celsidas launching an infantry attack at the front, and then swinging his elite cavalry round to attack on the flanks. With this in mind, he had placed the bulk of his battle-hardened royal knights on his flanks, mounted this time on sturdy war-horses. The idea was that the emperor's cavalry would charge them, expecting a battle of jousting, and then at the last moment, the royal knights would dismount and form a compact square of halberds. In this way, the king's heavy infantry could be everywhere at once.

He put his new recruits at the front, alongside more experienced and reliable troops. It was a lot to ask of them, but if he had guessed right, they would not face the heaviest attack.

He placed the Danz'kanari bowmen behind the front ranks (alongside his regular archers), figuring they would annihilate the poorly armoured Aristinian infantry, far before they even got into melee range. After that, who knew? Battle was always a matter of luck, as well as planning. He did, however, still have one last trick up his sleeve.

When the emperor's army came into sight, they were still in the formation described by his scouts. Xanstus breathed a sigh of relief. The Aristinian infantry let out a ragged cheer and charged the front line of the king's army. Before the Aristinians had even reached arrow range for their own skirmishers, the Danz'kanari, with their powerful war bows, were already taking them down.

Meanwhile, the emperor's Knightly Order did exactly what he had dared to hope they would do. Instead of hitting the flanks of his army in a massed charge, they continued to gallop all the way around to the rear. This was typically where a marching army was most vulnerable, and where the weakest and most unreliable troops were often placed.

As soon as the emperor's army had come into sight however, the royal knights, whose duty it was to guard the flanks and the rear of the king's army, were already carrying out their prearranged battle plan.

Dismounting as one, the royal knights formed into defensive squares the entire length of the army. The Aristinian knights, coming in at full gallop, quickly found themselves impaled by the bristling wall of halberds, while other battalions of the emperor's Knightly Order, rushing around to try and pierce the king's battle line somewhere else, quickly found themselves ripped to pieces by a deadly hail of arrows. In this way, the cavalry was defeated, and what remained of the Knightly Order was recalled by Imperial Guardian Kalsos to join the regular cavalry, reforming for another charge.

The emperor’s infantry was breaking. They had been rushed onto the field under the notion that the Knightly Order would carry the day, and yet here they were, being shot to pieces and facing heavy resistance. The Knightly Order had yet again been slaughtered, and the king's army was still in good shape!

The second wave of horsemen thundered forward. Instead of heading directly towards the rear, the Knightly Order directed the regular cavalry at the flanks, hoping that if the rear was well defended, they would at least be able to salvage victory by rolling up the king's battle line from the sides...

As they came upon the flanks, however, the pikemen, trained by Prince Celdon specifically to handle cavalry, held their positions bravely. Before too long, the horsemen found themselves in the exact same position as before.

Unlike the Knightly Order that came before them, the regular cavalry quickly lost the stomach to fight.

As they smacked against the wall of pikes, the cavalry was once again torn to shreds. The regular horsemen made an effort to escape the carnage under intense arrow-fire, and the remaining Knightly Order rushed to escort the emperor and his imperial guardian to safety.

Seeing this unfold, the Aristinian infantry broke ranks and fled. “Let them run, men.” Xanstus said. “If we show them no mercy, they'll think us no better than their emperor.”

*

After two days' marching, the king's army was camped outside the walls of Dosonarmon. They had taken only light casualties and very few deaths in their recent battle, and the mood amongst the regular soldiers was cheerful.

Older and more experienced soldiers were starting to get worried. Winter was drawing in, and a prolonged siege against Dosonarmon seemed unwise. For one thing, it was the regional hub of all the Aristinian Empire's north-western grain supplies and sat astride a mighty river. The city's defenders and citizens had no reason to fear starvation or thirst. Then too, the emperor's remaining infantry and bowmen were now secure behind the city walls.

The emperor's cavalry had regrouped, and although they remained at a safe distance from the king's army, still in their thousands, they remained a viable threat. Above all, the approaching winter freeze was the thing the men feared the most. If they failed to take the walls, they would simply freeze to death.

Just out of bow shot from the city walls, secure in their stockade for the time being, Xanstus called a council of war with the tribal leaders and generals, and he listened patiently to all their gloomy advice and predictions...

Half a mile away, on a hilltop overlooking the city, General Kalsos was making the same calculations and having similar arguments. With no sign of any siege engines or siege towers, he could see no way Xanstus could hope to capture the city. He advised the emperor to sit tight and let nature do the work.

As they both watched the besieging army below them, they noticed a sudden swirl of activity in the king's camp. From their vantage point, it had been easy for them to observe the gathering of the tribal leaders and generals, in what they assumed must have been a council of war. Clearly, a decision of some significance had been made – but what?

Down below, King Xanstus had finally revealed his plan to take the city. His camp boiled with activity, as he set his plan in motion. While his tribal leaders and generals mustered their troops up into rows, Bulvon and his royal knights threw off the brown linen tarpaulin from three of the baggage wagons, revealing respectively: a huge stack of ten-foot-long sturdy ash wood poles, a wagon full of steel pipes, and a third wagon full of cargo netting.

Even as the emperor tried to make some sense of the activity unfolding before his eyes, Bulvon's men joined the ash poles together using the steel sleeves and commenced nailing the cargo netting to the sixty or so, suddenly forty-foot-long ash poles, using the "U" shaped nails he had forged months earlier.

When the sudden flurry of activity paused for a moment, the emperor finally realised the purpose of the completed structure. It was a siege ladder, forty feet long, by sixty ash poles wide, each ash pole separated by a ten-foot-wide stretch of cargo netting.

Down below, all two hundred of Bulvon's men raised the structure above their heads and set off at a fast run towards the city walls. The Danz'kanari tribesmen raced after them and sent up a barrage of arrows against the bewildered guards on the city's battlements.

As the top of the giant siege ladder crashed against the castellations, King Xanstus addressed the rest of his infantry, who seemed as confused as everyone else by the sudden commotion. "Do you all want to spend winter in a tent?" he roared in question. "If not," he continued, "Get over that wall!"

Within minutes, over nine thousand of the Kings' Union's infantry had swarmed over the battlements. There was a brief moment of resistance by the gate tower, as the guards protecting the mechanism that lowered the city's drawbridge mounted a gallant defence, but when Bulvon arrived at the top of the siege ladder, puffing and blowing, he started, almost casually, grabbing the last of the defenders by the scruff of their necks and yeeting them, screaming, off from the top of the city's battlements.

Within moments, the drawbridge fell open, and the king's army streamed through to take possession of the city. Dosonarmon, after all his soldiers' worrying, was his.

Chapter 6 Part 1 – Transitions.

*

Over the next three years, Panthalassa would see less and less of his father and brother.

After the king's stunning victory at Dosonarmon, the snows had set in, and the king's army had no choice but to settle into the captured city for winter, and when spring came, Xanstus simply continued his campaign, pushing further and further into the heart of Aristinia.

Although the king continued to be victorious, there were no more quick wins. The Order of Tiius had declined to take part in any further battles after the capture of Dosonarmon. As they saw it, the king's people were safe now, and any further expansion would only result in unnecessary bloodshed and suffering.

When the king heard of the Order's imminent departure, there was a heated discussion in his private quarters between him and Sir Ardwyn. "You must remember that we are not bound by your laws, good King," said the High Paladin. "We joined your war to ensure that innocent lives would be protected from the emperor's blade. The Order of Tiius exists to protect the world from evil, not to further the ambitions of vengeful kings." At these words, the Order of Tiius made their leave.

As the king's campaigns dragged on, the Aristinians fought with fierce desperation, and their emperor, naive as he was, continued to press more and more of his people into conscription.

Before too long, it had become a stalemate. Each walled city now only fell after a prolonged siege, and the death toll on both sides was horrific.

On Xanstus's infrequent visits home, the atmosphere in the castle grew increasingly strained. His family home, once a haven of security and love, was now beginning to feel more like a cauldron of repressed emotions. For Panthalassa, it felt as though those happy childhood memories had been nothing but a dream.

Whatever the queen's private feelings about the war, she always supported the king in public. Behind closed doors however, she made no secret about her hatred for the war. The young prince would often hear his parents arguing bitterly in their private quarters, and in the morning, his mother's red-rimmed eyes would show that she had been weeping.

It broke Panthalassa's tender heart to see his parents fighting like this. He wished that he could find a way to be a peacemaker, but the gap between them was beginning to seem too wide. Even worse, their differences seemed to force him to pick a side, and although he loved both his parents dearly, having to make that decision was tearing him apart...

Panthalassa was struck by how tired and old the king looked now. He had once thought his father was invincible, but now his dreams were haunted by images of his father falling in battle...

Ever since Panthalassa had broken the toy figure of his father, he had been unable to shake the superstitious dread that his actions, in some way, were linked to his father's fortunes in battle. In a way he could not explain, he still blamed himself for his father's wound.

No matter how much he longed for peace and yearned for the comfort of his mother's arms, he decided, eventually, that his father needed him more. If he was ever going to stand in battle, especially next to his father, he had to overcome his peaceful nature.

*

Panthalassa spent more and more time away from home as he got older. With Xanstus's permission, once Panthalassa had reached the age of fourteen, James started taking the young prince, along with his bodyguard of royal knights, on minor skirmishes in the more remote, lawless regions of the kingdom.

As the war with Aristinia dragged on, there were more reports of bandits and outlaws who were causing mayhem in neighbouring villages, committing arson and daylight robbery and murdering travellers. Worst of all, as James dealt with these bandits, he and his men began noticing that some of them carried symbolic runes, made for worshipping *Odall*. Evil was afoot. Now Panthalassa's training got serious.

Since the bandits had been seen carrying runes of *Corruption Magic*, the royal knights assigned to James by the king would often join forces with the Order of Tiius. As well as dealing with the bandits who had been caught worshipping Odall, the Order of Tiius was also locked in battle with a demonic cult, that now, with the war having dragged on for four years, was rumoured to be getting even stronger. This cult, since its members were bound by magical oaths of secrecy, was simply known as the *Cult of Odall.*

Under James's tuition, the young prince would learn much more than just how to fight. The boy had long since become skilled with a bow, with a sword, and on horseback, and now James was teaching him how to fight as part of a unit. Whereas the regular cavalry would fight on horseback, royal knights only used their mounts to travel round the countryside swiftly. In battle however, thanks to their new training, they would dismount and form closed ranks, wielding formidable double-handed halberds.

As long as they all stood firm together, the long and sharp weapons made an almost impenetrable wall of steel. Panthalassa, while he learned to fight in these formations, felt a sense of security and belonging. It gave him a certain sense of comradeship to be part of such a wall. Standing shoulder to shoulder, knowing they all relied on each other for protection, made them close friends.

Chapter 6 Part 2 - Meeting Death.

Somewhere in the vast woodlands surrounding Pla–Kingus, in early spring.

*

The first day of spring came with an icy wind. The sun blazed down from the heavens and had melted the snow, and the skeletal branches on trees that had been stripped of their leaves last autumn were now slowly budding into life once more.

Panthalassa allowed himself a brief moment to observe the beauty of the land around him. He watched as the water from a nearby stream trickled gently over the rocks and underneath low-lying ferns and willow trees. He saw the deep blue sky, alive with small white clouds, which stood in stark contrast to the dull grey skies of winter he had become so used to.

Nearby in the surrounding trees, wood pigeons and other birds hooted and chirped eagerly in the midday sun, going about their business without a care in the world for the royal escort just below their beaks.

Below them, Sir Ardwyn Keyscarre and a troop of paladins had agreed to let James and Panthalassa accompany them on a small reconnaissance operation in the heart of the forest. Although James had taught the fourteen-year-old prince how to fight as part of a formation, the boy still had a lot to learn. He was beginning to gain mastery over his fears, but from time to time, he still showed signs of weakness. *'A few more of these missions will see the lad through,'* James thought. They carried on marching.

Continuing along the well-trodden dirt pathway, they soon approached a section of the forest so densely packed with pine trees that the ground was covered not in grass, but with the brown needles that had fallen from the trees.

Then they walked over a low hill and came to a sudden halt. “How beautiful,” said Sir Ardwyn, looking down into the enormous crater below them with a coolness that amazed Panthalassa, who himself had shrunk into a kneeling position, grasping onto a low branch on a huge tree that soared above them. He did this even though the land he was stood on was secure. Below him, the roots from the trees acted as a kind of stabiliser. Even a hurricane would have struggled to uproot trees as mighty as these.

“If we hadn't been looking where we were going, we could have fallen to our death!” Panthalassa gasped, and his eyes were wide as he looked down into the depression. It plummeted down for what seemed at least two hundred feet.

“If we weren't pressed for time, I'd have loved to paint the beauty of this,” Ardwyn continued.

“You paint?” Panthalassa asked him. "I find it odd that you have the stomach to mention artistry while glancing down into a crater deep enough to kill you!"

The high paladin gave the young prince a warm smile and nodded. “Aye, I paint. It's a passion of mine I've had since I was not much older than you.”

The paladin recounted the great many battles he had fought over the long course of his lifetime. "And it's not the first time I have stared death in the face either, young Prince..."

James squinted his eyes as he spied some movement on the opposite side of the crater in the far distance. To his amazement, he realized that some local Danz'kanari tribesmen had erected a sort of wooden elevator. It went all the way down to the bottom of the cliff! “That must have taken a lot of work!” he said.

Taking a moment to imagine how dangerous it would have been for the tribesmen to build such a thing, James went to ask him a question. “Did you pay these Danz'kanari to build this? Surely they would have built it for a good reason?”

Ardwyn shook his head. “We didn't ask them to build this.” the high paladin replied. “They've been working with the Kad'aeri for many months. They think they've found kenthril in the cliffs.”

“So... Ardwyn?” mumbled Panthalassa, interrupting them. “Remind me,” he went on, “who is our enemy here? Are we just dealing with bandits again, or are we finally getting to the root of the problem?”

“Well,” Ardwyn sighed, “the clues have all been leading here. Every group of bandits we deal with seems to leave a trail of runes and symbols carved into trees and rocks,” he said. “Lately, we've even seen evidence that some of them have been performing blood rituals. The Kad'aeri miners were the ones that called upon my men to investigate this crater, and after hearing what they had to say, I think we'll be getting to the root of the problem this time, young Prince.”

James looked at the high paladin uneasily. “Does this mean that we'll be fighting the Cultists *themselves* today?” he asked.

"Aye," Ardwyn replied, nodding his head gently. "It might."

Turning to his left, Sir Ardwyn began walking along a pathway that wound around the top of the crater. He raised his hand in gesture, and immediately the two hundred men behind him marched on.

Despite the tension visible on the young prince's face, a quiet part of his mind actually screamed with excitement, for he had often been told of the epic tales from long ago, tales that portrayed the heroism and valour of the Order's paladins as they dealt justice to evil forces far and wide. Many of these tales featured *demons* and other mythical beasts the *Cult of Odall* could supposedly summon.

He realised that, for some odd reason, he was able to ignore the fear bubbling inside his stomach far easier than before.

"I wouldn't worry too much, though," continued the high paladin. "This is merely a scouting mission. We'll only be here for as long as it takes to locate them. In fact, they might not even be here at all."

"Ardwyn?" asked Panthalassa. "What exactly *did* the Kad'aeri say to you?" and as he spoke, his tone trembled with interest.

"Well to start with, young Prince, you must understand that this whole area beneath our feet is riddled with tunnels," he said. James was listening to him too. "Some of the tunnels are natural, which is because these cliffs are made of limestone, which over time is dissolved by the rainwater. There are many rich seams of minerals here too, and so this place has been the focus of mining operations since the ancient times. As a result, these cliffs are honeycombed with abandoned mine-workings and tunnels." he said.

"There are many dangers for the inexperienced, as you might imagine," he went on. "But the Kad'aeri are well used to these dangers, because mining is in their blood. They have recently discovered what they believe might be a rich seam of kenthril near the base of the crater, but since the start of their latest operations, there have been a string of accidents and deaths. Some men have even gone missing, in fact the situation in the tunnels has become so dire that they have taken to building a wooden fort at the base of the cliffs, to shield them from the danger. I was called here because they believe the forces of Odall are at work."

"So don't you have any indications of their strength, Sir Ardwyn?" James asked, raising an eyebrow.

Ardwyn shook his head calmly. "They are not strong," he replied. "The Cult of Odall hides underground to ensure its own survival. If they could defeat us, James, they wouldn't be cowering in tunnels."

Panthalassa tapped his arm eagerly, interrupting their conversation yet again. “Ardwyn?” he asked.

The high paladin smiled back at him. “Yes, Panthalassa?”

“Will you teach me to use *Pure Magic* while we're down there?”

Ardwyn looked into the crater. He felt his heart sink. “Young Prince,” he sighed. “The Cult of Odall can sense when someone who uses that magic is nearby. For your own good, I cannot say yes. Not only would it endanger you, but your father would likely punish James and accuse him of being irresponsible.”

Panthalassa huffed sadly. “Very well.”

They approached the elevator. A half-naked bowman of the Danz'kanari stood to attention beside the thick wooden platform, and far down at the foot of the crater, a hundred or more tribesmen stood at the ready, holding tight a thick, and immeasurably long rope that brought the wooden platform down to the ground.

James eyed the rickety wooden elevator nervously. “You're sure there is no other way down?” he asked.

Ardwyn chuckled dismissively. “It's sturdier than it looks, James,” he reassured. “This elevator was made for carrying tonnes of heavy rocks. I'm sure it can handle you and I.”

It took several hours for all of them to reach the foot of the crater, and when the last of them had arrived, it was getting dark. When they had all been brought to the bottom, the rope-workers who had toiled to bring them down fell to the floor in exhaustion, breathing heavily and swigging water.

Panthalassa looked straight ahead and saw that there was a large wooden encampment. To all purposes, it looked more like a small, fortified village in and of itself. To his left, ash trees no thicker than his arm densely surrounded a giant lake at the foot of the crater, their branches still untouched by the growth of early spring, and they soared into the sky, each of them desperately competing with the others for what little sunlight ever reached this low, rock-strewn hellhole. On the ground itself, barely any life could be seen, in fact, it occurred to him that there was actually more life on the cliff-sides, where countless ferns and even small trees seemed to grow in abundance. *'You know, that really is the last place I'd expect to find a tree...'* thought Panthalassa.

"Well," said James, "if ever there was a place to expect evil to lurk, this is it." He beckoned the young prince over. "Come on."

When they went through the gate in the centre of the wooden palisade wall, a tribesman introduced Panthalassa and James to the layout of his tribe's encampment.

As Panthalassa walked past tents and crackling fires, he observed the small fortress village in all its functionality. Fletchers made fresh arrows for the Danz'kanari bowmen, smiths hammered steel on anvils beside the fireplaces, cooks prepared food and freshly hunted deer were being skinned and butchered. Beside one of the tents Panthalassa walked past, he momentarily gave attention to a conversation one of the miners was having with his apprentice.

"Why have you made this handle from pinewood, you idiot! Don't you know anything about wood?" he asked, recognising the freshly chopped wood from its distinct smell. Panthalassa listened in closely, for he himself wasn't too sure why it mattered.

"Here," said the miner, holding out a fresh piece of ashwood for his apprentice. "Hold this for me and watch." The man snapped the pinewood handle clean in half as he pounded it against a nearby boulder. "Now you try doing that with ash-wood and you'll find it much harder," he said. "Pinewood is used for construction because it keeps its shape in cold weather and is lightweight, but it splinters and is easily broken."

He handed his apprentice his carving knife. "Make the handle out of that long ashwood branch, because ashwood is springy and strong, making it ideal for tools with wooden handles. Don't let me catch you using pinewood again!"

'I never knew that each wood type had different uses. Then again, I suppose I never gave it much thought,' Panthalassa reflected.

Soon they reached the other side of the encampment. This was where the Order of Tiius had hastily erected their tents. Rather than finding a large tent that had already been pre-erected for him (as he had already become accustomed to on his other missions alongside royal knights), and rather than finding a slightly larger, or even differently coloured, tent that signified his social class, Panthalassa was greeted by Sir Ardwyn, who handed him the very same yellow linen tent coverings he had observed throughout the rest of the Order's camp. Lying on the ground at his feet, he saw a bundle of sticks and tent pegs, which the high paladin had placed there. Panthalassa quickly realised that he actually had to make *his own* tent!

"I'm the prince! why hasn't someone -" Panthalassa was suddenly struck by his sense of inferiority and seemed to be at a loss for words.

"The Order of Tiius has a code that each man must share the same hardships as his comrades, no matter the social class or rank," Sir Ardwyn stated, and his tone was as still as the lake-water beside the camp. He meant every word.

"Even for a prince?" Panthalassa asked him.

"Even," said Ardwyn, dropping the linen rags onto the floor beside the tent pegs, "for a prince."

James raised his eyebrow at the high paladin – even he was struck by this disregard for rank; he respected it and understood the moral necessity, but it came as new information. *'Oh well.'* he thought to himself, hiding his amusement, *'I suppose it will do the lad no harm being put in his place once in a while.'*

Panthalassa looked at Ardwyn again. "I would like a--"

But Ardwyn had turned around. He was a busy man, and the standard had been set. "A word..." Panthalassa mumbled on...

James helped Panthalassa to erect his tent in darkness. As they looked up, the sky looked nothing more than a deep blue circular silhouette above their heads, with the high cliffs blocking out any wind that may have otherwise blown about the canvas and chilled their tent. But as they finished their work, they were suddenly struck by an intense flash of light from behind the camp...

Looking back towards the elevator, they saw that the whole structure had suddenly burst into flames! And the colour of these flames was not orange, nor even blue, *but they were violet...*

A group of paladins hurried from the camp and stopped at the foot of the elevator. "Curse Odall. Curse him!" shouted the officer commanding the group. He could see no fire-starters around him. Whoever had started the fire, the officer concluded, must have been working their evil magics under cover of darkness somewhere far away.

Panthalassa watched with trepidation as the structure crumbled into charcoals and ashes and wondered, *'What then, if the Cult of Odall can destroy things so easily, is stopping them from burning down our entire camp?'*

This was going to keep him awake all night, and he could already tell by the frantic hurrying around in the camp that something was about to happen.

Sir Ardwyn Keyscarre and his men eagerly manned the defences, keeping their eyes peeled for signs of movement amongst the shadows. Veteran royal knights sent by the king himself stood side-by-side with the battle-hardened paladins, and they grasped their weapons with iron fists, alert for any danger.

For several hours nothing happened, but the men stayed at their posts. An eerie silence fell upon the camp, but even through this silence, the men would occasionally hear the rattle of pebbles crumbling down the cliff-sides in the night shadows. Sometimes, the sound of twigs snapping set the men on edge, and as the night wore on, a violet mist shrouded the woods surrounding them, followed by an icy chill creeping over the camp, which was unseasonal for spring...

James braced the young prince's hand and smiled at him in comradeship. He could feel how the boy trembled in his grip, trying his best to hide his fear. It eased James's own mind to know that Panthalassa felt safe under his supervision.

"James..." the prince whispered... "I want to see what's happening. Take me onto the walls."

James gave him an uncertain look. "Are you sure?" he asked. "It's unclear what will happen. You're safer here."

Panthalassa nodded firmly, setting his fears aside. "I'm sure," he said.

When they reached the platform on the wall, they saw a scene of mysterious calmness. It was unnerving to say the least, for amongst the darkness shrouding the trees, a purple aura of Odall's magic weaved between their trunks like so many wraith-like snakes. The golden glow of pure magic from the paladins on the battlements shone a light into the woods that flickered like a candle, and each paladin and royal knight beside the prince and his training instructor could see a white fog emerging from the ground amongst the trees...

The paladins manning the wall then felt *Tiius, the God of Justice* filling them with his holy power. Panthalassa looked to his left as he saw the eyes of each man glow a vibrant gold. Never in his life had he seen a man's very limbs glow with magic, for he had only ever read of such things happening in the *Chronicles of Sir Vorn the Demon-slayer,* which featured stories from a thousand years ago, telling its readers how this paladin from a bygone age put an end to the first Cult of Odall, and it ushered in an age of prosperity for all life on Fulminia.

Now the white fog, combined with this mysterious violet magic of Odall, began to materialise into form... This energy they were witnessing, this raw power, began to resemble the shape of a man...

As Panthalassa watched the paladins, he didn't have the courage to ask anyone the questions he so desperately wanted answers to... He watched as tears trickled down the faces of every last paladin and assumed that Tiius *himself* was observing this unholy figure through their eyes. These tears were clearly ones of immense sadness, tears that seemed even heavier than the ones he had wept for his father last winter – for although no man wailed or clearly displayed his sounds of distress, these men who cried were under the spell of Tiius himself. Not only were these the tears of grown men, but these were the tears of a god.

The evil shade that stood in front of the camp seemed to grin with pleasure, and for a moment it was as though the blackness in this shade's mouth was a portal into the vast nothingness of the universe itself – and then – it vanished.

Chapter 6 Part 3 – Beastly Encounters.

The following morning.

*

Panthalassa was sat on a rock just outside his tent, watching as the dark blue sky gradually grew brighter, and all night long he had stayed awake worrying about what he had seen...

Often, he would remember the odd page from stories told long ago about the Cult of Odall's ability to summon the dead and bring forth beasts from strange portals underground, and these tales would set him off worrying again, to questioning whether he was truly in the safest of hands, and so his night went...

It was a trumpet call that finally shook him out of his trance, and after the initial wave of shock wore off, he realised that he had ran out of time to sleep.

Already Panthalassa could hear James rousing himself awake in the tent behind him, and before too much longer, every paladin in the camp seemed to emerge from his quarters in roughly the same minute.

He marvelled at their discipline, and he was even more impressed by the speed with which the paladins donned their armour. They outpaced even the king's own veteran soldiers in their speed and efficiency. The young prince doubted whether they had even wiped the sleep from their eyes.

Another trumpet call sounded through the camp, and the paladins immediately set about packing their tents to leave, and it was about halfway through this process that the king's own veteran royal knights emerged and began doing the same thing.

Finally, James emerged and immediately waved off Panthalassa's offer to help him fold away the tent. "You're too slow!" he snapped, while quickly packing away his things to leave.

Only a few seconds later, the paladins and royal knights were primed to leave.

Sir Ardwyn Keyscarre marched in full armour into the centre of the encampment, and a drum-roll sounded beside him, to the sound of which every man (including James) hurried into a vast rectangular column of listening ears.

Panthalassa approached the column uneasily. He was astonished by the lightning speed efficiency of which the Order of Tiius could operate, and he could hardly believe that less than three minutes ago, this flat plain of rocks and pebbles was a sea of sleeping men.

"Alright men!" Sir Ardwyn Keyscarre, the high paladin, shouted, inspecting his paladins and the king's royal knights with narrow eyes that missed no detail. "You all saw what happened last night. Most of you have read the tales, and those of you who *have,* will know how serious our situation is," he continued.

"The manifestation of that *demon* indicates that the Cult of Odall is growing in strength, and I must also point out that demons haven't been seen in Fulminia for over two hundred years. We must find the hiding place of the Cult's necromancers and cut them down."

There was a silent acknowledgment amongst the men as they steeled themselves for the day's work.

“But we can't do that unless we get into the mines,” he said. “So for now, we will be guarding the Kad'aeri miners while they work to clear a blockage in the main tunnel.”

Sir Ardwyn turned and nodded to the tribal headman stood beside him. “Will you lead on?” he asked the grizzled old miner, who simply nodded and strode off through the woods, followed by his men.

"Right turn!" Ardwyn commanded. "Forward march!"

And at that, the Order of Tiius marched into the rocky woodland.

After a few minutes of marching, they came to a halt just fifty feet away from the cliff side. A rockslide from the cliffs above had completely blocked the entrance. The miners got straight to work. As they toiled to clear the boulders, the army stood by and watched.

The tribesmen worked in grim silence. Their suspicions had been confirmed, and now they knew that evil was afoot. The day was cloudy and overcast and served to fuel their gloom.

Suddenly the miners stopped working, and there was a chatter of voices. Some of the miners put their ears to the rock and began to listen intently. Even from twenty feet away, Panthalassa could faintly hear the sound of iron pickaxes meeting stone. Sometimes, voices would rise to swear or curse at one another, and from a distance, the voices sounded deep and gravelly.

One of the miners turned around and explained the commotion to the soldiers. “We should soon be through now lads! We can hear the other team working to clear the blockage from the inside!” and with that said, they got back to work.

A few short moments passed them by. The miners were yelling words of encouragement to one another, and for a while, everything seemed to be going smoothly.

All of a sudden however, there was a tremendous roar from within the tunnels, and the birds nesting in the trees atop the cliffs fled in terror. As the troops hurried into battle formations, the encouragements ceased, and a deathly silence filled the air...

Panthalassa clung onto James's arm. He looked for reassurance in his expressions, hoping that things would be okay - but he found none. Even James Ashenworn, his old veteran training instructor, looked scared. This roar was like nothing they had ever heard. It seemed to come from three different animals all at once - although neither of them could quite make out what any of them were. *'I've never heard anything like that in all my life...'* thought James.

At the front of the columns of paladins and royal knights, Sir Ardwyn, to the great confusion of James, suddenly went and sat himself beside a tree trunk. He appeared to actually start meditating!

'What is he doing?' James wondered. *'He should be giving* orders!' but Sir Ardwyn carried on meditating, and the men began to seem restless.

“Can't someone wake him up?” James asked, to which a paladin in close command with him replied “We must defend him, James! He's communicating with the druids behind the Kad'aeri miners! Without their help we may never escape!”

“Druids?” James asked, “What do miners need druids for?”

“Healing injuries,” the paladin replied. “Mining is dangerous work.”

As Panthalassa listened closer, he could hear the beast thundering down the Kad'aeri mine. He tensed his muscles harder around James's arm, and watched the area the noise was coming from with wide-eyed trepidation – most of all, he feared what would happen to those miners who were trapped between the sheer rock and the beast they had all heard.

Like a tremor in the earth itself, the beast shook the ground with its ferocious thudding footsteps. A boulder hurtled down the hillside behind the Order's columns and, to their great relief, crashed into the vast lake behind the old encampment, leaving the army untouched.

While this was happening, High Paladin Ardwyn Keyscarre finished meditating with a sudden jerk of shock. He froze for a moment as though he had just been awoken from a terrible nightmare; yet then, when he looked around himself, he saw that he was still alive. "The Druids are dead!" he shouted... "Defensive positions men!"

What happened next made Panthalassa's skin crawl with fear, for suddenly there came a sound which he had never had the misfortune of hearing before... It was one of the Kad'aeri miners, being tore limb from limb...

The beast ripped at the miners in a savage lust for blood, chewing on their bones and biting deep into their stomachs and vital organs. Some of the miners screeched in agony as the beast cut them down, and then at the height of the monstrous thing's onslaught, it crashed through the remaining blockage with its sheer strength.

Rocks and huge stones simply bounced off the beast's powerful back like arrows against a stone wall, and then, with tremendous speed, it charged forward towards the Order's formations.

White rock dust and Kad'aeri blood covered its three evil faces. The fangs of the three-headed beast snapped together in a bloody frenzy, and in the face of such a strong enemy, High Paladin Ardwyn Keyscarre and the Order's soldiers stood their ground.

James braced Panthalassa's shoulder. He could tell that the prince was utterly terrified, and he could feel him trembling in his grip. As the young prince looked up at him, James gave the boy a reassuring grin. “This is how history is made, boy,” he said.

Although Panthalassa wanted to run home, he steeled himself by James's word. Clenching his jaws to prevent his teeth chattering with fright, he nodded his head and held formation.

Panthalassa would have had nowhere to run in any case, because the formation was packed tight. As he stood his ground, his legs quaked beneath him. This, he knew, was where he would die.

The beast crashed into their formation with a terrible power, tearing through thick steel armour as though it were paper. Panthalassa watched with mounting horror as the beast threw the entire bottom half of a man into the air. It spewed with blood and was wearing the steel leg-plates of his father's veteran soldiers. This was one of the palace guards!

“Cangrunarkaei!” roared High Paladin Ardwyn, his eyes glowing with the golden

might of Tiius's power, and at those words, holy fire radiated from his war hammer and shot through the beast's body upon impact, yet rather than empowering the beast as the holy magic did to mortal men, this time the fiery glow of Tiius burned the demonic beast with a righteous fury, hissing and roaring like normal fires would when encouraged by hot tar. The beast growled in pain, its own eyes glowing red, then violet, then red again, and it snapped its jaws around the waist of a paladin, ripping his chest in half even through his armour, licking blood from his gushing body and then throwing him backwards into the middle of the defensive square.

Panthalassa looked at the corpse with horrified eyes. He was frozen with fear. As the young prince braced his halberd firmly in his hand, he was convinced that he was about to die.

He watched as the Order's paladins struck the beast with their spiked kenthril war hammers, piercing deep and bloody holes in its skin. He watched as the beast burned alive in the angry flames of Tiius, and even after this, it seemed to retain enough energy to fight on... The king's veteran soldiers were breaking. He could see it in their eyes. If even one man decided to run now, the whole expedition force would follow, and the beast would win the battle.

But despite the terrible carnage, the troops held firm. Gradually, this three-headed monster seemed to be losing strength.

Instead of ripping men in half or launching them into the air with its massive physique, the demonic monster now simply snapped its jaws into ribcages, crushing bones and vital organs alike, and although this ending was still a terrible fate, the beast did this with a sort of weariness. The flame had burnt out around it, and its skin was charred and bloody.

Paladins carried on pounding their war hammers against the beast's muscular body, spikes piercing deep into the beast's own vital organs. The king's veterans sliced at it with their swords, and finally, it collapsed at their feet in a pool of its own blood.

For a few more minutes, the king's royal knights carried on hacking at the loathsome creature's frame, hardly able to believe that the thing was dead. The paladins however, stepped back and marshalled into formations, ready to move out.

All around the fallen monster's corpse, men lay in bloody pools of carnage, their intestines hanging loose from their stomach like nothing Panthalassa had ever seen. Even some of the paladins seemed shocked by what they had just fought through. This was clearly a beast from long ago... a beast that men had previously attributed to old myths, exaggerations or even lies...

"Well men," murmured Sir Ardwyn, his armour covered in the blood of the beast, and of his comrades, the spike on his war hammer dull from overuse. "If this doesn't prove that Odall is getting stronger, I don't know what can," he said. "I am proud of all of you – we have each lost someone very close to us in this battle, and as for the young prince, I am sure he will remember this day for a very long time."

Ardwyn took a deep breath and faced the opening in the cliff. His shoulders sagged and felt heavy with the new burden placed upon them. This power that the Cult of Odall had now regained would surely spell destruction for many of the weaker kingdoms in Fulminia.

"But for now we must press on. We have a mission to complete. Move out!"

*

As Panthalassa and James worked alongside the Order of Tiius to root out the evil within the tunnels, the day dragged on. Often, they would find traces of *corruption magic* drifting through the air in wispy violet clouds, but all they would lead up to were dead ends at the end of cave tunnels. Blood-stained symbols were etched onto the cave walls, and it was clear that *necromancers* had indeed been here. "Blast it! They've escaped!" barked Ardwyn, finally at the end of the tunnel. One of the royal knights looked confused. "Escaped?" he asked. "But we've been on their tail all afternoon! Surely we would have found them!"

Ardwyn glanced at the soldier in resignment. "These Cultists have other ways of escaping," he sighed. "By summoning portals and communicating with Odall, these villains can sacrifice their own blood to be anywhere they want. For all we know, by now they could be hundreds of miles away." With this, their scouting mission was now complete.

The rest of their day was spent burying the dead. Each time Panthalassa looked at the fallen carcass of the beast, his whole body shivered, but after a few hours of digging and mourning, their day was finally over.

When he finally got to bed, Panthalassa spent long hours staring at the roof of his tent, his mind tormented by the horrific scenes he had witnessed that day. He finally slipped into a fitful sleep, only to awaken bathed in sweat from a terrible nightmare. He had seen his father's army being ambushed by beasts like he had seen today.

What Panthalassa wanted more than anything else at this moment was to see the prideful twinkle in his father's eye once he told him of his adventure... and to see his older brother, and to know they were both safe.

As he lay there in the dark, he made a promise to himself, that come what may, he would find a way to join them. With that decision made, he drifted into a long slumber.

Chapter 6 Part 4 – A New Quest!

City of Pla–Kingus.

*

A flurry of trumpets shook the young prince awake, and he immediately remembered the decision he had made last night. Reaching for his clothes, he got dressed quickly and made his way out of the tent.

When he left, he saw that the paladins were already assembled in their formations. All of them looked just as solemn as each other, and he himself was no different. His heart strings felt as though they were being ripped apart by the memories of those that had fallen.

James emerged from the tent behind him. “You're very alert today.” he praised. His tone was sanguine. “I bet you're happy that we're done here, aren't you?”

Panthalassa finished buttoning up his red silken shirt, then made his reply. “I'm not done,” he said irritably. “I'm going to see my father. I need to know that he is safe.” He began walking towards the paladins. He could see that Sir Ardwyn was drilling them. *'I wonder why the Order of Tiius sometimes decides not to support my father's wars?'* he thought. *'They've supported him before. Perhaps I can convince them to come with me.'*

James urged him to stop. “Wait, boy,” he said. “Think about what you're asking me to do. Are you sure this is the right decision?”

“It's the only decision,” the prince replied, continuing towards the high paladin. “You can choose to stay if you like, James, but I'm going.”

“The king asked me to keep you safe, boy,” James snapped. “I can't let you do this!”

Panthalassa raised an eyebrow at him sarcastically. “Well, do you call what we did yesterday safe?”

James frowned deeply. “I suppose you have a point there.”

As they approached the drilling soldiers, High Paladin Ardwyn called for his troops to stand to attention. “Good morning, young Prince,” Ardwyn greeted. He wasn't quite sure what to say, but he knew the prince wanted to ask him something important. “I'm going to see my father, Ardwyn,” Panthalassa said. “James doesn't like the idea, but I'm determined. Will you come with me?”

The high paladin mused over this for a moment, then nodded slowly. “I myself have some matters to discuss with the king,” he said. “Yes, we'll escort you.”

He looked at James and considered his disapproving expression. “I understand your hesitation,” Ardwyn said, “but if we set off now, we're likely to catch up to Xanstus quite quickly. With any luck, we'll meet him while we're still in the Tan'gran'ne'se, so there will be no harm done.”

James nodded his head reluctantly, but he had one last thing to say to the prince. “Once we meet up with the king, Panthalassa, all he'll do is send us back home.”

“I know,” the boy replied, “but at least I'll have a chance to say goodbye to him.”

Chapter 7 Part 1 – War Awaits.

Far eastern woodlands of the Tan'gran'ne'se, near the Aristinian border.

*

Thanks to the expertise of James Ashenworn, the king's veteran royal knights and Sir Ardwyn, young Prince Panthalassa was eventually able to find his father.

Travelling two days in the Tan'gran'ne'se, local guides had led him through rocky streams and across trackless moors. Often, the land they went through was densely forested, and so on occasion his followers found it easier to actually dismount and make their way on foot.

Last of all, when they were near Dessii, a passing merchant told them that the king's army was near and directed them down a steep wooded slope back onto the main pathway. According to this merchant, the king had garrisoned Dessii as a rallying point. The gossip was that several armies from all across the kingdom would be arriving here in the next few days...

During this journey, James had seen Panthalassa push himself harder than ever before. In fact, far from wanting to sleep early as the boy had done in other adventures, Panthalassa seemed to actually grow restless as the night drew on, only sleeping for a maximum of four hours, then waking up seeming eager to carry on.

James watched this change in his attitude with a certain pride. Although he knew that Panthalassa had adopted this sudden change as a result of great emotional distress, James reflected that perhaps it would be for the best. He knew that the king would be proud of Panthalassa's new-found determination to toughen up, and he also understood that in times of war and instability like these, it was never wise to sleep for too long in any case.

“Open the gates!” called one of the guards in the stone watchtower, and as Panthalassa trotted through into Dessii, he was struck by the buzz of activity. Blacksmiths hammered out fresh steel, the scents of ale or metal grease floated through the air, and very often he would trot past taverns already raging with old tales and bar-fights...

The inner section of the city, however, was protected by another stone wall, and the streets here were far quieter. The houses inside this section were tall and grandiose buildings made of brick and thick wooden beams, and some buildings even had statues of deceased family members (or so he assumed) in their gardens. On one occasion he rode past a house with the shutters open and was immediately hit by the smell of seasoned food. He recognised the fresh smell of basil, the tenderness of the salted lamb meat, and he also recognised another smell... freshly baked bread.

Panthalassa then reflected that, in his eager race to catch his father before he set off again, he had neglected to even eat a meal this morning. He was very hungry.

Last of all, Panthalassa came to the city square, where, in front of the huge mansion that was usually reserved for the mayor, he was surprised to find only a few battalions of royal knights gathered in formation. It seemed as though the entire army was missing! Standing at the front of one of these battalions, to Panthalassa's delight, was Bulvon Bravesoul.

James however, understood that the army was *not* in fact missing, but would no doubt be camped somewhere outside the city walls. Almost none of the king's soldiers lived here, and it would be unwise troubling the population with thousands of new men suddenly demanding a place to sleep. Dessii *did* have a barracks, but even the barracks didn't have the space for fifteen thousand men, which was the number that James assumed the king had brought here.

On catching sight of the young prince, Bulvon was struck with a sense of worriedness. Much like James, Bulvon feared how the king would react to his presence here, and he tensed his shoulders at the very sight of him. "My word," he mumbled to himself. “What is he doing here?!”

"Bulvon!" called Panthalassa, making his way towards him with an air of relief that startled the giant champion. "Is my father here?" he asked.

James sighed quietly at Panthalassa's naivety. Demanding an audience with the commanding officer, on active campaign, was a high-risk business, even for a prince.

"Erh-- he is! He's a little busy now though!" Bulvon answered. "Why have you come here? don't you see we're about to go to war?!"

“Where are all the soldiers? These are just my father's knights!”

Panthalassa's question was completely ignored.

"Bulvon," James murmured. "I've tried convincing him not to come, but he's determined to see his father. He's been through a lot recently; will you take us to him?"

Bulvon shot an uncertain look at the mayor's mansion, and wondered how the king would react. He took a deep breath and turned around to face the battalion standing behind him. "At ease, men," he said. "Now listen, I want all of you men to stay on your best behaviour while I take these two to see the king. I'm not entirely sure how he'll react, and the only reason I'm even considering it," Bulvon said, glancing back slightly towards James and Panthalassa, "is because the king has a right to know where his son is."

He then led the pair into the mayor's mansion. They climbed a flight of white marble stairs and opened a door to their right. Standing at the back of the room beside a dead fireplace, the king was hovering over a map on an oaken desk.

Without even so much as turning his head, King Xanstus raised his hand. "Thank you Bulvon, you can return to your men now. James, leave me and the boy in peace for a moment, will you?" he said. His tone gave no impression of anger or surprise. In fact, he seemed to have adopted a matter-of-factly tone that suggested he was actually happy his son was here. Xanstus turned around to face Panthalassa. "My son..." he sighed, sitting down on the seat beside his desk.

The young prince ran towards him in relief, hugging him tightly. "I have so much to tell you father," he said hesitantly.

The king smiled. "Word of your adventures has already reached me, my son. I have eyes everywhere, and I am very proud of you." This made Panthalassa smile.

"So... you know about the beast then?" Panthalassa asked. He couldn't help feeling a cold sweat trickle down his brow when he thought back to all the lives that had been lost that day.

"Yes, my son. I know about the beast," Xanstus replied. "The reports I have heard make it sound like something from those old legends, and now you have lived to see one of them die."

He smiled proudly at his son. "You are beginning to face your fears like a true warrior. Like a true Lordborn prince."

"Thank you, Father," the prince replied.

"In truth, I didn't think such a creature even existed," said Xanstus after a moment's thought. "It makes my blood run cold just thinking about you facing that beast while I was too far away to protect you. All I could do was put my trust in the men I left you with, and that seems to have paid off, but I am glad you are here now, where I can keep an eye on you."

The king began to walk towards the door.

"Wait, where are you going?" the prince asked.

Xanstus glanced back towards his son. "I need to talk to James for a moment. You can stay here."

Panthalassa sighed with disappointment. He had almost forgotten how uneasy his father seemed to feel about showing emotions. As the door closed behind him, the prince fell silent, wondering what would happen to him next.

*

In the corridor the king greeted James warmly. "I want to thank you for bringing my son to me. It makes me feel at peace that his safety is in my hands again. I don't trust anyone to keep the boy safe in the Tan'gran'ne'se, especially after what has happened!"

James was shocked.

"Don't you trust me? Or your wife?" he asked. "Don't you trust the Order of Tiius? Or the garrison you left in the city?"

"It's not that I don't trust them, James," the king responded... "It's that I'd prefer him to be with me, with my whole army guarding him, than be at home - out of my reach – and still in danger of being attacked by the Cult of Odall. Those priests and holy men in the Order of Tiius have started a war that will drag my kingdom down with them if I'm not careful!"

James listened in astonishment. Was the king mad? Did he really think the battlefield would be a safer place for his son? And did he really blame the Order of Tiius for the rise of the Cult of Odall? Could he not see that this long and unnecessary war was to blame? James fought to keep his emotions under control, and he answered the king softly. "So bring your men home, my liege. Surely the people would thank you for it, and your kingdom would be all the stronger," James said.

"Bring my men home?" Xanstus asked, suddenly taking a sour tone to his voice. "Have you been sent all this way by my wife? If I sued for peace now, they'd call me 'King Xanstus the Cripple!' I can't stomach the thought of peace with the emperor, that vermin! He was the one who put this scar on my face, he was the one who had my close friend's head tossed into the crowd like some dusty sack of rubbish, and he will pay for it personally!"

'Better a cripple than a warmonger...' James thought to himself, but he forced himself to answer calmly. "In any event, Xanstus, you have my loyalty," he said.

"Well I should hope so, James!" the king chuckled. "You're one of my eldest son's closest friends!"

James nodded. “So, is there anything else I should be told?” he asked.

“Yes,” Xanstus quickly replied. “You and Panthalassa are coming to war with me. My army is set to leave in three days.”

James sat bolt upright, suddenly realising that this would mean his own son, Foxeny, would be without his protection for many months. He scanned the king's expression and saw that he had broken into a sudden smile.

“My word, James! calm your patriotic fever! We have three days' wait yet!” Xanstus laughed.

James felt relieved that the king had misunderstood his actions in this way. “One worry is this, my liege...” James said, keeping his tone calm and under control. “My son, Foxeny, is the same age as Panthalassa. With me gone, I fear for his safety.”

The king smiled. “There is nothing I wouldn't do for a warrior as close to my sons as you are! Foxeny can have a room in my castle until we return. I'll send word out this instant."

"Thank you, my King."

Before James went down the staircase to depart, Xanstus called to him once more. “And James?” he said. The old veteran turned towards him. “Please inform Sir Ardwyn that I am ready to give him an audience.”

*

Once Panthalassa had been shown to his room, King Xanstus gave the word for the high paladin to enter. “Your Majesty,” Ardwyn greeted, bowing his head in respect. “I'm honoured to be in your presence once again.”

Xanstus turned away from the maps on his desk. “And I yours,” he said calmly, smiling warily. “What news do you bring?”

Ardwyn slowly lifted his head. “I will assume you've already been told about the monster?”

“I have,” the king replied with a nod. “It sounded like quite the battle.”

“Well,” Ardwyn went on. “I have come to shed some light upon the reason why beasts like that are appearing,” Ardwyn said. “When mortal men are locked in war, it serves only to sow chaos and despair. When the farmer is away from his land, weeds and poisonous plants flourish. Chaos and despair are the weeds of war, good King. As men die, they grow. This is why the Cult of Odall is getting stronger.”

Xanstus paused in thought for a moment. Shaking his head in disbelief, he made his reply. “I have ruled this land for thirty-two years,” he said. “My wars have never caused such beasts to arise in the past. I see no reason why this war is any different.”

Ardwyn looked at him grimly. “The war is dragging on. Dead bodies are piling high. I ask you to consider a ceasefire, or the situation in the Tan'gran'ne'se may very quickly spiral out of control.”

“A ceasefire!” he laughed. “You've been sent here by my wife! I will not let that woman meddle with my plans.”

“Meddle with your plans?” Ardwyn asked. “Your wife is an Arch-Druid! If it wasn't for the queen's philanthropy, your situation would be far worse.”

“Bah, I suppose you're right there,” the king sighed. “I'll end the war when Celsidas is dead. If you leave me to fight my war, I'll leave you to fight yours.”

Ardwyn nodded his head and reached for the door handle. “We'll fight our war, Xanstus. As we speak, men like me fight the forces of Odall across your Kingdom.”

“Then it's settled,” the king said. “I wish you good luck.”

Chapter 7 part 2 – A Grand Army.

City of Dessii, south-eastern Tan'gran'ne'se.

*

When Panthalassa first discovered that he would be coming to war with his father, his initial reaction was shock.

He had witnessed the carnage of battle less than a week ago, and his first instinct after seeing such a thing was to avoid seeing it again at all costs. When the young prince had impetuously embarked on his quest to find his father, he had fully expected to be ordered home at once. Now however, he wondered fearfully what he had got himself into.

He was only fourteen years of age. A boy of his age shouldn't be heading off to war this early, but King Xanstus didn't care. In his eyes, his son being here with him was far more preferable than being kept at home, where it seemed to the king's mind, that the Cult of Odall and the Order of Tiius were determined to wage war on one another, in a vicious crusade to see the other destroyed.

Even so, the king was intelligent enough to see the value of having the paladins protecting his kingdom from evil. With this being the case, he had sent word to every garrison in his kingdom, telling them that they should lend their support to the Order of Tiius. To keep the Cult of Odall at bay.

Even as the king's army prepared for war, the Cultists were busy summoning the dead and opening gates into the black abyss of hell – and no man, aside from the necromancers who summoned them, could truly know what manner of wicked beings lay behind those gates...

Xanstus had battles of his own to fight. He wasn't going to let his son's safety impede his ability to defeat the emperor. He had to get revenge, and over the next three days, while Xanstus and his top generals stewed over the map in their endless war planning, Panthalassa finally found time to train with his brother.

When they trained together, Prince Celdon was filled with pride. He witnessed the fact that his brother's attitude towards training had completely changed. Whereas before Panthalassa was clearly afraid of training, now, he threw himself into the fray with an urge to learn combat like Celdon had never seen before.

Panthalassa still didn't exactly enjoy his sessions; his heart had always been one of a peaceful nature, and the thing he cherished above all else was the opportunity to spend time with his brother, but at least now, after all he had seen in the last few weeks, he saw the need for it.

Fear was his reason. Fear for himself, and above all, for his family. Panthalassa trained because of fear.

Although Celdon could still defeat his brother, he realised with surprise, that he could no longer take that for granted. Panthalassa's attacks were beginning to have a certain flow to them and were lightning fast. Above all, they were totally unpredictable. Celdon felt sure that James's training was paying off.

*

One morning, when Celdon and his younger brother were busy sparring, they heard the huge inner gates of Dessii slam open. A vibrant golden glow of *pure magic* filled the main street below them, and through them marched a huge detachment of the Order's forces.

At the front of the army rode *Paladin Commander* Garren of *Calligii.* He was a striking figure with a stern forbidding countenance. The grey stallion beneath him was coated in rich yellow fabrics that radiated pure magical energy. His hair flowed like smooth chestnut in the gentle wind behind him, and his kenthril armour glinted sunlight brilliantly from the many decorations and rubies inlaid into it.

Despite him being a Calligian, this paladin commander was someone of great importance to the holy Order of Tiius; formerly a desperate boy suffering under the tyrannical rule of the Calligian emperor, Garren Kraeksoul had resorted to thieving to simply help his family survive.

When he reached the age of twelve, he was drafted into the imperial army to serve as a drummer boy until the age of fifteen, but then, in a battle along the *Wall of Straeum,* his father was killed by a ballista round, and the emperor's legions were defeated.

Left on the desolate field of carnage to die or be eaten by the crows, a young Garren Kraeksoul had limped pathetically towards the giant iron gate in the middle of the wall before him, wishing to either die or be taken hostage by the Straeiian king's men-- and when he did this, rather than taking him hostage, the king of Straeum then *personally* delivered him to the Order of Tiius, and then, when he had arrived, fifteen year old Garren finally found the love and peace he had been starved of for all his life.

Tiius, and all his children, welcomed him with comforting arms.

And now, at thirty-one years of age, Garren Kraeksoul had climbed the ranks of the Order through countless battles, serving his god selflessly after repenting his sins. He marched into King Xanstus Lordborn's second capital with an army behind him, to bring evil to justice once again.

In the Order's force, four units of hand-picked paladins, each consisting of one hundred men (with high paladins commanding each sub-division) moved on horseback in the vanguard, and behind them, further thousands of Order-Knights marched in chorus with a steady drum, shields swaying hypnotically, emblazoned with the symbol of the Order of Tiius, which with three simplistic gold lines, bore resemblance to both the holy sceptre of the god himself, and the capital letter "Y".

The *Grand Paladin* was in direct communication with Tiius himself, and Tiius had decreed that an end to the war was needed, now that he could see how Odall *himself* had grown in strength in Fulminia.

Ending this war, the Grand Paladin knew, might involve fighting even more cavalry, and so even though a holy force of this magnitude would usually be reserved for battles along *The Wall of Straeum,* the Grand Paladin had made an exception for this occasion, and he sent one of the largest detachments of the Order's troops the continent had ever seen, commanded by one (of four) of his paladin commanders, to aid in King Xanstus's cause.

The weapon of choice for the Order of Tiius's knights was the spear. Spears, when used by a highly disciplined (and flexible) force, are perfectly made for fighting cavalry, and King Xanstus knew that. So, in his mind, as long as these men were on his side, victory was certain.

At either side of the paladin commander, two banners, each bearing the symbol of The Order, flew elegantly in the wind, and during the course of this day, many more soldiers from across the king's country would enter the city.

Arriving from *Satia,* a great many more spearmen marched under a methodical drum. They marched under a pink banner that had a black horse in the centre, and their uniforms were made of simple leather. Their discipline, however, matched that of the king's own royal knights, and their spears were 20 feet long. These men were bulky and short, and only their leader, Lord Adragon, was on horseback.

From *Adaria,* Lord Aleric, who (as well as the Order Lords) had attended the king's banquet at Winter's Hope, marched his troops under a banner symbolising the land

and the sky. The lower part of the banner was coloured green and was made jagged so as to symbolise grass. In the middle, a tree was roughly painted, its trunk planted in the soil, and all around that tree, shades of blue flowed out into the heavens, portraying the sky.

Lord Aleric's men were more numerous than those of the other lords, and they came in three separate detachments. First came the cavalry.

Trotting at the front of the force, Lord Aleric's knights pierced the sky with their lance tips, their steel helmets glinting in the sunlight wonderfully. From the neck downwards, their whole bodies were covered by full suits of chainmail, which allowed for more flexibility than plated armour would have. The chainmail also took less away from the natural speed of their steeds.

Their discipline, however, seemed lacking, and they openly talked with one another in their high, pompous accents, as they made their way towards the city square.

Behind these two thousand horsemen, a larger force of swordsmen appeared. These soldiers, while also wearing full chainmail, carried large rectangular shields at their sides. These troops seemed slightly more disciplined, yet by their facial expressions, and by the sluggish way they marched, their morale was lacking. Each one of their shields was made of thick poplar wood, and they were coated with a plain, bright green linen. Apparently, Adarian shieldcrafters weren't so creative.

Last of all the Adarian forces, after the five thousand swordsmen, came the skirmishers. These were men who didn't even share a common uniform, and their weapons included bows, crossbows and javelins. Even slings were used.

Most of the skirmishers looked half dead. Many of them were sweating profusely through their multitudes of clothes, and they had clearly been force-marched to exhaustion. Some of their clothes looked torn, and it occurred to Prince Celdon that they may have even joined battle with the undead. On one of the skirmisher's sheepswool tops, a large patch of what looked like stale blood was visible. Another man, while he trudged past the less than amused prince, unknowingly dropped a severed finger from his back pocket, straight onto the pathway.

A few moments later, another skirmisher eagerly picked the severed finger up with his bare hands, plucking a silver ring from it, then tossing the finger to the side once more.

'So this is the "great" army of Adaria? How far the mighty have fallen...' Celdon thought, harking back to the history lessons he had learned as a child.

He remembered hearing of a time when an independent Adaria, along with its allies, once defeated the Calligian Empire's onslaught on the border of Straeum. The Adarian army, at least in those days, was said to have had the best discipline in the known world, and if the legends were true...they had half a million men.

These tales were from five hundred years ago, and yet now, this undisciplined force of perhaps ten thousand 'soldiers', was all that remained of their old glory.

Last of all, stumbling into the city square with drunken laughs and slurred singing, the Istarians joined the king's army. These men were once the cream of King Nassarrod's fighting force, that fallen, recently conquered ruler of Istaria.

Prince Celdon remembered Bulvon's tales of ferocity, when he had beaten three thousand of these foes, with no more men than his own battalion of two hundred. Now that these *axe-sentinels* were here in front of him, he could finally believe the stories.

They reeked of crude ale and gone-off milk. Their wolfskin tunics that covered chainmail gowns made them look no more civilised than the Kad'aeri berserkers already in the king's army. These men seemed more like bandits than soldiers, and Prince Celdon actually felt ashamed that his father was letting these men join their most glorious campaign.

At the end of the day, and after a long head count, King Xanstus Lordborn concluded that his force now numbered (leaving out the camp followers and supply wagons) forty-one thousand men.

In the morning, the army would move out.

Chapter 7 Part 3 – Bloody Diplomacy.

Outskirts of Dessii.

*

The march started with a heavy rain. All the way through the city, the hammer of tramping feet was equalled by a roar of droplets pelting against the roof tiles. As the army reached the outskirts of the city, the rain stopped abruptly, and the sun broke through. Yesterday, the prominent smell was the stench of the city, today that odour was now pushed aside by the wonderful smell of *petrichor,* that earthy smell that so often accompanies spring. The verges on either side of the road had now flowered into abundance at the presence of rain.

The shower seemed to have brought out all of the best features in what little wildlife existed by the pathway. The dandelions' vibrant yellow flower-heads were spread out to their fullest, the grass seemed greener than it had the day before, and even the pathway itself, as Panthalassa was beginning to see, would have been overgrown with greenery, including the very hardiest, most determined of sycamore saplings, were it not for the constant thrum of soldiers' feet.

How much more miserable then would the ants beneath the pavement be, now that their tunnels of dirt had been soaked into oblivion by the lashing rain? With their only hope of escape being the cracks in the cobblestone, which had now been overrun by swarms of humans pounding endlessly above their heads, with bodies so heavy and powerful that they could have crushed an entire colony under their feet, if only they wanted to...

Panthalassa was always the type of boy to wander into a world of his own in thoughts like these, and all of a sudden, it struck him... *'That's it! That's why I'll never be a good warrior. I care too much. I'm too soft hearted...'*

He tried to catch a glimpse of James's expressions, who rode proudly beside him and his older brother, Prince Celdon.

James was smiling. He had always said that he loved the rain, and he loved the smell of *petrichor*, too. It reminded him of brisk summer days, where he could simply lie back and enjoy the fruits of his labour in peacetime... Although at the moment he was mounted on a horse and suited in thick war leathers, he too, seemed to be in a world of his own, picturing himself under the shade of a tall oak tree munching on a fresh apple just plucked from the orchard... *'Yet, James seems to venture into his own world too, and he is no less a warrior for it...'* Panthalassa thought on...

After the king, leading from the front, had led the army out of Dessii, he then took his forces down a road that he and his veterans knew all too well.

Bulvon closed his eyes as he marched his men past the fortifications. All those hidden traps and surprises that had so masterfully defeated the emperor four years ago, but he couldn't help feeling a sense of guilt when he was here at this moment. *'I must never forsake the king's plans again...'* he thought. *'The king would have never been injured if we had stayed put.'* he scolded himself for the king's injury, which at least in his mind, was completely his own fault... *'When battle next arrives, I will never leave his side.'*

Celdon felt exactly the same as Bulvon. He smiled at Panthalassa but felt a sincere sense of loss. "Brother - if you can sense something about me and the other men at the moment, you are correct," he said.

Panthalassa looked back at him and gave an uncertain smile. "What do you mean?"

Celdon pointed to the mounds of earth at either side of the pathways... those same ones that had been placed there to conceal death traps beneath holes overgrown with brambles and ivy. "You see there, brother?" he asked. "That is where the Aristinian Knightly Order met their defeat; and all around us, if you look closely, you will see felled trees overgrown now with moss and brambles; you will see mounds of earth not too dissimilar from these ones, and you will realise that this was the place where our father beat the emperor."

Panthalassa took a moment to observe the land around him... Already a more spiritual sense was beginning to fill his mind... a sensation of blood, of slaughter... men dying by the thousands... misery... and fear... so much fear...

"I can sense it..." Panthalassa breathed.

There was silence for a few moments.

"Is..." he mumbled... "Is this where Father earned his scar?"

Celdon nodded slowly. "Earned? No..." he sighed. "He did not 'earn' his scar, it was inflicted upon him by a cold and soulless emperor, who deserves nothing but a quick death to make up for what he has caused."

James nudged Celdon's arm. "He earned it alright, lad," he insisted. "You're looking at it the wrong way. Do not think of this scar as something that will turn your father into a cripple; rather, look at it as something that he lived to tell the tale of; a page in history. A memory. That scar, Celdon, is something that you should be proud of him for."

King Xanstus smiled as he overheard this part of their conversation. "Very touching, James," he said. "Although I must admit, I do miss my right eye!"

Some of the men laughed at this. There was a certain humour that suggested they were laughing with him, rather than at him, and the sound of the soldiers' laughter broke the atmosphere of sadness.

"I'll tell you what, James. Perhaps I won't kill him after all!" Xanstus continued. There was silence among the front ranks as they waited for the king to finish his sentence.

"Maybe I should thank him for giving me such a pleasant memory! Oh how I love the emperor for tearing out my eye!" he called, and as he said this he cast his arms wide to face the sky, smirking at James wryly. The men roared with laughter.

James smiled and peered off to one side, appreciating the humour for what it was. *'Every joke that is made in this fashion must have its victim,'* he thought. *'Thank the gods I'm old enough to take this roasting in my stride...'*

They marched on through the woods, soon making their way through the gap in the mountains that separated the Tan'gran'ne'se from the Aristinian plains.

King Xanstus glanced uneasily at the clifftop, where four years ago, the Kad'aeri berserkers had levered an enormous boulder down the side of the hill and caused an avalanche. He remembered the deathly screech of the men who towed the emperor's supply train just before they met their end, how the horses screamed in their helplessness, and he knew that now, if the emperor's men were somehow beside them on the clifftops, his army was in that very same precarious position. All it would take, King Xanstus noticed, to slay countless hundreds of his men in this moment, would be perhaps twenty men loyal to the emperor (armed with no more than pickaxes and crowbars), and Celsidas would already have won the day.

After several minutes, the army had marched through the gap in the hills onto the plains. Within the next few hours, they would reach the old village of the *Varnixye,* that same one that been sacked by the emperor four years ago. Although the village had since been rebuilt, Warlord Zalxorr grimaced at the memory of those he had lost. He tightened his grip on his sword, seething with a lust for Aristinian blood. *'I will avenge you, Father,'* he thought. *'As for all our young and middle-aged, who still live on, I will make them proud.'*

Killing the emperor's men was not enough for him. The king's early victories had only served to prove that the Aristinians could be beaten. It was not just the emperor's soldiers that Warlord Zalxorr hated, it was Emperor Celsidas, of the *Baeres* bloodline, himself.

The king would march past many more towns and villages over the course of the next few days, and although they had all been rebuilt and doubly fortified, each one reminded Xanstus why the war must continue. *'So much effort has been spent, conquering and holding these territories...'* he thought. *'But if I don't kill the emperor, it will all have been for nothing. I'll be remembered as a cripple, and I'll never live down the shame...'*

On the fourth night, the king's army had got to a hill, less than twenty miles away from *Aokron*, which was the next city he intended to take. "Make camp here!" the king called into the fog. "We will march again at dawn."

*

While the rest of the army slept, Bulvon, as he liked to, took first watch, and through the darkness of the night sky, he saw a man with a torch making his way on horseback towards the camp.

'One of the emperor's messengers...' he thought to himself.

The rider pulled down his rough linen hood and held his torch up to try and identify the banners on the encampment.

"What do you want? It's three in the bloody morning!" Bulvon called.

"I wish to speak to the emperor!" the rider replied.

"Well it's me you've got!" Bulvon answered. "And who are you?"

"I am Haerris of Straeum! Messenger under authority of King Larbaeris Sajj! And I wish to speak to the emperor!"

Bulvon laughed heartily. "Do I look like an Aristinian to you?!"

"I can't identify the banners, sir! It is too dark!"

"We're Unionites! We are invading Aristinia! Now come inside the camp and I will take you to our king."

"A messenger from Straeum, you say?" asked Xanstus, sitting upright, shirtless, in his bed of furs.

The young messenger entered the tent. As he entered, the king immediately noticed his hair. “My word, you're as young as my eldest son and you've got hair as white as a crone!” he chuckled.

White hair was a physical feature that almost everyone from Straeum shared. It was genetic.

The boy was lost for words. He had never seen a king shirtless before, and his jaw had dropped.

“Well don't just stand there looking at me like you're an imbecile! What was your message?” the king demanded.

“I-- I'm sorry! I've just never seen—”

“Never seen someone without a shirt on, boy?!” The king laughed. “Gods be good, the emperor’s allies are virgins too!”

Bulvon snorted with laughter.

“Yes, your Majesty! I just wanted to--”

“Yes, your Majesty! He even admits it! Ha ha!” the king carried on.

Bulvon chuckled with childish glee.

“Your Majesty, my message was this! The *City of Straeum* has fallen under siege! She is calling her allies to aid her!”

“Aid Straeum, eh?” the king asked, placing a hand on his hip sarcastically. “And why exactly did you come here to deliver this message? The emperor is in the opposite direction.”

“I was lost... I got told that the emperor had an army camped somewhere in these parts, and I saw your camp. This is my first time delivering a message,” the boy replied.

“Then why didn't 'his Majesty' send a more competent messenger, Hmm?” Xanstus asked.

“All of the king's old messengers are dead. They died trying to escape the Calligians who have surrounded the city.”

“So you're not a *real* messenger, you're an escape artist,” the king grumbled. He shook his head. “You are wasting your time here. I will not accept peace from the emperor, and with that being the case, the emperor can't help your city.”

The messenger stood in awkward silence for a few more seconds, lost for what else he might say, until the king broke the silence again. “Put him under lock and key, Bulvon. We'll keep him there until we can find a use for him.”

*

At the break of day, just as the camp was starting to stir and the birds were singing their dawn chorus, another body of men approached the camp. *'Aristinian knights...'* the sentry in the watchtower thought to himself, taking in their gleaming armour and the fine horses they rode.

The leader of the group of about twenty horsemen approaching the camp was wearing a brilliant silver-silk cloak and was coated in gold-trimmed bronze plate armour from the chest downwards. *'And that one's a nobleman, or even royalty if I'm not much mistaken... I'd better tell Bulvon at once!'*

Climbing down the ladder, the sentry then ran towards the large red canvas tent, in the middle of the camp, beside the king's own. But before the sentry reached the tent, he saw that Bulvon was sat beside a campfire, munching on some bread with cheese.

“What's the matter? Who is coming?” the giant champion asked.

“Aristinian knights.” the sentry replied. “Maybe some kind of royal escort...”

Bulvon stood up. “Let me see this for myself!” he grunted and climbed up into the watchtower.

As the escort drew closer, the sunlight began to brighten. Bulvon could just make out the man's clean-shaven face from atop the tower, and observed his handsome, youthful smile. This was clearly someone of noble birth. “I think you're right.” he said. “Royalty, I would say, and under a white flag! Go tell the king at once!”

But no sooner had Bulvon given the order, that Xanstus Lordborn emerged from his tent, already fully dressed in his plate armour. It seemed as though he had had very little sleep. “No need to say anything. Send him in,” he said calmly. “But his guards must stay outside.”

After a minute or so, the gates were opened. The emperor’s messenger made his way into the centre of the camp square, where the king was waiting for him, grinning crookedly.

The Aristinian nobleman dismounted, then gave the king a deep, respectful bow.

“Speak your words, prattler. I have little time to spare,” Xanstus spat. He could feel a headache coming on.

Ignoring the insult, the envoy pulled an ornate scroll from a leather container and carried on. “Greetings, good King! I am Lord Zakron Baeres, first cousin of the emperor himself. His Imperial Majesty has entrusted me personally with delivering this message to you, rather than send some common messenger. He hopes by this gesture, to try and convince you of the sincerity of his desire to achieve peace between our peoples. I am honoured to meet you.”

The king pulled the scroll from his hands and gave it a quick read. *'Peace on my terms, he writes.'* Xanstus thought...

He chuckled slightly... *'Well, I'll make my terms nice and clear!'*

Xanstus walked towards him and gripped his shoulder. “These are my terms.” he growled. Unsheathing his sword, King Xanstus plunged his blade cleanly through the envoy's stomach, aiming high so that the weapon would slice through his heart.

There was a deathly silence, after the initial gasps of horror. Bulvon watched as the envoy's blood spurted down onto the king's leg-plates, and dropped his mouth in astonishment... This wasn't the king he once knew... Had he gone mad?

As Xanstus released his grip, Lord Zakron's corpse flopped backwards onto the ground. As a final act of barbarity, King Xanstus severed his head.

“M... My liege?” Bulvon murmured in a shocked whisper... “He was under a flag of peace!”

Xanstus looked at him sternly. “Go fetch that boy from Straeum. I have a task for him after all.” He gripped the envoy's head by the hair and tossed it towards Bulvon. “Tell the messenger that he is to take this to the emperor, and that he is to tell Celsidas, that *that* is my answer to his peace offerings!”

The blacksmith opened his mouth to protest... but Xanstus met his eyes with a look of daggers, and Bulvon remembered his guilt... *'I might not always agree with the king's decisions, but I will not fail him again...'* he thought.

Bulvon sighed in despair. “I'll send the lad away with the retinue outside.”

When the messenger from Straeum was handed the grisly contents, he gagged, trembling with shock. “I'll go right away!” he blurted, fearing that if he failed to obey the command, he too, might share his fate.

Chapter 7 Part 4 – Exciting Discoveries.

The Plains of Aristinia.

*

Minutes after the messenger from Straeum had departed, the Order of Tiius, in their usual disciplined fashion, packed their tents and prepared to march out. A moment later, their entire force was stood to attention before their paladin commander, Garren.

Xanstus was impressed. *'At least they're keen to march,'* he thought.

But when the king heard what Garren had to say, his mood swiftly changed.

"Here we stand, men!" shouted the paladin commander. "The crossroads between Aristinia and The Kings' Union, two human kingdoms locked in combat… "We have all heard the king's answer to the peace offering, and with that being the case, it is clear that so long as we remain in this army, we defy the very god we serve."

Whispers blew about the camp as the king's men heard these words. They were shocked to hear what seemed like a desertion so early in their campaign.

"The Order of Tiius follows the will of Tiius alone," Garren continued. "And since that means battling evil, our holy order will continue to help King Xanstus purge the Cult of Odall from the Tan'gran'ne'se, but we cannot take part in an unjustified war of invasion."

The king seethed with rage and gripped the hilt of his sword while he listened to this. *'Trust a Calligian scum like him to make such a betrayal... the Order of Tiius are nothing but mercenaries and pirates posing as holy men!'* he thought, and yet he was also struck by the fact that there was nothing he could do...

While they may abandon him in this campaign, the king was acutely aware of the fact that they were not bound by his laws.

They *were* holy men, and without their help, the Cult of Odall would simply overwhelm his defences back in the Tan'gran'ne'se. He could not afford to quarrel with them.

The king gritted his teeth, listening on in his silent fury, to the filth that this Calligian paladin commander was spewing.

"Our mission now then, must lie to the east." Garren continued. "We pledge our service to Tiius and pray that he gives us the strength to free Straeum from the grip of the Empire!"

"Honour for Tiius!" replied the paladins, pledging their service to his cause.

"Forward march!" commanded Garren.

*

Morale was low that day.

All morning, the king's army would march under the grey sky, rain pelting their helmets and soaking the cobbles under their feet, and the soldiers miserably trudged on, knowing full well that ten thousand holy warriors had just abandoned them.

Tiius had abandoned them, and they could all feel it.

In midday, in the middle of spring, even despite the obvious warmth, it was raining. Not the fresh rain that quenched the plants' thirst, not the usual rain. This was *miserable* rain. They were just wet. And they carried on marching along this endless line of cobblestone that made its track through the Aristinian plains, wondering if they would ever reach a destination.

The army was silent and subdued, with each soldier preoccupied with his own gloomy thoughts.

The king noted the soldiers' mood but made no effort to cheer them up. He was too entangled in his own worries. *'And so, however inconvenient it may be, the kingdom of bloody Straeum has finally found its aid,'* thought Xanstus. His face was set into a grim frown. *'I wonder what will happen now that the Order of Tiius have left us...'* his train of thought continued. *'If Straeum is getting ten thousand reinforcements from Garren's paladins, will that encourage Emperor Celsidas to finally bring his Knightly Order home?'*

Xanstus made a mental note to dispatch his most trusted spy, the one he had nicknamed 'The Watcher,' to the Wall of Straeum, with instructions to warn him at once of any such troop movements.

'Thankfully though, we've dealt with the bulk of his Knightly Order in Aristinia,' he concluded. *'Even if those treacherous paladins do choose to desert me, this time,*

the emperor's army is finished.' At the back of his mind, the king knew more than anyone, that the poor morale of the army was a serious problem. This, more than anything else, was his concern, and now, as if he needed more to upset him, Prince Celdon began his woodpecking.

"If I may ask, Father, what exactly is our plan?" he inquired, "for it seems like you're just marching the men forward aimlessly... until we meet the emperor's cavalry."

"Cease this at once, Celdon!" Xanstus snapped, "I am more than just a simple fool, and you of all people should know this by now. I would never lead thirty-one-thousand soldiers into the vast plains of Aristinia, without first having devised an intricate plan. Let me concentrate."

"What is your plan then?" Celdon asked.

Usually, the king would never have tolerated such apparent disregard for his authority, even less so from his own son, but right now, he understood perfectly why Celdon was doing it, and it was for the simple reason of worry. Celdon feared that if the emperor had even half a chance of killing Xanstus again, he might just succeed, and so, as a father, rather than a king, he felt a sense of shame wash over him for his outburst; and Celdon noticed now, how the king's shoulders had slumped.

"I will tell you the plan in due time, my son," he sighed, "but needless to say, the enemy is far away enough for us to carry on marching. Please let me concentrate."

"Yes, Father."

Bulvon looked up to the king and saw that his shoulders had sagged, and although this only happened for a brief moment, it was enough to bring his spirits low. *'No one else must abandon our king at this hour,'* thought Bulvon... *'When the time for battle arrives, we must fight like cornered beasts to preserve his honour, for if we fail to defend him again, all will be lost.'*

James saw the king's expression too and thought that the king was feeling doubt. *'Whatever happens next,'* James thought, *'even if the king is unsure of his odds for victory, I will defend Panthalassa with my life.'*

Panthalassa, who was the youngest boy in the army, saw his father's expression and turned pale. Never before in his life had Panthalassa seen his father breaking under pressure, and although this was in fact *not* what Xanstus was feeling, the mere fact that he had interpreted it in this way played something evil with his mind.

The reality? The king's scar was draining his presence of mind, and he hated the sense that his eldest son had seen weakness in him.

He needed to maintain a clear mind. To shut the pain out. For once, King Xanstus felt like he needed to toughen up *himself.*

*

Night was falling upon them, and they were approaching a town. One of the king's scouting parties drew up their horses beside the king and bowed their heads low. “Greetings, Sire,” spoke their officer.

Xanstus stared at the man through the creeping darkness. “What news do your scouts bring?” he asked. The officer raised his head and gave a slight smile. “Aerikennos appears to be empty, my lord. The doors were cast wide open. Me and the men were able to get through the gates – without so much as a single arrow being fired.”

The king raised an eyebrow sceptically, suspending his disbelief.

“We checked every building, sire, and every tunnel. It's completely empty.”

'I wonder what the emperor is up to?' Xanstus thought...

“Very well,” he responded, stroking his beard. “We'll rest inside the town. Carry on officer.”

As the scouts rode off to join the marching army, Prince Celdon was flooded with incredulity. “Father,” he murmured, “this is very strange. Are you sure we can still trust his word?”

“My scouts have never lied to me before, Celdon,” sighed the king. “They are hand-picked for their trustworthiness. It just unsettles me that the emperor would abandon such an easily defensible town.”

“It could be a trap,” Celdon continued. “What if Celsidas wants you to take it?”

Xanstus shook his head and glared sternly, implying that no further discussion would be permitted. “The town is strategically unimportant,” he said. “Even *had* the town been garrisoned, my initial plan was to simply march around it.”

Within minutes they had crossed the river, climbed the hill and arrived. Not only had the Aristinian military abandoned the town, but to their surprise, so too had most of the civilians.

The king told his men to get some rest, for he knew that tomorrow would likely bring plenty of surprises. While the army slept, Xanstus had his scouts take him and the quartermaster to the town's armoury. “It's full, you say?” he asked. “Well then we'd better see what's inside!”

Panthalassa and James came with him.

As the giant doors creaked open, revealing the sheer size of the cache, the king's mouth curled into a satisfied grin. “My word,” he chuckled. “We'll make good use of all this!”

But suddenly, his train of thought was interrupted.

“What are these for, James?” Panthalassa asked, his voice reverberating through the hall. He picked up a metal object with four spikes and inspected it closely.

“Caltrops,” James replied. “Whichever way you throw it down, one of the spikes will always face the sky.”

James picked one up, glancing gingerly at the king - “and they're especially useful... against cavalry.”

Chapter 7 Part 5 – Devastation.

Half a day's march away from Dosonarmon, Plains of Aristinia.

*

When the king's army left Aerikennos the following morning, the rain subsided. The sun was bearing down upon them from the heavens with a newfound heat that made it seem more like summer than early spring, and as the soldiers drummed their feet over the Aristinian plains, they soon ran into a river.

The surface of the water flickered sunlight like glitter, casting an air of calmness through the army that seemed strange for what felt like the eve of battle, and Panthalassa, who was at the front of the force with James, Bulvon, Celdon and the king, was especially moved by the beauty of the riverbanks.

Although the vast majority of the Aristinian plain was filled with light yellow grass blades, the banks of this river were alive with countless explosions of greenery, with flowers and balsam, saplings and old trees filling the land around them.

"James, I have something I want to ask you," said Panthalassa, still keeping his eyes fixated on the beauty of the emperor's countryside, watching as the river trickled eastwards, flowing ever further away from the Tan'gran'ne'se with every passing second.

"Yes, young Prince?" James replied, his eyes also wandering around the scenery.

"I no longer feel as concerned about my own safety. Is that normal?" he asked. "I feel much more worried about my family and friends."

James cast Panthalassa a gentle smile. "Yes, it is," he replied. "I think that when you look death in the face enough times, the prospect of feeling scared for your own sake begins to feel rather silly, and so - instead of feeling scared for your own sake, you begin to feel doubly scared for those you love."

Panthalassa thought back to his expedition into the crater... he remembered how the beast had torn men in half and thrown them into the air as though they were nothing more than empty skins of water.

He remembered how convinced he had been that his death was imminent; that such a beast like that could never be defeated, and that even despite all the men who were guarding him, he, in that moment, had felt completely vulnerable.

"Do you remember when the beast threw that soldier into the middle of the formation?" Panthalassa asked him.

"Yes, I do," replied James. "I remember it a lot better than I'd like to, in fact."

"I think that was my 'looking death in the face' moment," the prince commented. "After that moment, I've felt scared almost constantly – but not for myself..."

Bulvon reached over to the young prince and patted him on the shoulder with his meaty right hand. "Then you're braver than you give yourself credit for," he assured the young prince, smiling with his many years of battle experience, to guide his words. "Now that you've seen the blood of battle, Panthalassa, you'll find it harder to let those you love suffer on the front lines."

Bulvon sighed gently and looked at the king, and even though all he could see was the back of Xanstus's head, just seeing the mere outline of it took him back to the very moment the emperor's lance had almost killed him... "What drives me into a battle fury, young prince," he continued, a tear trickling down his face as he contemplated his failure to protect his friend, "is the thought of the ones I love being harmed."

"And perhaps, Panthalassa, since you and I are men of sincere emotion, you will become brave through comradeship."

Celdon suddenly felt moved by Bulvon's wise words. "That's beautiful..."

Two more hours of marching ensued after those words were exchanged, and after those two hours, the king had found his position.

The army had been arrayed in battle formation, stretching across the land for half a mile.

On their left flank, the river still flowed into the distance, now being hidden behind what had become a lush forest surrounding the banks. Over the river, just behind the army, there was a bridge.

The king knew that the river here ran much too fast for the emperor's forces to outflank him.

From his viewpoint on the open plains, the bridge, and even the river, were now completely invisible because of the dense forest. There was a thin path of dirt that wound towards the bridge, but so far as the king was aware, this pathway, after the bridge, led only towards the peaceful trading kingdom of Jaldana, and as such, so far as the king was aware, had no relevance to this battle.

On their right, the plains continued, and here, the king noticed, he would have to place a few thousand caltrops to help guard his flank. As far as the eye could see, yellow fields of grass interwoven with the occasional stream or small hill, covered the landscape.

And in front of the army, to the king's great joy, was a steep hill. *'I'll make him think he has the advantage of higher ground,'* he thought. *'And when his men charge down the hill, my caltrops will devastate them.'*

"Alright men!" he commanded, "The emperor's army has been sighted marching towards us, and even now they are only three hours away. They march at a speed of five miles per hour, I am told, and in these three hours, I expect each man to pull his weight and fill the land in front of us with the spike traps."

Celdon gritted his teeth nervously, looking up at the hill before them with cavalry in mind. *'If the emperor can bring thirty thousand horses into the field as he did last year, a few thousand caltrops isn't going to slow their charge... we're doomed!'* he worried...

"I can see that look on your face, my son," the king whispered to him.

"Let me tell you something. The Aristinian Knightly Order has been greatly weakened by their defeats, and right now, as our scouts have confirmed, the only ones that remain in the emperor's army have been assigned to his personal bodyguard," he said. "The bulk of Celsidas's force, as you should now be made aware, does not in fact consist of cavalry at all, but of light infantry. Levied farmers. And when they then see that we have arrayed ourselves at the bottom of this hill, they will charge with all their might down towards us, thinking that their momentum alone will be enough to break us."

"Ah..." Celdon replied, watching as his father's soldiers deployed the iron caltrops all across the field. "So you've positioned us at a disadvantage to encourage the emperor into folly-- so he will charge downhill and try to break our lines... and then his own troops will lie in agony all across the field, where the Danz'kanari will nock their arrows and finish them off?"

"Precisely," Xanstus agreed.

The rain was creeping in again, and a dark cloud hung low over the field like a swarm of evil spirits waiting to haunt their mortal prey.

"It's getting cold," Panthalassa complained, straining to keep an eye on his father through the fog, as the vast defensive square in the rear guard kept him safe.

"Cold?" James inquired. "This isn't cold. Perhaps you're just sick with the suspense – nothing has happened for too long."

The three hours had passed, and despite the sound of marching feet in the far distance, all seemed a deadly quiet.

The caltrops had been placed, and all the men were waiting in their formations. Bulvon, Celdon and the king were in the middle of the formation, surrounded by wooden stakes and royal knights. They were in a position that seemed perfect to observe the battle around them, while also seeming close enough to lend support if their own strength was required.

Xanstus peered off to his left flank, where he had positioned the fierce warriors of the Kad'aeri and the Varnixye. He saw that while the earth vibrated from the force of the emperor's march beyond the hill, Warlord Zalxorr was busy giving his men a passionate speech. "He'll get his chance today..." Xanstus said.

Peering off to his right flank, he saw Lord Adragon, from Satia, whose highly disciplined spearmen would provide a mighty defence, along with the caltrops, to keep his battle line from rolling up, should the emperor attempt to flank him.

The other warriors, he then reminded himself, the axe-sentinels from Istaria, the green-shielded swordsmen from Adaria, and Lord Aleric's household cavalry, were all in reserve.

Then, when all these men had done their work, and the emperor's army was beaten, the Danz'kanari, who were inter-weaved with the regular archers, would finish them off...

"The emperor won't escape this time..." he mumbled... and then, seeming to follow his words, the rain began.

A bolt of lightning struck the field in front of the king's formations, and for a moment, as Prince Celdon peered back towards his father, he saw his disfigured face.

The lightning bolt lit up his terribly scarred facial features with a ghostly white flash, and the king's one remaining eye suddenly seemed aflame in madness. "Today, my son, I will kill him!" he growled, and through the gloom of the storm cloud hanging above the army, it now seemed, at least to Celdon, that Tiius had fully abandoned them.

Celdon shuddered in a superstitious dread. As the hellish lightning lit up the landscape, it seemed as though Odall was laughing wickedly, taking great delight in the bloodshed that was about to ensue.

As the king glared onward in his angry lust for vengeance, the emperor’s army finally arrived.

Announcing their presence with a burst of trumpets, the emperor arrayed his Knightly Order on the hilltop, now seeming to number only a few hundred strong, yet still appearing menacing on the open field.

“Good, he's here,” said Celsidas.

The emperor made a hand gesture and rallied his Knightly Order behind him. Galloping off to his west flank, he gave the order. “Ready the ballista!”

As the king watched the emperor's men wheel the machine to the top of the hillside, he squinted in his ultimate confusion... “Just one?” he murmured. “One single ballista?”

With a crack that echoed across the field, the ballista fired an object towards the king's platform. At first it seemed to be a rock of some description, as though the emperor had fired it to break down some imaginary gate – yet as the object fell to the ground at the king's feet, he noticed, with wide eyes, that it was a severed head...

He lifted it up by the hair to try and identify who it belonged to, yet unfortunately, due to the excess of open wounds, of filth, and of bruises, the face of this man was battered beyond recognition... *'I don't like this,'* thought the king, *'obviously the emperor is trying to tell me that I've lost somebody dear to me... But who?'*

Emperor Celsidas drew his sword and gestured it forwards, and at his command, thousands upon thousands of infantry soldiers, dressed no more neatly than peasants who worked in the field, charged down the hill towards the king's formations.

In their hands, their weapons ranged from axes and spears, to farming scythes and even pitch forks, and in their sheer numbers, they shook the ground with their thunderous assault, roaring with the anger built up in their hearts, stemming from thousands of years of oppression under the tyrannical rule of their monarchs. All these furious cries, as they rushed down the slope, were turned to howls of agony as they charged over the king's caltrops.

The emperor’s mob bled for every rage-filled step they took and roared curses to the gods, tripping over mounds of their own injured, and men were trampled to death under the sheer weight of the bodies rushing over them.

The clatter of steel against shields split the air, and all along the king's battle line, men roared their anger and added to the fray.

“Nock!” came a command from behind the king's line, and all along the rear, the Danz'kanari and the regular archers were fixing arrows onto their strings and positioning their fingers to do bow work.

"Draw!" the voice then continued. "Loose!" And at that order, thousands of arrows whistled through the air and squelched through the open flesh of their opponents.

Levies fell dead in great numbers, their bodies adding to the already heaping masses of dead filling the slope, and yet, even despite all this, the frontal charge carried on, the ear-ringing clatter of steel echoing loud.

"Now!" Commanded the emperor, and as he raised his sword for a second time, his mercenaries joined the fight.

Bearing down upon the king's right flank, a great horde of axemen wearing fur coats and chainmail thundered forwards. They roared with their fearsome deep voices and whirled their weapons through the air, and by the looks of them, the king assumed that men as tall as this could have only come from the icy tundra of *Yoxharia,* where unruly tribes still coated the land, still unbound by any unifying king or government, and many of these tribes, much like these hulking monsters of men who were aiding the emperor, were hired by foreign commanders to participate in wars far away.

As all these warriors and levies pushed against the king's line, Panthalassa, who was still well protected in the rear guard, had become eager to join the battle. "Let me go James!" the young prince protested, the clamour of war battering his eardrums, his heart racing in a desperate fear for his father. "I have to join the fight at the front-line!" he cried. "I can't just wait here while my comrades die!"

James tugged him firmly backwards, pulling the prince back into formation. "Are you mad, boy?!" he shouted, coinciding with another lightning bolt that struck the ground behind the battlefield.

"You are here under the king's protection!" James stated. "He has placed you in the rear-guard with me, and I will not put the king's battle plan at risk by letting you simply rush off to your death!"

But as James finished his sentence, a tremendous fanfare of trumpets echoed suddenly over the battlefield from behind them. *'It seems as though the boy will get his wish sooner than I had hoped...'* he thought with a sigh. "About turn!" he roared.

The king spun around to locate the source of the sudden fanfares. He could already feel the ground rumbling...

He grasped the severed head with both of his hands. *'The Watcher!'* he thought. *'My spy, who was supposed to tell me about the emperor's veteran Cavalry! Celsidas has brought the full twelve thousand home!'*

And as the Aristinian Knightly Order galloped onto the field, he was flooded with dread. Now the cavalry formed their lances into rows of steel.

'I placed my son in the rear guard...' he remembered, instantly scanning the battlefield for battalions that could slow their advance. *'My boy isn't ready to face such an assault!'*

And the charge began.

The defensive square that formed the rear guard now reformed into a crescent to face the on-rushing cavalry. "Brace for impact!" one of the knight centurions shouted, yet in reality, all the royal knights knew that without sufficient cavalry to counter charge them, the infantry would be easily overrun.

"Lord Aleric! Get your horses over there and stall their charge!" the king roared. "Bodyguard!" he cried. "On me!" At that command, Bulvon raised his axe into the air in salute, following his greatly scarred king through the field.

Panthalassa watched as all this played out. "I don't believe it," he mumbled, his voice trembling. "My father is going to be defeated, isn't he?"

Yet James didn't have time to think about this question.

Like a hammer against an anvil, the Aristinian knights crashed into the rear guard. Their impact was of such force that it shattered the defensive crescent almost immediately, and only because of Lord Aleric's counter charge were Panthalassa and James allowed to live through this. "Make for the bridge, men!" Xanstus commanded, and suddenly, for the first time since he could remember, the king's trumpets sounded the retreat.

The king waded through the thick of battle, cleaving the emperor's men with his greatsword as he rushed forward. "Follow the King!" Bulvon roared, chopping through the enemy forces like a knife through butter, and his two hundred battle-hardened veterans followed behind...

Emperor Celsidas watched the slaughter from atop his hill.

"So, Kalsos..." he asked, watching as the king's army reeled from the impact of his assault. "Shall we join the fray?"

"Let them run," the imperial guardian replied. "For even rats will fight like lions when cornered."

"Yes," replied Celsidas. "Well perhaps now, at least, he will think twice before he attacks us again."

Back on the plain below, the king had regrouped with James and his youngest son. The battle was descending into chaos, and the only thing the Unionite forces could do at this moment was struggle, with all their might, to reach the bridge.

“Stall their assault!” the king commanded. “We will be able to defend ourselves if we can fight our way over the bridge!”

The Knightly Order was reforming for another attack. Their first charge had been a success, and they had suffered almost no casualties. As the king's men fought their way over the river, the Aristinians began to realise that they had already won.

The emperor’s trumpeter blew a long, sustained note, and at that, as the emperor's reinforcements joined his personal bodyguard, King Xanstus Lordborn had been defeated.

*

When the king returned to Pla-Kingus later that year, he ordered that the taxes on the poor should be raised.

He couldn't afford his lords' disloyalty after this defeat, and he decided that the best way to keep them to their obligations was by enriching them at the expense of his own people.

His next decision was that his youngest son, Panthalassa, would cease in accompanying him into battle. Although it had been his own decision to allow the boy to join the army, he saw now, in defeat, just how close his bloodline had come to being erased. He needed one of his sons to remain at home, even if for nothing else, just to keep things under control. “I know you're young, boy,” Xanstus would tell him, “but you're turning into a fine warrior. You've faced bandits and cultists before. You've even battled their hell-beasts. I know you'll make me proud.”

On Panthalassa's return home, he and his retinue came by James's farm. Alongside many other farms in the area, it had been completely destroyed. The roundhouse lay in ruins, the wall had crumbled, and the timber frames were burned to char.

James dismounted. He took a moment to mourn his tragedy and wandered in desolation through the fields. All the animals had gone, and others were rotting in the open. He saw a man butchered by the side of the road, who he instantly recognised as one of the tenant farmers. James closed his eyes and began to weep. *'At least my son is safe inside the king's castle. Foxeny will be devastated once he finds out,'* he thought.

Panthalassa wept too. He remembered those happy years spent fishing, harvesting and enjoying the fruits of his labour. He had made friends here and learned many things. This place was a part of his childhood.

Eventually, they tore themselves away and made for the capital. When they finally returned, James arranged a new home for him and his son, inside the city. "It's far too dangerous to go back to farming now." James told his heartbroken son. "Everything on our old land has been destroyed, and there are much greater threats to our safety than there were before. We'll have to get used to living in the city."

Fortunately, James had accumulated a small fortune serving the king. As such, he was able to purchase a home within the upper district and had a large enough garden to carry on growing his food, albeit on a smaller scale.

While James and Panthalassa had been away, the Cult of Odall had grown to even greater strength, and now had unleashed the armies of the undead to plague and ravage the land around them. The Order of Tiius was locked in combat with them every day.

Besides all this, with the king away for so long, law and order was starting to break down. Banditry flourished, and even full-scale rebellions were becoming increasingly common. Although James continued to train Panthalassa, more and more of their time came to be taken up with trying to keep order.

The kingdom itself had embarked on a slow road to death, and even despite this, with the king's rage at its very pinnacle, peace seemed utterly impossible.

The next four years would see a bitter stalemate develop in Aristinia. While this year had seen the king defeated, the next one would see him rout the emperor's army completely, dealing another crushing blow to his infamous Knightly Order.

After pushing the emperor back to Aokron, however, his levies and mercenaries would break the King's siege and force him back home again – and yet, the very year after that one, King Xanstus would levy his own farmers, his own labourers and peasants, training them as much as he could, before hastily arming them and throwing them into battle.

And that year, after finally taking Aokron, the blacksmithing capital of Aristinia, the king came home victorious.

Rather than accepting peace however, King Xanstus still seethed with rage, insisting that he would not let his people rest, until he had personally slain the emperor. "King Xanstus the Cripple!" he would roar, "If I can't complete my conquest, that is what they will call me!"

And so, the year after that, when Panthalassa had reached the age of seventeen, King Xanstus left, once again, for war.

After losing Aokron the year before, the emperor decided to pull back his forces and garrison his fortress city of *Oioidamon* – the bottle-neck citadel that defended the

Aristinian *Circle of Mountains*.

While the king's siege of the fortress city lasted from early spring until late autumn, it was eventually broken, reaching its conclusion at long last, when the king's Kad'aeri miners tunnelled under the walls, crumbling them into ruins from the very foundation stones.

Slaughtering the emperor's remaining mercenaries and levies, King Xanstus then left Bulvon, along with some two thousand royal knights, to guard Oioidamon over winter...

And that winter, as the emperor’s resources grew ever smaller, he sought aid (once again) from his allies.

Sending messengers far and wide, Celsidas begged the king of Straeum to join his cause.

Yet after debating this request long and hard in *The Senate,* King Larbaeris Sajj, along with many other leaders west of the Calligian Empire, decided that Celsidas would fight alone.

When Emperor Celsidas of Aristinia read his allies' replies, which re-stated the urgent importance of defending their eastern borders from the Calligians, he turned, in his own desperation, to the one force he knew would still help him...

The emperor, in that dark moment, had vowed to ally himself with Odall.

Chapter 8 Part 1 – A Weakened Kingdom.

City of Pla-Kingus.

*

Every year, King Xanstus would ride to war on his black stallion, his army trailing behind him with all the best metal and rations the kingdom had to offer them, and every year, the king, Panthalassa's father, would return with more rage.

It seemed like an endless cycle. Would this war never end? And what, as his son, could the young prince do to stop him?

'The emperor almost killed my father!' he would remind himself. *'And if my father is unlucky again, Celsidas may yet succeed!'*

These fears drove him into loyalty.

How could he betray his father in his most pressing hour of need? He couldn't; and so instead of seeing that peace would ultimately save his kingdom, Panthalassa dug his head in the sand, supporting his father blindly, and refusing to see what was truly happening to his people.

His father was right, and the rest of his kingdom was wrong.

War was good, and peace was bad. The emperor and the Cult alone were to blame for the kingdom's suffering, and nothing was going to convince him otherwise.

*

It was a midsummer's day. The king had already been away from Pla-Kingus for three months, and Panthalassa was waiting for James just outside the keep.

He heard the squeak of cartwheels coming from behind him. The queen was setting off on another of her missions to help the poor, with a grain-laden cart following behind her, and he knew that at any moment now, he would be on the receiving end of yet another of her lectures.

She pulled up beside him, and before too long, they were arguing.

"No I'm not coming with you!" Panthalassa protested, pacing down the pathway in between the yew-tree hedgerows. "I have much more important things to do!"

"Panth, you're not ten anymore," Dranah responded, her tone more calm than his. She was stood beside a wooden cart full to the brim with grain and rations brought forth from the cellar of her own castle. "It's time you learned that what I am doing is just as important. I want you to help me feed the poor, to support the people your father is fighting for."

"So that's what you *'druids'* tell yourself is it?" her son asked. "You tell yourself that giving the poor more food will help the kingdom, but it is the soldiers that will need it the most! You're just taking food from them!"

"How dare you!" The queen snapped. "What I'm doing, Panthalassa, is making sure the people don't starve to death! This war has affected the kingdom in more ways than you allow yourself to notice!"

Panthalassa sighed loudly and looked away from her. His face was tense with a bitter understanding that she was right. He was silent for a moment.

"You're a young man now, Panth." Dranah continued. "You're old enough to make your own decisions; but before you rush off to please your father, think first about his people."

The clatter of horse hooves echoed over the drawbridge. It was James.

"I'm going to train, Mother. It's what father would want."

She watched him leave. The sadness in the queen's heart tugged at her every breath. *'It's a shame that you've become this way...'* she thought. *'...but maybe one day you will remember the value of compassion.'*

"Take us into the lower districts," she told the cart driver, and as he cracked his whip over the horses' backs, eight royal knights accompanied her on horseback.

For some months now, on the queen's instructions, her servants had set up a soup kitchen in the poorest district in the city. That way, even the poorest person in the city could be sure of at least one hot meal a day.

From today onwards, the poorest among them would also be given enough grain to take home to help feed their families.

Dranah made a point of meeting her people *in person* rather than leaving her servants to do all the work for her. She knew how important it was for the morale of the people, for them to see that the royal family cared for them.

“Bless you, yer' Majesty! How can I thank you enough?” asked one woman after she was handed a scoop of grain. This particular woman had three children at home and was struggling to feed them with the markets being virtually empty.

“You don't need to thank me,” Dranah replied gently. “Just make the grain last as long as you can... this war has taken a heavy toll.”

As she carried on distributing the grain, the crowds began to gather. Huddled masses of desperate citizens so thin that their bones showed through their skin were surrounding her; the guards had locked into defensive positions to hold them back, and each time she handed one of them a scoop of grain they would do one of two things, either they would disperse from the crowd and hurry into the safety of their homes, or in some cases, when their state was too unbearable, they would hold the seeds to their mouth, and eat them raw...

She looked into their eyes... Their dull hopeless stares seemed to pierce straight through her. *'This is what war does to the populace,'* she concluded. *'This madness must end soon, or we won't have anyone left to draw up.'*

Later that day, returning home, she noticed a party of soldiers accompanying a tax collector. He was dressed in fine yellow silks and had a bright red tabard that signified his association with the king. The queen’s lips pursed in a frown of disapproval. She was ashamed to see tax collectors working in this poverty-stricken part of the city.

As the queen approached the group, the tax collector knocked on one of the doors loudly. “War taxes for the king!” he demanded, his tone a deep bullying bray.

A man who looked to be in his late seventies eventually opened the door. “I don't ave' any money left Sire,” he begged, leaning against a solid oak branch he had fashioned to help him walk.

“Yes you do!” The collector insisted. “Hand it over. The king demands it.”

“What ‘ave I done to offend his Majesty?” the man asked. “I was a soldier before ee' was even on the throne!”

One of the troops standing beside the tax collector edged his spear-point closer. “Stop wasting time!” he shouted.

The man leaned backwards at the sight of the soldier's weapon. “Tiius ‘ave mercy!” he snapped. “You rats ‘ave no respect!”

“Enter the house,” the tax collector ordered his men. “Take everything of value.”

“No! Get back!” The elder protested, barring the way with his walking stick, yet the collector kicked his feeble weapon aside and threw him to the floor.

“Enough!” The queen's voice rang out like a whip crack. She urged her chestnut mare forward, and her eyes fixed onto the collector with grim displeasure.

“Help him up again,” she ordered.

The collector, now startled by the situation he found himself in, looked around and saw that the queen's royal knights had surrounded him. “Very well then,” he replied, his voice now trembling in discomfort as his own soldiers recognised higher authority in the queen's men.

Swatting his own soldiers aside, the tax collector helped the elder to his feet.

“Good,” the queen continued. “Now. Give him some coins.”

“Y... Your Majesty?” he asked.

She glared at him. “Would you dare to disobey royalty?” she asked, her tone casting dark shadows into the collector's soul. “Give the man some coins!”

Reaching into his purse, the collector tossed the old man a golden piece, his face turning red with disgrace.

“Right. Now go away!” she snapped. “This is the poorest district in the kingdom. Only an idiot would think it worthwhile to try and raise taxes for the king in such a place. Go and tax the rich!” she added. “And give word to your colleagues, if I hear reports of any of you in this area again, I will have you flogged!”

Quickly departing with his soldiers, the collector grumbled under his breath and tried to recover his damaged pride.

The old man had watched the whole scene with his jaw dropped in amazement. “Thank you!” he mumbled.

Dranah smiled at him. “We are a kingdom of justice, not a kingdom of bullies,” she told him. “If that man bothers you again, be sure to tell one of my guards.”

'I... love you...' the man thought, yet as the queen trotted off into the distance, all he could do was watch her in silent gratitude.

Chapter 8 Part 2 – Deathxia.

The Order of Tiius's Stronghold, City of Pla-Kingus, later that day.

*

After returning to her keep, Queen Dranah had decided to have some rest. She felt satisfied that she had spent the day giving hope to her people, but she knew that her work was far from over. Recently, there had been a report that one of the capital's main graveyards had been desecrated, and she was going there personally. *'Tonight I'll be helping the Order of Tiius,'* she thought. *'If my druids and I are to be of any use, I need my focus to be clear.'* To this end, she rested her head.

The Order of Tiius had specifically sent for the druids. The unholy defilement of the graveyard was of such potency that the very trees around the sacred place had begun to wilt and die. When the queen awoke from her slumber a couple of hours later, she quickly got changed into her druidic robes and set off.

The order-knight standing guard beside the drawbridge bowed his head low in respect. "Welcome, *Arch-Druid,*" he said.

As the queen entered the Order's stronghold through the *portcullis* (the lifted iron gates), Queen Dranah was struck, but not for the first time, by the magnificence of it all.

Upon entry, Her Majesty observed a golden mist, which seemed to hang over the whole enclosure like a cloud, shimmering above sacred shrines and druidic groves; and then, intermixed with these clouds of pure magic, Duella had also blessed the zone with her own magic of nature, casting a gentle green aura around the stone monolith circles at each of the four corners of the stronghold, ensuring the long life of the flowers and trees which sprung into life along every pathway with unimaginable beauty.

In the centre of all this was the Order's holy barracks. It was a giant, stone walled structure surrounded entirely by ancient trees, with beams of light shining down upon them from the heavens, and the watchtowers soared into the sky, flying high the banners of their Order.

After seeing all of this, the queen rode along a pathway that stretched on to her right, heading towards the largest monolith circle in the enclosure. All along the pathway beside her, green mists weaved peacefully between the large pear and hazelnut trees, their sprawling roots forming hills of their own as they weaved through the flower-carpeted soil.

The druids bowed before the queen as she entered the circle. Dranah smiled at them in satisfaction. “I'm pleased to see that so many of Duella's devotees have answered my call,” she said.

"Is everything ready?" Dranah asked.

"It is, Arch-Druid," replied Sir Ardwyn Keyscarre, who had, in earlier years, aided the king in his first battle against the emperor.

Sir Ardwyn Keyscarre was one among many other paladins who practised Duellan magic alongside his sacred duty to the Order of Tiius. Since these two magic types often complemented one another, it was not at all uncommon to find men who were both paladins and druids at the same time.

The queen raised an eyebrow at the high paladin, insisting by her gesture that he should continue.

Ardwyn indicated by hand towards a pathway that wound directly north of the monolith structure, to which any visibility to the queen, from her position, was hidden behind the lush excesses of the forest.

She trotted towards Sir Ardwyn and peered off down the pathway; and here, to her delight, she saw four hundred paladins, organised into columns of one hundred and suited in fine kenthril armour. "Their weapons have been enchanted in the grand paladin's own cathedral, your Majesty," Ardwyn told her. "If anyone can defend your druids while they heal the decay of the land, it is them."

"Inside the *Cathedral of Straeum* itself, you say?" she asked, sounding rather impressed.

Sir Ardwyn nodded his head in confirmation. "Aye," he replied.

"Well let us make haste then!" she spoke, swiftly turning her brown mare to face the pathway she had just ridden down. "For the Cult works best in darkness, and our daylight is fading fast!"

"Forward march!" commanded Ardwyn.

As the druids joined the advancing force, they prepared, with strong hearts, to face the Cult of Odall.

*

Night had crept upon the holy warriors as they advanced into the dark forest. There was a dead quiet that chilled men to the bone, for not a single owl or night bird made a sound. It felt as though the very life of the forest had been extinguished.

So absolute in fact was this silence, that the queen's ears rang to leave her mind something to focus on, for the noiseless air felt so thick that it almost muffled the very sound of marching feet.

Above the force of paladins and druids, wicked branches from dying trees sprawled into the dark blue sky, adding to the feeling of unease now weaving through the army like an evil shade.

“There is evil in this place,” High Paladin Ardwyn declared, halting his force in the middle of the vast graveyard.

"Yes, I can feel it too," spoke the queen, narrowing her eyes as she scanned the foggy surroundings for suspicious activity.

Whilst Sir Ardwyn organised his men into defensive positions, the druids and *battle-priests* began their attempts to re-consecrate the graveyard. Quickly however, as the magical energies flowed through the earth, searching for souls, there were cries of horror. “This grave is empty!” one of them wailed. “The dead have been raised!”

Feeling for any signs of the soul through the power of her magic, the battle priest had soon made this terrible discovery...

"Raised?" Ardwyn asked. “But this place was under the protection of a fire blessing! The necromancers would have been reduced to ash!”

Queen Dranah, after caressing one of the dying trees with Duella's nature magic, also felt something... "The forest is being drained of its life by a mysterious illness," she said.

She walked around the base of the tree slowly, her gentle green magic illuminating the ground below her. She widened her eyes at that moment. "*Deathxia...*" she spoke grimly... "The black jelly..."

One of the royal knights standing guard beside the queen let out a hacking cough, at that moment, and spat from his mouth the same dark substance... "Agh! Apologies, your Majesty!" he said.

Dranah then looked at him, as a cold sweat ran down her face... "How are you feeling?" she asked, holding close to the man's face a glowing ball of Duellan magic.

"I'll be fine, my Queen," the royal knight assured her. "Just a belly ache, that's all."

But the queen's magic revealed a dark ring around the soldier's eyes. "You're suffering from Deathxia, soldier!" she gasped. "Report to the high paladin at once!"

Upon hearing these words, Sir Ardwyn made haste towards the pair. "Show me your eyes, soldier," he mumbled on. Holding a ball of Pure Magic to the man's face, he soon confirmed his own fears. "Blast those cultists!" he cursed, realising at that moment, the sheer scale of his problem. "They have summoned one of Odall's own demons! The fire blessing was broken!"

"So this illness is demonic?" the royal knight asked him, trembling. "Will I die?"

"You will recover from this illness, you're in capable hands," Sir Ardwyn said, "but if you weren't under the supervision of such skilled magic users as ourselves, the Deathxia weaving its way around your body would have drained you to the point of exhaustion, magnifying your belly ache into sickness and eventually killing you."

The soldier's face turned pale. The black rings around his eyes stood out from the rest of his skin like the terrible marks of death they were... "And... would anything have happened after I died?" the royal knight asked. "This is a magical illness, after all..."

"After your death, soldier, the Deathxia would have vaporised into Odall's Corruption Magic, airing its way through your rotting skin until it hit your brain," he replied, "and then, it would have raised you as a living corpse. To serve Odall."

The royal knight was standing wide-eyed. He couldn't believe what he was hearing. "So, who do I see?" he asked.

"I'll see you off to a druid and a priest. They will know what to do," the high paladin answered. Oh, and one more thing... Deathxia bursts into flames upon its first contact with Pure Magic," he sighed. "I'm not entirely sure how the priests manage to cure people without causing excruciating pain, but I've been told the druids make it completely safe. Don't be afraid."

Patting the man on the back, Sir Ardwyn saw the soldier off to one of his most talented priests. *'Poor lad,'* he thought.

"So..." Queen Dranah spoke, edging her way closer to the high paladin as her soldier left her line of sight, "to ask you a question..." she continued. "What exactly will become of the other towns in my kingdom?"

The high paladin turned around to face her with a worried frown.

"What I mean is this," she added. "If the Deathxia can spread faster than we can keep up with, is it, in that case, unrealistic to imagine whole towns being plagued into undeath?"

Ardwyn clenched his fists at the very thought and held his breath short. "Not at all, your majesty," he said... and his voice trembled with the heavy duty placed upon him.

"In fact," he struggled on, "there is something that I must tell you about Deathxia, your Majesty," he continued. "Deathxia jelly, more like a kind of mushroom than anything else, emits spores from the very thing it latches itself on to... and these spores are the corrupted remnants of the living soul..."

Queen Dranah then fell to her knees and pressed her head against a gravestone, lost in thought. "So you mean to say that..." she murmured, "...that Deathxia is a plague that not only kills your mortal body, but one that condemns your eternal soul to serve Odall?"

"Yes," sighed the high paladin. "That is exactly what I mean to say..."

Ardwyn looked into the queen's eyes. He saw her tears glistening in the moonlight as they rolled down her cheeks. "That's awful," she said - and yet, almost as soon as she said this, she lifted her head and looked at him, seeming to regain a portion of her royal determination. "Is there a way to fight the spread of these Deathxia spores, then?" she asked him. "Besides simply purging them with Pure Magic?"

Ardwyn smiled at her with a passing sense of pride. *'If only Xanstus fell in battle,'* he wished, the thought carrying on further. *'If only he would just die, and then this beautiful woman could be her peoples' true leader...'*

"Yes," Ardwyn finally replied to her. "There is a powerful ritual that we can cast. It combines the strength of Tiius, and the love of Duella into one force, flowing like a tidal wave through the soil and cleansing the life growing from it. Such a spell requires immense concentration, though - in fact, people have died from exhaustion simply by casting it, but if we eliminate the root of the problem early enough, we have the manpower to do it."

"Ardwyn?" Dranah asked. "How exactly is Deathxia spread?"

"The necromancers vomit the stuff up from their plague-riddled stomachs," Ardwyn sighed.

"Why don't they turn into the undead too?" she asked.

"Deathxia vomit is a side effect of their addiction to Corruption Magic, your Majesty. Odall doesn't let his servants rest as Duella and Tiius do. Perhaps the reason they take longer to become undead is because Odall benefits greatly from their endless suffering."

"I see." Dranah nodded her head slowly as she took in all of this new information. "So they're not quite alive *or* dead... they're somewhere in-between."

Standing up, she spoke further. "Then the best way to combat the Deathxia, if the necromancers throw the stuff up, is by killing the necromancers themselves. Then, after the root of the problem has been dealt with, the ritual of cleansing can be performed."

"The necromancers must be killed using Pure Magic." Sir Ardwyn stated. "For only that way will they be truly free from being risen into undeath."

Turning around to face the pathway before him, the high paladin unsheathed his sword. "Alright men! Form up!" he commanded, and the paladins quickly arrayed themselves into a square column.

"Now I trust that I've known you all for long enough to not require a speech before every manoeuvre," he put in, to which the men gave a slight chuckle.

"From this point onwards, we will move into the deep forest, following the trail of the black jelly." Ardwyn said. "Expect to fight the undead, and together, we will stop the Cult in their tracks."

He gestured forward with his sword and ordered his paladins on. "Move out!"

Chapter 8 Part 3 – Blood and Darkness.

Deeper in the forest.

*

After an hour of marching, the paladins had finally found their enemy.

Seeing the Order's massed columns, the Cult's necromancers had fled back into the shadows of the forest, leaving the undead to stall Ardwyn's assault.

The ghoulish hordes sprang upon the Order's paladins. Leaping onto them from the darkest corners of the forest, skeletons and zombies clawed at their armour in a vicious frenzy, aiming for their eyes and chewing on the open flesh.

Battle-Priests rained golden fire from the skies, incinerating the living corpses where they stood and turning the dead wood surrounding them into piles of ash and charred remains, and while they did this, the paladins sliced and hacked with their swords, the crunch of steel breaking bones sounding loud through the air.

“Defend the queen!” commanded Sir Ardwyn, spearheading the advance through the thick of the forest, his enchanted blade striking down all who stood before him as corpses fell to heaps of ash, perishing under the judgment of the holy flames. “Chase those necromancers down!”

After another half-hour of intense fighting, Ardwyn's men had backed the necromancers into a corner.

Surrounding them against the wall of a cliff, the paladins arrayed themselves into a defensive crescent, battling the undead on the forested side, and pressing the necromancers tight against the cliff on the other.

“Your gods lead you astray, paladin,” croaked one of the necromancers, trembling beneath his torn, black cloth robes, his face pale with sickness and malnutrition, his body withering away under the harsh demands of his cursed god. “Death is inevitable. You fight for nothing!”

Ardwyn held his sword-tip to the man's neck, the fierce glow of Pure Magic burning his corrupted skin. “I fight for justice, necromancer, which is more than can be said for cowards like you, who choose darkness!” he spat, then plunging his blade into his neck. “Kill them all. Burn their bodies!”

And at his command, the battle-priests shot a wave of Pure Magic across the field. The eight necromancers who they had chased through the woods burned alive in the zealous, golden flames, their cloth robes and hoods glowing orange from the sheer heat, as the stinking men inside them crumbled into dust.

Now Sir Ardwyn joined the fray. Queen Dranah and her druids stood behind the defensive crescent, weaving their Nature Magic through the formations of paladins, healing their battle wounds as they hacked and slashed on, leaving only ashes and charred bones in their wake.

After an hour of intense fighting, this small victory was theirs.

Ardwyn sighed deeply as he eyed the chest-high pile of bones and ashes on the ground before him. “It always saddens me to fight the undead,” he spoke, his voice carrying on the night air, like the gentle rustle of autumn leaves.

“Saddens you?” questioned one of his men, raising an eyebrow.

Ardwyn looked back at him. “Every one of these corpses, paladin, was once loved by men like you and me,” he replied. “Once sons, once daughters, mothers and fathers. Never blame the corpse. Blame the magical force that raised it. Everyone who we fought just then was innocent.”

“...Even the necromancers?” the paladin asked.

Ardwyn sheathed his sword. “No, soldier. They deserved it,” he answered. “Damn the necromancers!”

A violet glow in the far distance then suddenly caught his attention. “Follow that light!”

Then, reforming into their marching columns five abreast, they continued their advance through the dead of night. It was widely understood by the men that the druids would save their healing of the land for *after* the mission was completed... and while they marched on, a demonic shade watched them coldly from afar...

With two necromancers by its side, it watched the paladins' advance through the woods without expression. The wind on the high moorlands appeared to blow right through it, almost as though it wasn't really there...

"They are too late, Master," spoke one of the necromancers, his stomach turning sour as he uttered this uncertain statement. "The ritual is almost complete."

"They will never reach the enclave in time," mumbled the other.

Phasing its head into two, the demon looked at both necromancers simultaneously, its figure shifting through the air like a moving shadow.

'It doesn't matter whether the Order succeeds here or not...' it replied, the words entering both minions' minds telepathically, its mouth unmoving.

Demons are manifestations of Corruption Magic. They can choose to appear in any form they wish. Their magical power is of such potency that they can even choose which parts of their decided form are solid, and which of them can be passed through, just like air.

'The Deathxia has already affected many settlements across this kingdom,' the demon continued. *'The undead forces, which these puny paladins 'battled' today, are nothing compared to the sheer numbers they will have to face in the months yet to come.'* The demon's tone slid into their minds like shifting paper...

"What now then?" grinned one of the necromancers.

The demon seemed to fold in on itself from the feet upwards, morphing through its own eyes and mouth until it had become nothing more than a dimly glowing ball of violet energy. *'Join the others in the enclave below,'* the demon answered, meaning both of them. *'Die.'*

And with that, the demon hovered to the ground, sprawling its purple mass of Corruption Magic thinly across the moorland, circling around the necromancers' feet and then liquidising.

As the demon's liquid form bled into the soil, the grass turned a pale grey, and the two necromancers, accepting the will of their unholy master, walked back down the slope, into the forest.

*

The dead woods had fallen into an eerie silence.

Since withstanding the first onslaught of the undead, Sir Ardwyn and his men had pressed further into the woods, pursuing the dim violet glow in the distance, and now, although the soundless air carried gently on the wind, it was still broken by the occasional rattle of bones in the far distance... and the moisture, which was so thick in the stagnant air that it made them sweat... “What are they playing at?” growled one of Ardwyn's paladins. “They know we're here. What is suddenly making the dead so cautious?”

“Just stay on guard, soldier,” Ardwyn replied, marching on. “They could strike again at any moment.”

As they moved further along the hardened dirt pathway, they came upon an open space within the forest, with mists hanging low over the withering plants, a shallow stream ahead of them trickling gently beneath an old wooden bridge... and standing on this bridge, lost in a trance of chanting, stood one of the necromancers.

Torn black robes coated his body, muddy from over-use, and his hands were folded into his sleeves at his chest. Although the Order's expedition force approached him in full formation, he seemed to remain calm.

Ardwyn unsheathed his sword, and the other paladins under Ardwyn's command drew swords as well. The golden glow of their blades lit up the darkness through the thick fog.

The shine of Pure Magic lit up the necromancer's face, shaking him out of his trance. He looked at Ardwyn, who was moving towards him at the front of his massed columns. “You will accomplish nothing by killing me.” he croaked, his mouth curling into a wry grin.

Ardwyn gave the signal for his men to halt. He walked alone towards the cultist, sword in hand. “What do you mean!” he barked.

The hooded man laughed, sounding genuinely amused. “You can win here, paladin!” he crowed... “It doesn't matter!”

At that, Ardwyn plunged his blade into the necromancer's heart, Pure Magic shooting through his body with a surge of fire. “Damn their evil games!” he sighed.

Turning back towards his men, Ardwyn then gave the signal to continue the advance, and as they moved over the bridge back into the thick of the forest, they found themselves at a crossroads. One of the pathways was long and straight, littered with leaves that had fallen from the trees above them, and the other pathway, which turned off to their right, stretched further into the darkness, the hard dirt stained red with what seemed like fresh blood - and at either side of this pathway, corpses lay sprawled on their bellies, holding hands with one another for the entire length, the black jelly, Deathxia, weaving its way over their bodies and circling around... something... at the end...

Looking down this route, Sir Ardwyn then noticed what that *'something'* was. A bloodied skull, sitting beneath a wooden sceptre of Tiius, which was flipped on its head, to symbolise his death. “I've heard about this kind of ritual before,” Ardwyn growled, his eyes narrowing as he tightened his grip on his sword. “This is the way we must go.”

They pressed on.

“What is this ritual for, then?” asked one of the queen's druids fearfully, her eyes filling with tears at the gruesome sight.

“I've seen rituals like this before. It looks as though they're plaguing the capital city,” Ardwyn replied. “If it succeeds, our small numbers will no longer be enough to stop the spread of the Deathxia here. Thousands will become undead...”

The queen's mouth curled, her heart sinking deep. “If they are performing this ritual here,” she murmured, “wouldn't they be performing it elsewhere too?”

The tremble in Dranah's tone resonated with his own feelings. Turning to face the queen with soul-felt compassion, Ardwyn made his reply: “Elsewhere, your Majesty, they have likely already succeeded,” he sighed. “If Xanstus refuses to bring home his main army for just one more year, he may find himself, all of a sudden, king of the ashes.”

One of the royal knights serving the queen as her bodyguard shot the high paladin a glare. Those words, if spoken by an officer loyal to the Lordborns, would be considered high treason!

Ardwyn held the soldier's gaze. “We are paladins, not your king's subjects, bodyguard,” he said. “In any case, is it treason to speak the truth?”

The knight stayed quiet. He knew Ardwyn meant no harm, and by now they had reached the skull underneath the reversed sceptre, which burst into a mass of violet flames before their eyes...

“Despicable!” Ardwyn lashed, striking the thing with his glowing blade, and this action snapped the unholy sceptre in half, the skull beneath it crumbling into ashes before him. “Onward!” Ardwyn commanded.

As they moved, the low white fog at the paladins' feet slowly began to shift colour, changing hue into a dark purple... Once again, Ardwyn called for his men to halt. “Form up men,” he ordered. “There is a demon among us!”

'It is not too late to join us...' whispered a mysterious voice, sliding into the minds of each man and woman in the Order's task force.

“Ignore the demon's wicked words, men!” one of Ardwyn's paladins shouted, “Anything it tells you, block it out!”

'Your presence here merely serves to aid our cause, mortals...' the demon went on... *'If you fail, you will simply deliver your souls right into our hands...'*

Before the paladins' very eyes, the violet fog shifted along the forest floor, sweeping over the hand-holding corpses at either side of the path, morphing into a single form in front of them... the form of a man-sized ant.

'And if you succeed,' the demon choked, now appearing to speak through its huge *mandibles... 'then you will have done nothing but postpone the inevitable!'* it said. *'This kingdom is doomed!'*

“Enough words!” one of the younger paladins beside Sir Ardwyn roared, breaking formation as he shot a ray of Pure Magic towards the beast.

“No!” Ardwyn cried, “Don't!”

'Foolish paladin!' the demon laughed, effortlessly launching a jet of Corruption Magic in return, blasting it forward from its antennae.

In a mere second, collapsing to his knees and then falling flat on his face, the young paladin was vaporised by the demon's greater power. Ardwyn took a moment to consider this man, who just this morning had sworn the paladin's oath.

Rising through the ranks of order-knights, this young man had easily been one of Ardwyn's toughest men, physically stronger than almost everyone here at the moment... He took another moment to consider, at that point, his bravery, which clearly had not been lacking.

'Another one to fill my ranks,' the demon chuckled. *'You mortals know nothing.'*

And at that, the demon's ant form dissipated in a burst of violet energy, shooting into the sky in all directions.

Ardwyn turned the corpse around by his shoulder... *'The poor lad was fried to the bone,'* he thought, looking into the helmet of his old comrade; this young paladin, who was now nothing more than a skeleton in a suit of armour. *'Words cannot describe the tragedy of naive youth,'* he thought on.

Arising from his inspection of the body, Sir Ardwyn moved back to the task at hand. "Alright men, we've all seen the power of that demon, but we can't let it dissuade us from pursuing the last of these Cultists!" he sighed. "March on!"

As they advanced further, the putrid stench of burning blood filled their nostrils, coinciding with a persistent, droning incantation...

As they came to an open cave, Ardwyn looked down into the rocky enclave and saw the necromancers' ritual.

The bodies at either side of the pathway now wound down into this opening, holding hands, and connecting both sides at last at the cave floor, being placed in a circle around the central cauldron.

"They've sacrificed one of their own!" Dranah whispered, looking at the cone-shaped fire beneath the cauldron, which had burned straight through the stomach of a necromancer, spread-eagle on the hard rocky ground.

"Yes. The Cult of Odall does that quite often," Ardwyn replied...

Watching on, Ardwyn then realised that the blood was actually inside the cauldron! And as he observed for a little while longer, he saw the boiling blood rise up from out of it, leeching over the sides of the cauldron and pooling beneath the other necromancers' feet – who stood in a ring around the circle of corpses.

As they harnessed corruption magic in their palms, they chanted with a jarring lack of rhythm, growing louder and louder as the ritual began to reach its final stage.

As the blood from the cauldron was fully emptied and pooled at the necromancers' feet, it then shot back towards the cauldron in a burst of violet magic, lighting the face-down corpses aflame one by one.

"Now is the time, paladins!" Ardwyn called, raising his long-sword high into the air, the glow of Pure Magic piercing the night sky. "Charge!"

Thundering down the slope into the rocky enclave, the Order's paladins dealt justice, slaying necromancers as they fled their terrible wrath, and purging the ritual fires where they burned. "Follow them into the cave, men! Do not lose them!" Ardwyn roared, chasing them as they ran.

These were the last eight Cultists. As the paladins rushed through the dark caves, they barely had time to notice the creeping dampness, the stalactites growing from the ceiling, nor equally the stalagmites growing beneath them. Instead, wading through the knee-deep pools of water in full plate armour, the paladins continued their charge...

Slaying the necromancers one by one, they breathed a sigh of relief when they were finally hunting the last one of them.

"The water over there is red, Ardwyn!" Dranah pointed to her right, towards a winding corridor in the cave that sloped upwards...

"Perhaps our last enemy has committed suicide," one of the other paladins laughed.

Ardwyn went first up the slope. Leading from the front, he clambered up the slippery cave floor on all-fours, often having to use his own sword to stab at something to hold on to... After he had done this, the other men followed behind, with the last of them tossing their swords to the queen and her druids, just so that they could stab for grip too.

Searching the dark corridors of the cave under the dim golden glow of their weapons, they turned their final corner... and, grimacing in utter disgust, they now beheld exactly how the necromancers got their blood...

Chained against the cave wall for the length of the corridor, a hundred children, maybe more, who seemed no older than nine or ten, had been stripped bone naked, and defiled by the Cultists.

Lost for words and in utter disbelief, Queen Dranah sobbed openly, casting aside her royal composure as she absorbed this sickening sight.

Even Ardwyn, whose many years of battle experience had hardened his face to not weep at such gruesome, heart-breaking sights, was distressed by this horrific act.

"Look for the ones that are alive," Ardwyn instructed, his voice soft and breaking. "In fact, unchain them all. Even if they are dead. Nobody deserves to rot in a place like this!"

"Least of all, innocent children!" Dranah cried.

Tightening his grip over his sword, Ardwyn alone pressed on towards the cultist, who by now was backed against the wall at the end of the cave, chanting frantically with his hands glowing a dark violet.

Echoing from behind Sir Ardwyn, the rattling of chains intensified, now coinciding with a high-pitched shrieking coming from the lungs of some of the dead children...

The necromancer had risen the defiled dead into undeath...

"You monster!" Ardwyn roared, breaking into a charge as his anger boiled over into blood lust.

After stabbing the necromancer in the stomach, he then concentrated his power, harnessing the Pure Magic with twice as much zeal as before. Just before the last necromancer's body was overwhelmed by the power of Pure Magic, he managed to choke one last sentence, into those dark, echoing tunnels...

"The blood... this was only for the blood!"

With that, cackling madly, the final necromancer was slain.

Turning his back to hide an almost overpowering moment of grief for the innocents, Sir Ardwyn forced himself to keep his emotions in check.

"We need to take those who are still alive back through the woods," he exhaled. "Until we can discover which families these children belong to, they will be cared for, and raised gently in our stronghold."

Slogging their way back through the deep water, they all soon began to fully feel their exhaustion. Water dribbled through cracks in the ceiling and their voices echoed like haunting spirits.

The druids hugged the devastated children, carrying them the rest of the way through the cave. “You'll be safe now,” soothed Queen Dranah, holding one dejected boy's head to her chest. “My druids will look after you.”

Sir Ardwyn moved closer to the queen; his footsteps brisk but subtle. This part of the cave seemed to be on the verge of collapsing. A large boulder had already fallen from the ceiling of the cave, and jets of water were streaming out from cracks in the rocks. “I don't mean to hurry you, your Majesty, but if you'd look behind you,” he murmured, “it might be a good idea to move along...”

The queen suddenly understood the situation they were in and began to hurry her group of druids on.

Finally, with relief, they reached the entrance to the cave. Weary and footsore, they made at last for home.

Chapter 9 Part 1 – The Burden of Tyranny.

The next day.

*

Panthalassa walked over the drawbridge into the royal district of Pla-Kingus. The morning sun shone brightly, casting an orange hue over everything, and the air, which was crisp and fresh, filled his lungs, sending wake-up shivers the length of his body.

With James by his side, he had prepared himself for another day of training, and now, walking down the pathway towards the *High Market Square*, which one had to walk through in order to reach the royal sparring grounds, James had decided to start the day with apples.

“These two look juicy!” he said, picking the finest apples he could see in the crate, on the market stall, holding them in his hands, checking them for holes, looking at their bright red coat streaked with green lines, as they gleamed from the sun.

“They're the best apples in all the land, Sir!” the stallholder replied, his voice strong and cultured. “Picked from the most bountiful, sun-baked orchards in the north!”

James rolled his eyes. “Spare me the descriptions, merchant. I've harvested apples like these myself.”

Although it was not the first time he had shopped in this district of Pla-Kingus, James was taken back by his accent. Far from sounding a like farmer, or even like a normal merchant for that matter, this man sounded positively well-spoken.

“Ah!” the merchant continued, pointing his finger rudely. “You're a farmer!”

James nodded. “I was,” he replied grimly, giving the man a handful of coppers for the apples...

“Tell me, merchant,” he asked, still wondering about his accent, “why is it that *you* sell the apples here, and not the farmers?”

“Oh, please,” the merchant scoffed. “The farmers sell their produce in the lower districts. This part of the city is no place for peasants!”

“But tell me, why?” James persisted, trying his best to ignore the insult.

The stallholder narrowed his eyes and paused for a moment. “Alright, I'll tell you, “ He agreed. “Two hundred years ago, my family served King Kransus Lordborn in the war against Adaria,” he said. “During that war, my ancestors distinguished themselves in high places of rank, earning recognition, and even close friendship with the king. After the war ended, Kransus and his courtsmen ruled that no farmer should be allowed to sell their produce in the Royal District. Since my family had become close friends with the king, he gave my great- great- great grandfather an official license to control the markets here. Between my family, we hold a monopoly.”

“Ah,” James spoke. “So you buy the farmers' produce at their fair prices, then after you have their goods, you resell them for extortionate ones?”

The merchant grinned like a snake. “Be on your way, James.”

Handing Panthalassa one of the apples, James met the man's grin with a dirty look. *'It's people like you who contribute to the peoples' suffering,'* James thought. *'How on earth would you expect a normal person to pay twenty coppers for two apples?!'*

They continued through the High Market Square.

Ducking through the crowds in a ragged grey robe, a woman of uncertain age lurked about suspiciously, looking to see if anyone was watching.

She didn't know it, but Prince Panthalassa himself was observing her every move.

Then, believing that no one was scrutinising her, she snatched two loaves of bread and hurried off down a dark alleyway.

“Leave her, Panth,” James mumbled, “the poor lady is likely starving.”

But Panthalassa, recalling his father's angry rants about thieves and robbers, had other plans.

“Stop, thief!” he shouted, to which two guardsmen in iron chainmail hurried to see what was happening. “She went that way!”

As the guards chased after her, James grabbed Panthalassa's arm and tugged him round to face him. "I said leave her!" he sighed. "What's happening to you?"

Panthalassa looked at James with a puzzled expression... "Why do you defend the thief?" he asked.

Tugging his arm free, Panthalassa then ran off to watch what the guards would do, with James following shortly behind. *'I'll have to go along with this...'* James knew, heaving a painful breath... *'If I follow my heart here, I'll end up losing my head.'*

And when they turned down the dark alleyway, they saw the thief again, with her hood down and both arms held by the guards. They were dragging her along the pathway. Her knees were bloody, and she was unconscious.

For a moment, when Panthalassa saw the state the woman was in, his heart sank. *'This is too harsh,'* he thought...

But then he hardened his heart, for these were his father's laws. There was a war on, and this was no time for softness. He couldn't betray him.

The woman had come around and was gazing around wildly. "What will her punishment be?" Panthalassa asked, adopting a calm voice that betrayed how he really felt.

"She stole two loaves, your Highness," one of the guards replied. "So she will lose two fingers."

"No!" she screamed, looking up at him pitifully "I was only trying to feed my children!"

'Children...' James thought to himself... *'Without their mother, they will likely starve!'*

“I don't make the rules, lady,” the Guard replied. “Just obeying the law."

Staring at the men in disgust, James spat a question to them. "Do either of you have children, I wonder?"

He coughed loudly and shook his head. "Of course you don't," he sighed.

The guardsmen shot him a glare. One of them opened his mouth to speak. "Even if I did, Sir, I wouldn't want them to be raised by thieves!" he answered back.

James closed his eyes and breathed deeply... *'Just stay calm...'* he reminded himself... *'These are royal soldiers, obeying the king's laws.'*

"Come on, you," the guard snapped, turning his head back to the woman, and within a few seconds, she had been dragged away.

Looking up at James, Panthalassa noticed that his shoulders had slumped. "Are we still training?" he mumbled, still shaken by the punishment he had forced onto the woman.

"No." James declared, setting himself straight again, his tone sharp. "You need to see something."

Despite his wish to be shown no more, Panthalassa secretly knew that he was in the wrong, and decided to follow him... "Where are we going then?" he sighed.

"To the lower districts," James answered. "So you can see the truth."

Panthalassa was accompanied by a bodyguard of four royal knights.

When he and James passed through the stone wall which surrounded the Royal District, the iron gate clanked shut behind them. *'Those gates seem to have become very symbolic,'* James thought to himself, frowning. *'Just as the nobles ignore the plight of the poor, so too do they cage themselves in; just so they can carry on, in their ignorance.'*

From this moment onwards, the houses were smaller, and less impressive. The smells of sickness and poor hygiene drifted through the still summer air, and the marketplace in the far distance looked almost barren.

Glancing around for signs of life, Panthalassa looked down one of the alleyways, and here, laying inside a broken wooden box, lay the stinking remains of a dog, which looked as if it had been gutted on the spot, eaten, and simply left to rot in the open air.

He gagged at the sight. "I..." Panthalassa coughed to clear his throat... "I don't see why this is part of my training James."

James sighed at him. "Today's lesson is different from the others, young Prince," he said. "A good warrior must also be aware of how war can affect people."

"Are you trying to suggest that my father is to blame for all this?"

"You can make your own decision on that, Panthalassa," James carefully replied. "I'm just making sure you see it."

Entering the marketplace, Panthalassa was then greeted by a sight he had not seen before...

At the corner of the Lower District Market-Square, a huddled mass of skeletal citizens had crowded around an open cart at the end of a pathway.

"Here you go sir," spoke one of the Order of Tiius's order-knights, his voice soothing the masses like honey... "Your rations for the week."

The order-knight handed the man a scoop of grain.

"Bless the Order's kindness," said James. "Always leading by example."

"Yes..." Panthalassa muttered, "bless them..."

The prince's voice was almost a whisper. On the surface, his expressions showed pleasure at seeing such philanthropy, yet this superficial mask was betrayed by his tone, which even as he spoke to James, betrayed his confusion.

'I can't allow myself to show compassion!' Panthalassa thought, remembering his father's desire to see him toughen up. *'I must remember the soldiers. They need it more.'*

"But..." he continued, and James knew full well that when the prince said this, he was looking for ways to justify what Xanstus was doing. "But we are at war, James," Panthalassa concluded, his expressions turning grey. "Their suffering is necessary for the greater good."

Looking at the young prince with eyes like daggers, James asked him something else. "The greater good? So what is the end goal? Peace?"

Panthalassa tensed up at this question. He knew, deep down, that peace would solve many problems.

But he closed his mind to that way of thinking. “No, James.” the prince snapped. “Victory! Death to the emperor, that scoundrel!”

“Victory was won two years ago, Panthalassa, when your father conquered Dosonarmon,” James replied. “And again, three years before that, when he defeated the emperor’s cavalry near Dessii...”

Already, James could see his student's mouth opening, opening like the backside of a bull, to make more replies. “Yes, I hear you, boy. You've said it before,” James sighed. “The war can't end until Celsidas is dead. Come with me.”

For several more hours, James took the prince around the city, showing him several examples of the king's neglect.

The deeper they ventured into the poorer quarters, the more Panthalassa became aware of an atmosphere of tension and hostility in the crowds.

On one occasion, they were surrounded by a crowd of beggars and homeless citizens clamouring for small coins – and upon leaving the street, with no small measure of help from Panthalassa's knights, a fierce argument broke out between them.

“This isn't the fault of my father James!” Panthalassa shouted. “Work-shy peasants, who would rather resort to money-scrounging or robbery, rather than doing an honest day's work, is no problem that my father has to deal with!"

James growled a breath, looking for words that would seem less like treason to the knights... "I never said your father was to blame, young Prince," he exhaled. "I am simply trying to show you how war affects the people."

"Well," Panthalassa tensed, "it's not my father's war! The emperor invaded us first! Didn't you mention Father earlier?"

"I merely stated that there have been two occasions where he could have ended the war, young Prince," James replied. "How you interpret what you see is entirely up to you.'

After they had walked a little further, they saw another cart thundering towards them from a distance, which was heavily guarded by royal knights and carrying barrels of honey.

Wheeling closer and closer, the smell of the sweet nectar from the cart drifted gently into the nostrils of the starving masses.

Moving aside so as to let the cart past, James and Panthalassa were then surprised to see the masses actually charging straight towards it! *'They'll get themselves killed!'* Panthalassa thought, biting his fingernails in trepidation.

But what followed shortly after shocked them both.

Leaping at the cart in their desperation, the citizens tried valiantly to pry open the barrels of honey – yet the royal knights, not allowing their cart to stop, carried on thundering forward, swatting their people aside with the flats of their swords, and in some cases, actually hacking off limbs.

Trampling some of them to death under the weight of their horses, the royal knights then passed their cart down the street, escaping the frenzied masses with their cargo still intact.

The cart was heading towards Castle Lordborn.

James rushed into the crowd, trying to help the people who had lost their limbs, tearing his shirt into ribbons to try and dress their wounds – and yet, it was in vain. James had little knowledge of how to dress wounds or stop bleeding, and so all he did, was try his best – and his best was not enough.

Panthalassa watched James as he tried hard to help the wounded. He felt ashamed of himself for not doing the same – but as James realised that he had done all he could, he reluctantly pulled himself away.

As the afternoon sun shone on the horizon, they started making their way back.

“So you see, Panthalassa,” James breathed, “when your mother gives food to the poor--”

“They shouldn't have got in the way of the cart!” Panthalassa cried, fists clenched at his side... yet James knew that Panthalassa could see the truth now.

On his way home, James thought back to a time when everyone had more than enough to live in happiness with one another. When King Xanstus was a fair ruler, who sought to bring harmony and peace.

He remembered a king who was not plagued by a brain-damaging scar, who could see beyond personal grievances.

James wondered to himself; how much longer would this war last? How many more lives would be lost before peace could finally return? He didn't know.

He sighed, thinking to himself: *'How far this kingdom has fallen.'*

Chapter 10 Part 1 – Aerbonitas.

Outside Aerbonitas, the Capital City of Aristinia.

*

It was nighttime. Bulvon, Xanstus and his eldest son were sat around a campfire, talking about the battle to come.

Since the king had seized Oioidamon a year before, the emperor, after hearing that Xanstus was on the march again, had pulled back all of his remaining soldiers to the capital.

And now, inside this final city, he was going to make his last stand.

"How many do you think they are?" asked Bulvon, taking a bite out of an enormous leg of boar, which along with the rest of the beast, had been roasting on the flames for hours now. He was holding the chunk of meat by the bone in his giant hands.

"No more than seven thousand, Bulvon," the king replied, eyeing the capital city, which to his great joy, had no walls. "We have the emperor bottled in now."

"Do we have enough men to take Aerbonitas?" Celdon worried. "There's been a nasty sickness drifting through camp recently, and many of the soldiers won't be able to fight at their full strength."

The king dismissed this. "Peasant soldiers drinking ale before battle is nothing new, Celdon," he snapped. "The sickness is probably nothing more than intoxication!"

Bulvon smiled to himself. "I could use a flagon of ale myself!" he chuckled.

The king smirked eagerly at him, pausing a moment for thought...

"In any case," the king carried on, "the city is poorly defended."

He glanced at the settlement. "And they are outnumbered three to one."

"I meant to ask you, father," Celdon inquired. "Why have none of the cities beyond Oioidamon had walls?"

Xanstus looked at his son with a dumb expression. “Because we're surrounded by mountains!” he laughed. “Oioidamon was the bottleneck! We're in their heartlands now.”

Celdon flushed red and realised the silliness of his question. “Oh,” he murmured.

“...And frankly,” the king continued, “I grow tired of slaughtering the emperor's armies.” He waved his scribe over to the campfire. He was a young boy with dark hair, not much older than thirteen.

“Write down this message, boy,” Xanstus spoke – to which the young boy hurried an ink and quill onto a flat stump, which was lit up by the glow of the campfire.

“Write down: To the emperor: I am writing to you, so that we may avoid unnecessary casualties in the morning. My terms are these...” King Xanstus paused for thought.

“In the light of such a long conflict, I have judged it necessary that Aerbonitas, your capital, should be surrendered to my will immediately...” he said.

“...I also demand that you hand over the rights to own the Aristinian Knightly Order, thus pledging their new allegiances to me...”

“And finally,” he concluded, “you and your imperial guardian will arrive in our encampment, before the sun reaches its peak, tomorrow morning. And you two will be alone.”

Pausing to look at the city, he saw the emperor’s castle in the far distance, which even at night time, towered over everything, its windows lit up by dimly burning candles in the hallways.

“Also, your Majesty, if you should refuse my terms, I will slaughter every last one of you, in cold blood.”

As the king peered off into the distance, he glimpsed the figure of a man standing in the light of one of the castle windows...

Stopping a moment to try and identify the man, he then realised it could be the emperor himself. He felt, if only for a moment, the heartbreak of a nation.

Although the emperor was too far away to properly identify, he nonetheless felt a spark of communication inside his heart, like the quick flash of light, when one strikes a flint stone with steel, King Xanstus felt the emperor's pain. *'He knows he is the last of his bloodline...'* he thought. *'He is looking down upon his people – his citizens who have suffered so much the perils of this war, and he pities them. How much more will I force him and his blighted countrymen to endure?'*

The king shook his head, clearing his mind of this unwelcome moment of pity. “Anyway, boy,” he barked to his scribe. “Give that letter to one of my messengers and have it delivered to the emperor at once!”

At that, the scribe did the king's bidding.

*

A fist knocked twice on the thick oaken door. “Your envoy, my noble liege!” echoed the voice of an Aristinian knight, who was on guard duty outside the emperor’s bedchamber.

“Is it from the king?” Celsidas asked with a sigh, hardly turning from his windowsill.

“The letter was taken from one of the king's messengers, yes,” the knight replied.

The emperor stood up straight and composed himself “Let him in,” he said.

Moving his sword away from the envoy's chest, the knight gently opened the door, and allowed entry. When the emperor's envoy entered the room, he bowed his head low, and handed his master the letter, not presuming to be worthy of looking him in the eyes.

“Thank you,” Celsidas spoke. “Leave now.”

Closing the door behind him, the envoy made his way back to the throne-room, where the king's messenger had been arrested until the emperor had received his message in safety.

But when Celsidas unrolled the scroll, his fists clenched in anger. “Hand over my capital and Knightly Order without an arrow being fired?!” he roared. “And he wishes for me to prostrate myself before him as well? To simply throw myself at his mercy in the morning? Does he hold my dignity in such contempt?!”

“Come to bed, your Majesty, I beg you,” pleaded one of his concubines under the furs, trying in vain to soothe his temper.

“Be silent, woman!” he snapped, stomping his feet back towards the windowsill, where he looked long and hard at the vast force surrounding his city and sighed.

“No, I will not surrender to these terms,” Celsidas growled in a low tone. “I would have gladly given him my northern territories for peace. I might have even considered giving him Oioidamon...”

He shook his head and rested it on the window. “In truth, there isn't very much I can do.”

The concubine hugged the fur quilts for comfort and mused over these words. "But you're the emperor!" she whispered fearfully. "Surely there must be some way you can win!"

Celsidas felt his hands tremble in suspense. He gripped them to calm his nerves. "Yes," Celsidas finally answered, his voice weighted with resignation, "I suppose there is."

He closed the shutters and imagined the dead crawling from their graves... He pictured the Cult of Odall's necromancers spreading the plague of Deathxia as they turned the populace of Aerbonitas into walking corpses... "But you don't need to hear it," he sighed...

He made his way towards the doorway. He was going to seek out the underground tunnel where he had secretly conspired with the Cult's demons.

"Wait, where are you going?" the concubine asked.

Celsidas clenched his fists tightly. He considered killing her on the spot, but then reminded himself that she knew nothing of what he had done. "I have military matters to attend to," he replied, turning away from her.

A tear rolled down his face slowly. "Sleep well."

*

The sun arose behind the king's battle formations. They had spent their first hours of sunlight hurrying around in preparation for what was likely to come. "Any minute now, if the emperor values his peoples' lives, he will appear before us," Xanstus said. He was mounted atop his stallion besides Celdon. Bulvon was busy sharpening his axe.

Prince Celdon looked upwards. He saw that the sun had almost reached its pinnacle. "Yet it seems more likely Father that we will have to attack after all."

Xanstus shut the visor on his helmet. "It does," he snarled. "And after the battle, my revenge will finally be complete."

Gripping the hilt of his sword, Xanstus then noticed a rider coming towards them from a distance. "Wait," he murmured. "Maybe the emperor has some sense after all! Let the rider through!"

Galloping up towards the king, the envoy tugged on his reins to bring the horse to a halt... "The emperor has dispatched me to give you this reply, King Xanstus," he said, handing him the scroll. "Hah, it won't take you long to read." And with that, the envoy rode away again.

"Insolent fool!" The king scoffed, reading the emperor's message aloud: "I refuse your terms. Let it begin!"

Chapter 10 Part 2 – The Fall.

Outside Aerbonitas, the Capital City of Aristinia.

*

The attack commenced with a great blaze of trumpets. The king's men poured into the city from all sides, and trebuchets rained hell from the heavens.

When the soldiers had rushed to within just forty yards of the first buildings, the sound of smashing windows ensued, followed by rapid volleys of crossbow bolts, which whistled through the air and simply slipped through the bodies of the onrushing men, felling them with such gruesome efficiency that one could see through the holes which the bolts pierced, remnants of shattered bones and torn organs hanging loosely from the other side, and yet despite these weapons, the Aristinian defenders were unable to stem the king's assault, for although by now more than half of Xanstus's army were of conscripted peasantries, they came onto the emperor's men with such numbers and determination, that their enemies simply collapsed under their charge.

This was the battle that would end the war, and if the soldiers had even half the chance of seeing peace again, to return home to their loved ones, it was a chance they were going to take.

"Storm the buildings!" Xanstus commanded. "Anyone you see holding a weapon, kill them!"

His strategy had been simple. Advancing shortly behind his levies with a crack battalion of royal knights, the king had planned to use his peasant soldiers as expendables. They would be the carrying force of this siege, swamping the streets with their massed numbers, absorbing the volleys of arrows and other projectiles the emperor might have in store for them, and then eventually, when at last this horde of levies lay slain on the field, his royal knights, the battle-hardened tribesmen and his subject lords' much depleted squadrons of veteran troops would finish the job.

"Push them back to the market square! Flank around the side-streets where you can!" the king continued, yet as they advanced deeper into the city, the king's levies were met with their first disciplined resistance. They were now faced with the emperor's finest infantry. These were his imperial pikemen.

As the thundering horde of conscripts came furiously upon the emperor's wall of jagged steel, they roared their war cries, adding to the din of the battle as sharp pike blade met flesh.

"Keep pushing!" commanded Xanstus, pressing into the rear of his levies with the finest troops of his own army. "Don't give them an inch!"

Yet as the struggle carried on, the imperial pikemen showed their resilience. Like a boulder fixed into the ground, the emperor's men held their position, staving off the roaring waves of levies one after the other, until their weapons were either snapped, or in some cases, were forced from their hands as the levies impaled themselves like meat on a skewer.

Reaching for their swords, they then slashed at the king's levies with skill and ferocity, churning the street into a pool of blood, as limbs and fallen soldiers littered the ground.

And eventually, after long hours of fighting, the pikemen were overwhelmed.

It was getting dark now, and the battle still raged on. All around them, the sounds of clashing steel were mingled with that of screaming civilians, occasionally made all the worse as flaming boulders crashed through ceilings and into the streets, flattening both soldier and civilian alike, as other houses caught fire and swept whole neighbourhoods into a blazing inferno...

Watching all of this from the fleeting safety of his private chambers, Emperor Celsidas drew his sword.

Earlier that afternoon, he had ordered his concubines and servants, alongside his imperial guardian, to be escorted away from the city, through a secret underground passageway underneath *Castle Baeres*, which came out, after many miles, at the other side of the mountains.

He had then ordered this secret passageway, which only he and the Aristinian Knightly Order knew of, to be sealed again; not just by closing the trapdoor, but before closing it, actually filling the hole with rocks, and he had then, to further secure their guaranteed escape, had the imperial blacksmiths pour molten copper over the rocks, sealing it away forever.

As the emperor drew his sword, watching over the burning city, he let the steel gleam in the candlelight of his bedroom. *'She's still polished to a high shine...'* he thought, letting out a heavy sigh. *'While my soldiers die horribly, bloodying their swords in battle, my sword still remains clean.'*

He looked out of his window again, and at first, considered suicide...

Then he looked back to his sword. "But that is not how an emperor dies." he spoke aloud. "Like a captain on a sinking ship, the emperor must die with his Empire."

He left his chambers.

Walking down the hallway towards the spiral staircase, he then saw the portrait of his great grandfather, Emperor Elgannos III, who in his day, had led his Knightly Order from the front, repelling three separate invasions into Aristinia, later proceeding to seize large swathes of the northern grasslands from the Kingdom of Jaldana.

As Emperor Celsidas II approached the painting, a sense of shame washed over him. Who was he to fail the Aristinians so greatly? What ruler in his right mind would ally themselves with Odall, just to overcome another mortal king?

Celsidas felt his great grandfather's eyes peering into his soul. In his portrait, he still wore the royal bronze, his chest extended proudly, his cavalry sabre held upright beside him, the golden bull, the symbol of Aristinian power, emblazoned into his breastplate.

"I will lead what is left of your Knightly Order, great grandfather," he murmured in a solemn tone. "I may have been naive, even foolish in my reign, but at least I will die like an emperor should," he sighed.

He looked up to the portrait again, and this time felt his great grandfather's grim expressions tearing at his heart. "I... will be the last emperor."

After leaving the keep, he prepared himself to fight to the last.

*

Deep underground, in tunnels beneath the Aristinian capital, a vast purple mist weaved through the air. *'Now is the time!'* spoke a deep, mysterious voice, that could be heard by all of the necromancers who were gathered in the darkness.

They began their chanting once again. For months without end, the cultists had been scouring the emperor's land for corpses, looting graves and even plaguing fresh towns with Deathxia, to boost their numbers.

They had summoned portals with their strange blood rituals of Corruption Magic, allowing other necromancers from across the continent to gather here, bringing with them whole armies of the already-risen dead.

Now, hearing the commanding whispers of their demonic master, whose ominous tone echoed through the enclave, the necromancers cast their spell upon the undead hordes, awakening them for the battle.

As they arose with such vigour, they seemed as numerous as the grains of sand on a beach, clawing their way out of the earth and then tearing at the support-pillars, which had held the ground above them, for the battle thus far.

As the support beams gave way under the vicious clawing of countless angry corpses, the ceiling of the vast tunnels collapsed, and the Cult of Odall's horde swarmed onto the plains surrounding the city.

Following shortly behind them, the necromancers saw that the ground was already littered with crossbow bolts and fresh corpses, many of which, to their wicked joy, were already riddled with Deathxia...

As the necromancers left the tunnels with their hordes of furious undead, they began harnessing their violet Corruption Magic once again, raising those brave soldiers who had died in battle – to fight their own brothers in arms.

"Ram the gates, men! This is the final push!" cheered King Xanstus, watching his men trundle the heavy battering ram across the narrow path, towards the emperor's castle gates.

At either side of the pathway, the land sloped steeply downwards, with grass blades, which were soaked with blood in the darkness, covering the slopes fully.

The darkness of night had fallen, and a low fog hung around their heads like an evil curse, broken only by the arrows, and other projectiles being rained upon them from above, which one knew were being fired from the enemy watchtowers, but seemed to simply appear from out of the mist like thick storms of steel hailstone, piercing the soldiers' armour and clattering against shields, as the men inside the battering ram raged against its weight and heaved their exhausted bodies into their work.

The emperor's troops had packed the stone watchtowers along the castle walls thickly with crossbowmen and men-at-arms, firing so many missiles towards the king's men that the pathway itself had broadened, simply by the sheer numbers of dead soldiers who had fallen down the slopes.

As the battering ram finally halted in front of the castle gates, the men inside began their attack, pounding the gates repeatedly, while the archers behind the ram fired countless volleys through the low fog, aiming, with little hopes for success, for the men in the watchtowers, with their arrows often snapping as they missed, and struck solid stone... that, or whizzing through the air aimlessly, sometimes straight over the structure and into the courtyard beyond, or in some instances, followed by a distant sound of smashing glass, which meant that the arrow had actually smashed one of the windows of the keep, and planted itself somewhere inside.

As the siege carried on, and the king's men toiled to breach the final defences of the emperor's own walls, the ground itself began to rumble.

“What's this! An earthquake?” Bulvon laughed, watching as the king's men battled on, readying his axe for the butcher’s work that lay ahead. “Well, it won't stop us!” he cheered, “The emperor dines with the dead tonight, hahaha!”

Xanstus peered around carefully, noticing a sudden flash of violet behind him... “This is no earthquake, Bulvon...” and he then realised the sheer scale of his situation... the violet flash was Odall's magic... and how numerous must the army of the dead be, to shake the *very* earth itself?

“DEFENSIVE POSITIONS!” the king roared, smacking his trumpeter with the flat of his sword. “Breach those gates!” he commanded. “Quickly! Defensive positions!”

All around him, the battlefield was now a hive of activity. Whereas before, his melee troops had allowed themselves a moment’s rest, thinking their work finished for the most part, save from the final bursts of energy that would await them inside the castle, now, far from resting, they were frantic.

They hurried about the city square before the castle walls, rushing to block off the pathways and form defensive columns. “Brace yourselves!” Bulvon shouted. “They've been killed before, they can be killed again!” he continued, raising his axe into the air in defiance.

And then the horde hit them. Like so many hornets pouring from their nests, the raging dead sprang from the shadows and the fog, smacking against shields and tearing at faces with their bony, claw-like hands, ripping at them until they were nothing but thin ribbons of bleeding flesh, dangling from their cheekbones like sausages on a rack.

“Hold your ground men!” Xanstus roared, hacking at the furious dead with his greatsword, eyes wide as he caved in the skull of one skeleton, wondering how the thing didn't drop like a fly, but instead - carried on fighting – as though nothing had happened! “Hold them until we can breach the castle!” he added.

Another wave of crossbow bolts pelted the king's line from behind!

“Why are the bastards still shooting at us?!” Bulvon shouted. “Can't they see who we're fighting?!”

The king shot a glance at the watchtowers behind him. The fog was lifting now, and he could just about make out the silhouettes of the emperor’s troops. “They can see us...” Xanstus huffed, sweating profusely from his exertions – and the emperor’s men were actually loading up for another volley!

Retreating a few paces from the battle line, King Xanstus gave himself pause for thought... Although the king was the type of leader to fight by his soldiers' side, in times like these, he needed to think...

All around him, his men were failing. The cream of his force – his royal knights – were being torn to shreds like thin paper against a mill of jagged rocks... were these monsters immortal? *'We need to fight on some kind of high ground...'* he thought... *'At least then, we'll be able to hold our position...'*

The stench of death was strong. He had never smelled anything as foul as this, even in his many years of battle experience... The smell of one rotting corpse was one thing – but hordes of them? – this was something else.

“Retreat towards the emperor's castle!” he shouted. “Quickly, everyone!”

“But they're still shooting at us Sir! We're--”

“I don't give a damn! At least the emperor's men bleed like we do! Get inside that castle! Move!”

The levies were the first to break. Losing all sense of reason or discipline, they shot towards the gates like shards of glass falling from a smashed window. First the levies, then the tribesmen, and before long, the whole army was falling back in almost complete disorder. Almost – apart from the king's royal knights, who even despite the odds, still possessed enough restraint and self-discipline as to fall back in an orderly, fighting fashion. They bought the rest of the king's army time, paying for it dearly, with their lives.

“Open the gates you son of a whore!” Xanstus boomed, his voice muffled but still audible over the clamour of battle. “This is no longer a war between me and you! This is between us, and Odall!”

“Pull the other one!” One of the emperor's men replied. “If we let you inside, they'll follow behind you!”

“Well can you at least shoot at *them,* instead of *us?!”* Bulvon roared, swinging his axe ferociously as he cleaved a zombie vertically from head to stomach.

“Open the gates!” called a voice from beyond the walls. Although the voice was barely audible over the ear-breaking noise of war, the king could just about make out that his voice was that of the emperor himself...

“Get that ram off the path!” Xanstus commanded. “Push it down the hill! Get inside the castle, now!”

But as the iron gates squeaked open, the king's men were met with quite another obstacle.

As the gates opened, they revealed the last remnants of the Aristinian army. Standing before them, they saw another battalion of imperial pikemen, and a small bodyguard of Aristinian knights, surrounding Celsidas himself...

Glaring onwards, speaking to his men only one command, the emperor gave just one more order. “Advance.”

“Advance!?” The king snapped.

He realised at this moment that he had been beaten. “Let us in, Celsidas! By all the gods, what are you doing?!” he carried on.

But this cry drew no response from the emperor. While Celsidas watched the king's men become surrounded, he hung his head in shame, thinking of only one reply that would give truth... *'Betraying the human race...'* and this, he was too ashamed to say.

“Let us in, right now!” the king roared on, who like everyone else in his army, was fighting for his very *soul's* survival.

“I don't believe it...” cried Celdon... “The emperor has allied with Odall...”

“We're doomed...”

Yet far off into the fog, a new glow was becoming visible, and this one was gold...

At the head of a vast force of paladins and Order-Knights, with each man mounted atop his horse, Grand Paladin Leonidas *himself* had arrived!

The ground trembled as they galloped into battle, their lances with kenthril heads tipped forwards, and when their wedge-formation hit the swarming mass of undead, they charged down the wide central pathway, their lances snapping from overuse, at which point they unsheathed their swords, glowing from enchantments in the *Holy Cathedral of Straeum,* and they slashed at their every wicked foe.

Fire was cast from the Grand Paladin's sword as he brought it down, turning countless scores of the dead into heaps of charred bone and ash, and their mission was simple. They had not come to join the king. They had come to end the war.

The emperor dismounted, and rushed onto his battlements... “It's over...” he murmured.

Falling to his knees and resting his chin against one of the stones, he looked ahead, witnessing the Grand Paladin's charge, with a heavy heart, that knew what he had done. “Nothing can save me now...”

“Fight on, men!” Xanstus boomed, swinging his greatsword with a renewed vigour, that had filled his army. “Celsidas, you bastard!” he also spoke. “I'll have your head kicked down my capital's streets like an empty wooden cup!”

But as the clamour of battle pounded their eardrums, Bulvon, who had been fighting like a wild dragon for the whole siege, was struck in the chest by an arrow.

“Arrggghhhh!” he cried, still mustering the strength to swing his axe one last time, his blade cleaving through the chainmail neck guard of one of the emperor’s finest pikemen.

“Bulvon! No!” Celdon bawled... “Take him into the centre!” Xanstus commanded, then moving to grasp his friend of twenty years by the shoulder. “You're not dying today!”

“Rrgghhh! I can fight on!” Bulvon coughed, blood dribbling from the corner of his mouth. “Let me at them!”

“Lie down, damn you! Won't you rest!” said one of the royal knights struggling to hold him down, who was surprised to see that even when injured, it had still taken three men to hold Bulvon down!

The giant blacksmith grinned from ear to ear, his teeth stained with blood. “I know I won't die!” he chuckled. “There's too much life left in me!”

And as he lay pinned to the floor, the three royal knights pulled him onto the grass, where he would be less likely to be trampled by the paladins – who were now coming directly towards them!

“Onward, my paladins!” Leonidas thundered. “Let the vengeful flames of Tiius breach these gates!” and charging ahead, the paladins' eyes glowed with the fury of their god, their weapons striking down the emperor's last battalion of pikemen.

And while the Order of Tiius stormed through his final lines of defence, Emperor Celsidas, in a last hope to save himself, ran inside the castle.

'I can't escape,' he panicked, wiping his sweat-soaked brow with his sleeve, *'I've sealed the tunnel...'*

He rushed to one of the windows in his throne room, '*Everyone is out there,'* he thought on. *'I'm the only one left inside this damn building!'*

He watched his men dying. Their weapons breaking, their shields shattering.

Still they fought on, with their hands and teeth, growling like old dogs, loyal even unto death.

The emperor’s tears hit the marble floor. *'I never deserved men like these. I'm not worthy of their devotion.'*

He slid his hands down the window, eventually falling into a sitting position. *'I am the last emperor...'*

As he sat there, his arms wrapped around his legs, like a teenager lost in the heartbreak of love, he sobbed his final tears and prepared to die.

Chapter 11 Part 1 - Parade of Death.

Ten days later, City Pla-Kingus.

*

When they left Aerbonitas, all that remained of the once great city was a sea of smoking ruins. Some of the buildings were still on fire, and the Cult of Odall's countless animated corpses had been left virtually unscathed.

Of all the undead that had been turned to heaps of ash by the holy flames of the Grand Paladin's men, only around three thousand of them had actually perished, and thus, for the most part, the undead had largely still been left to scourge the land around them, and even now, from the sacked villages around the war-torn capital, grew stronger yet.

When the king's army had finally returned to the Tan'gran'ne'se, all that remained of his force were two battalions of royal knights, the king and his heir, Bulvon (who was being treated by paladins and druids inside a carriage), Warlord Airen and one last tribal chieftain, Zalxorr. All the rest of the king’s men, lords, conscripts and tribesmen had been torn to shreds by the unrelenting hordes of the undead.

Before arriving in the Tan'gran'ne'se, the king had sent messengers on fast horses, in all directions, bearing orders to pull the whole garrison of each city and town, so that they might join his army. At first, Celdon was unhappy about this, and he gave a series of heated arguments – but Xanstus reminded him of the dangers that might follow if the people saw him as being weak. "After a war like this, my son, it would be suicide to march through our capital with such a shattered shell of an army. The people would overthrow us in an instant!" he reminded him.

So, arriving in his capital, with his borders almost completely undefended, King Xanstus Lordborn had the emperor’s head fixed onto a wooden pole behind the first column of royal knights and began his parade.

*

The city bells rang loudly from atop the main entrance to Pla-Kingus.

At either side of the long central pathway through the city, which led first through the common marketplace, then through the upper district, and eventually into the square beneath Castle Lordborn, the commoners had formed into vast crowds.

Most of them were women, the elderly, or children, and yet their numbers had swelled to such an extent that the royal knights, who had been kept inside the capital city as a garrison force, could barely hold them off the pathway.

The bells rang again, and this time, the ground beneath the citizens' feet pounded from the impact of ten-thousand soldiers marching beyond the city walls, marching alongside a musical fanfare of trumpets and drums, tramping the ground in cadence with their shields, swaying hypnotically in the late summer sun, their armour polished to a high shine, or in the cases where the armour and weapons had been bent or broken, had been completely replaced.

As the huddled masses of common people swarmed around the pathway, eager to spot loved ones who had been sent off to war, the air was tense, and now, possibly for dramatic effect, the music had faded away...

For a few moments, the crowds fixed their eyes onto the closed gates, waiting for the moment they would be flung open, and yet all they saw for these few moments were six trumpeters making their way onto the platform between the watchtowers, and an almost inaudible dialogue between someone on the ground, and a man inside one of the towers.

A moment later, a herald, dressed in fine silks of scarlet and gold, made his way onto the platform, and stood in-between the trumpeters.

“People of Pla-Kingus! Your king and his men have arrived at long last!” he exclaimed, smiling as he gave them the welcomed news, reading straight from a scroll. “With the death of the tyrant, Emperor Celsidas, His Majesty the King is proud to announce the formal end to the war in Aristinia!”

The air exploded with cheering at this announcement. James however, who was also watching the scene with Panthalassa, seemed unmoved. *'But at what cost, I wonder...'* he thought.

“Furthermore, His Majesty would like to thank his loyal subjects for their continued support, and he pledges that, with the backing of his victorious armies, this day will mark the beginning of a long and sustained era of peace!”

As the king's herald sauntered back into the watchtower, the six trumpeters played a short fanfare of high spirit and triumph, marking the moment with cheering crowds, as the gates were cast open.

Initially, the scene seemed like something of a cliche, the crowds cheering, the victorious king, music that sounded the very embodiment of glory. Everything was going as planned. Panthalassa, who in reality, was supposed to be training, couldn't understand James's scepticism. “The war is over, damn you!” he broke. “Why can't you just be happy? Now the peace will return!”

James looked into the king's eye as he trotted past, his sword was held forward in triumph, his one remaining eye was fixated on the tip of his blade, and he seemed to be mumbling something under his breath... *'He's gone mad,'* James thought.

Looking around himself, James also observed how the people seemed to dismiss the decapitated head of the emperor, which, he noticed, was hovering atop a wooden pole, directly above him...

“I asked you a question, James!” Panthalassa continued, but his voice was trembling.

James turned around to face the young prince. The boy was as pale as chalk. “You know why, Panthalassa,” he replied.

“The emperor... he deserved it,” the prince mumbled.

“It's not the emperor’s head I want you to see, boy,” James answered. “You see that woman in the window? Does she look happy?” he asked him.

“She's cheering!” Panthalassa said.

“If you listen closely, you can hear her children cry in the background. Look at her face, she's in tears!”

“Maybe they are tears of joy?” asked the prince.

“Or, maybe they're not,” James replied. “Look how the others in the crowd talk amongst themselves in despair. Perhaps their sons and fathers are in this battalion? No? Maybe the next one? Do they even know who these soldiers are? I certainly don't recognise any of them.”

“What are you saying, James?” Panthalassa asked. “Neither you nor the people could memorise the face of every soldier.”

“Draw your own conclusion, Panthalassa,” James answered. “But the cheering fades away once the king has passed by.”

As the army paraded through the market square, James and Panthalassa rushed through the crowds to keep up with the king. Along their way, they would hear the plebeians whispering among themselves, spreading rumours perhaps, and at one point they overheard a whole group of people, admitting to one another that they, like James, didn't recognise any of the soldiers. They were comforting one another, as each of them had failed to spot their loved ones within the parading army.

On another occasion, Panthalassa noticed a mother, with a baby in her arms. She was in floods of tears, and she was speaking with one of the paladins handing out grain in the market square, crying aloud that she wouldn't be able to feed her child, without her husband's soldierly wage. The woman had begged the Order of Tiius to take her child as their own, admitting that her babe would suffer – perhaps even die - if they didn't take him.

With a heavy heart, the paladin finally agreed to take the baby from her.

'At least there is peace now...' Panthalassa thought, shedding a tear of his own... *'Maybe my father will become like he used to be – and maybe now that the war is over, my parents will stop their dreadful quarrelling.'*

He allowed himself a moment of hope... *'And if the peace really does last long enough, maybe my people will begin to heal...'*

James tapped him on the arm and pointed into the crowd. Panthalassa fell back into reality, and looked in the direction James was pointing. "There, do you see her?" James asked. "Your mother is a wonderful woman, and even as we speak, she is comforting the poor."

"I see her..." the eighteen-year-old prince replied.

Observing the scene before him, Panthalassa watched the king's battalions trot past. To a man, each one of them seemed incredibly well-fed. They bore the muscular physiques of racehorses, marching through the thronging crowds in their polished armour, looking the very picture of wealth and victory.

In contrast to the royal knights, the civilians around them looked little more than husks of skin and bone, their cheekbones unhealthily defined through their faces, their children, of which not many remained, looking only slightly better for wear - moreover, most of their clothes were filthy, or torn beyond repair.

And there stood his mother, Queen Dranah, surrounded by paladins and druids, handing out grain to them, with eyes so deep in sorrow that she could no longer find the strength to compose herself... and so, she showed her emotions openly.

"She looks as if she's been crying," Panthalassa murmured, struggling to hold back his own tears, "but surely the people's situation will improve now? I thought the peace would have made her happy."

James sighed. "If it were just peace, it might have," he replied. "But too many lives have been wasted in this war," he continued. "She's heartbroken."

“Well let's try and cheer her up,” Panthalassa said. “The worst of her troubles should be over.”

“Well, it does look like she could use some comfort...” James agreed.

They followed the queen back to Castle Lordborn. Once she was inside the keep, she dismissed her bodyguards. She glanced uneasily at the pair. “What are you two doing here?” she asked. “I thought you were witnessing the procession?”

“We were,” Panthalassa said, “But you looked very upset... We came to--”
“I'm fine,” Dranah interrupted him. “I just have a lot to think about.”

“Why aren't you happy?” he asked. “All you ever talk about is peace! Now that Father has won the war, you seem even more upset than you were before!”

“You don't understand, Panth,” his mother asserted.

A few seconds of silence followed. Then the young prince sighed loudly. “I don't believe this nonsense!” he snapped, storming up the castle stairs towards his room.

“I'm sorry for his behaviour, James,” the queen sighed. “Although I'm sure you've got used to it by now.”

James lowered his head and smiled painfully. “I have,” he replied. “Should I leave you in peace? Perhaps following you wasn't my smartest idea.”

The queen paused for thought... *'There's so much that I need to get off my chest... James has hated the war just as much as I have... Maybe I can trust him.'*

“You may stay,” Dranah told him. They went inside an empty room, and James closed the door. "What's the matter, your Highness?" James asked. The fireplace was barren, and the room was cold. All around him, the scent of frankincense drifted through the air, although given the absence of burning incense sticks, the exact location of the smell was a mystery.

"You must swear one thing to me James," she spoke. "Swear to me, that you will not tell anyone what I know, until the word gets out."

"I swear it, Your Majesty," he agreed. "I--"

"Call me Dranah, Please," she sighed, interrupting him.

She moved to a dark corner of the room, sat down on a chair beside a wooden table, and rested her head in her palm. "I'm running out of hope," she admitted. "This peace. It is false."

James moved closer towards the table and indicated he would like to sit down. Dranah nodded dismissively. "Why is it false?" James asked. "Is it because of the famine? Because of all the lives that have been lost?"

"Because of the undead," she answered. "While my husband was away, the emperor signed an unholy pact with Odall, and it's all because my husband wouldn't accept his peace offerings."

James remained quiet while he took in the magnitude of this discovery.

"My husband's messenger was told to lie. There will be no peace now, and I don't know what to do."

"So... Was the king's army defeated?" James asked, raising an eyebrow, his heart racing with a tightly controlled sense of dread.

"No, he won," Dranah answered. "A messenger arrived in the castle two days before my husband did and told me everything. I've been silent about it this whole time."

"If he won," James pressed, "how many of the undead still remain? Was that head on a spike really the emperor?"

"It was," she nodded. "We have been unable to count the undead hordes, as of the moment. But if the rumours are to be believed, they could be anywhere between a hundred thousand, and... and..."

"And what?" James asked.

"And a million..." she breathed.

"A million? Surely not! Such a number could only be the work of doom sayers!"

"Let's hope so, James," she continued, "because there is something else I feel the need to tell you. Our borders have been left open. All of the garrisoned troops have been pulled into this city. Our kingdom is a hollow shell waiting to be cracked open like an egg."

"The people need to know this, your Majesty," James murmured.

"No!" Dranah flared. "When the people find out, all will be lost! We will be overthrown! And what's worse than that, James, is that when we're gone, there will be no one left to command our forces! The undead will run rampant!"

James stood up slowly and bowed his head low. "You have my word, Dranah," he solemnly agreed. "Not a soul will know. I won't even tell the prince."

Dranah clutched at her chest and sobbed for a few moments, eventually re-gaining her composure and moving to reply. "Thank you," she said.

As James opened the door to leave the room, he saw Panthalassa walking across the hallway. The young prince had decided that his reaction was immature, and he had come down to apologise. Now however, after overhearing James's last words, he had something else in mind. “What won't you tell me?” he asked.

“It's nothing important,” James replied, gently closing the door behind him. “Your mother is just upset. I think it would be best if you let her get some rest.”

The prince’s eyes narrowed in suspicion, but he nodded in agreement and returned to his quarters, brooding over the meaning of the incident.

Chapter 11 Part 2 – Fatal Training.

The following morning.

*

Panthalassa barely slept that night.

Laying awake, his eyes had wandered off into the distance, lazily observing the golden patterns on the ceiling, his mind trying in vain to shut out the questions that so pressed against him. Neither James nor his mother had made any secret of their disapproval of the war, so why weren't they happy about the victory?

What secrets had his mother been telling James? In the dark, Panthalassa thought back to some of the comments they had made in the past. Both of them had criticised the way Xanstus was running the kingdom – and had a commoner said some of those things, he would have risked being arrested for treason.

Again and again, Panthalassa's mind came back to their strange reaction to the king's victory. Was it possible they were plotting against his father? This is what kept him awake.

When morning had dawned, he heard the servants hurrying about the dining hall below him, and he realised that his opportunity to rest had gone. He needed to get out of bed soon to eat and then to begin his daily training. *'But I'm not even hungry!'* he thought. *'I just want to know what's keeping everyone on edge!'*

And so his morning had begun.

At breakfast, he had forced a few mouthfuls of his meal down, but he wasn't hungry. He just wanted answers.

His mother refused to discuss the matter with him, asking him to respect her privacy, and after pleading with her in vain for a while, Panthalassa gave up and left the palace in a foul temper. He went to look for his tutor.

James was waiting for him on the drawbridge. "Morning," he sighed, still troubled by the revelations of the night before. “Are you ready?”

Panthalassa shot him a frown. “I'm tired,” he answered, and his tone was laced with frustration.

“Well, we're all troubled by something,” James noted. “Come on, it's time we got over our troubles and let off some steam.”

“I just want answers, James!” the prince replied, walking with him across the bridge. “What did you and my mother talk about last night? Was it about my father?”

“I don't want to think about that today, boy,” his instructor replied.

They walked through the market square.

'I bet it was. It's about the king!' Panthalassa thought. “It was, wasn't it!” he barked.

“No.” James answered. “It was not!” He took a deep breath... “What we spoke about last night was none of your business, Panth. You'd do well to keep your nose out of it.”

“But she's my mother!” he snapped. “I deserve to know why she is upset!”

“Come on now, lad.” James tugged him by the arm, pointing to one of the bread stalls. “Are you hungry?”

“No, I'm not,” the prince stated. James bought some bread anyway. “Well I'll just save this for later, then,” he said.

And after a few more minutes, they had reached the sparring grounds.

The knights, who were on guard duty, opened the large oak-wood gates. It was a dreary setting. Panthalassa had become all too familiar with these sand-scattered grounds, these stone walls which enclosed the training place, blocking out the sun with their shadows, and the armoury.

Panthalassa was considered too old to use the weapons made of oak-wood, for they were reserved for the amateurs, for the younger ones of thirteen and under.

And so, ever since the age of fourteen, Panthalassa had been pressed into training with live blades instead. The edges of each blade had been blunted for safe use, although the tips were still sharp.

They grabbed their swords and shields and made their way onto the sparring grounds. “Alright, let's start,” James said.

He took a moment to observe Panthalassa's stance. His shield was raised high, slanted towards his left shoulder, covering his torso and the lower half of his head, while the boy's sword was held forward in the front, ready to launch an attack, or defend if necessary. “Good, you've perfected your stance,” James said. “Let's begin!”

Launching a strike against Panthalassa, James used his own shield to bash open Panthalassa's guard, creating an opening and moving in with his blade. “Come on! You know how to counter-attack! We practised those moves just two days ago!” James stated. “Try again.”

When the attack came around a second time, the young prince, acknowledging James, shifted his stance so that his shield was covering his right shoulder. He then attempted to manoeuvre his sword around his shield to close the gap before his torso, while simultaneously disabling James's shield on his left shoulder…

But his manoeuvre had failed. James anticipated the prince’s move once again, and rather than leaving himself open, he thrust his sword into the space before Panthalassa's stomach, ending the duel once again, just before Panthalassa could finish his move. “You're not concentrating, boy! Come on, wake up!” he snapped.

The prince sighed his frustration, and this time he went on the attack. “I'll show you!” he spat.

Attempting to bash open James's guard with his shield, Panthalassa threw his sword forward in several places, each time being effortlessly parried by James, alongside deft movements with his shield, to incapacitate Panthalassa's guard, and before too long, James had won yet again. “You wouldn't get this many chances in battle!” he shouted, and then he launched into a counterattack.

Panthalassa fell into a fighting retreat to avoid having his guard broken once again. Although his body ached in fatigue, he managed to parry James's blows one by one. Sometimes, his shield would be bashed aside, and other times, he would move around his instructor on the sparring ground, trying in vain to get around his flanks, until at last, after several minutes, Panthalassa found himself beaten yet again.

“What do I have to say to make you concentrate!” James barked, falling into his fighting stance once more. “Learn to overcome your weakness! Your enemy will not give ground just because you're tired!”

“But you're not my enemy, James!” Panthalassa replied, “And I haven't slept all night!”

“In this arena, boy, I *am* your enemy! Concentrate, and perhaps this time you'll survive!” he snapped.

Launching into another attack, James shot his sword and shield forward as one, aiming to bull through his student's guard, and place his sword at Panthalassa's neck, but Panthalassa fell back to absorb his instructor's charge, thrusting his own shield forward in an attempt to begin a counterstrike...

It failed. When James noticed Panthalassa's well-timed manoeuvre, he whirled around the counterattack with the force of a tiger, brushing Panthalassa's sword aside and moving in to close the distance, while Panthalassa, trying his best to withstand the assault, fell into a fighting retreat once again...

'This doesn't feel like training anymore!' the prince thought, desperately withstanding his instructor's attacks... *'Is he trying to kill me!?'*

He fought on, parrying James's blows while still trying to launch some of his own. "James!" Panthalassa called.

"Concentrate, Panth! Don't talk to your enemy!" His instructor snapped.

'He is trying to kill me!' he thought! And this flash of dread made him re-double his efforts...

'Good!' James thought, observing his student's sudden increase in alertness. *'The lad is starting to wake up!'*

As James picked up his pace even further, a flood of adrenaline rushed through Panthalassa's body. He felt as though he was actually fighting for his life...

His mind closed off all sensations of fatigue. Even his hunger left him. All he could think about in this moment, was winning the duel...

In one swift motion, Panthalassa threw his shield forward to block James's assault, casting open his instructor's guard and finally breaking through with his sword...

In the rush of the moment, however, Panthalassa's adrenaline reached a fever pitch, and rather than stopping short of James's chest, he followed through, right till the end... until the blood was flowing...

James looked at his student with an expression of utter shock! He dropped his shield onto the ground, placing one hand onto Panthalassa's shoulder. "Look down, young Prince..." he whispered...

Panthalassa's adrenaline ran dry, and in that moment, filling with exhaustion, he realised what he had done...

As he looked down, he saw his instructor's sword point, which was stopped short before his stomach, in the exact same place which he himself had been stabbed.

"Even now, If I had wanted to kill you, I still could," James wheezed... before dropping the sword to the ground. "But you are something worth protecting, Panthalassa," he said... "And I love you..."

"I-- I was scared that..." Panthalassa sobbed... "that's what you were doing..."

But he realised now, how stupid that thought had been. "I'm so sorry!" he cried.

"Panthalassa..." James croaked... "I have lived a good life, and it has been an honour to serve you," he said, still trying to console him. "Forget my harsh words, and just know that everything I have tried to show you, I have shown to you through compassion, and friendship..."

As James's life slipped through Panthalassa's arms, the young prince cried his tears and hugged him tightly, removing the sword from his belly. "Please, I'm sorry!" he sobbed... but nothing he could say would ease the pain...

"Be strong, young lion," James mumbled... "for I have cheated death many times before..." he continued. Blood began to spill from his mouth. "Allow me to depart this world with one last lesson, boy... that in order for evil to prevail, good men must become ignorant, and go against their own better judgment..."
"Now, young Prince, you can further your father's agenda, or stand against the shadow looming over this world, as I did... farewell..."

As Panthalassa watched the icy hand of death fall upon James's bruised body, he wailed his grief, and eventually tore himself away.

Chapter 11 Part 3 – The Sword of The First King...

Later that afternoon.

*

In a wave of regret, Panthalassa fled the city. Overwhelmed by surging emotions and impossible decisions thrust upon him, all he could think to do was run...

'Betray my father, or betray James?' he agonised, the tears still streaming down his face as he ran through the woods. *'How could I ever make that decision?'*

An icy wind blew through his hair, and as the sun set behind the forested mountain ranges of the Tan'gran'ne'se, he felt as though hope itself had been extinguished.

'He was my closest friend...' he thought, twigs snapping beneath his weary footsteps. *' Foxeny - he will never be able to forgive me...'*

As he ran, he re-visited his earliest memories with James's son. Those happy days of fishing and joking with one another in the fields. All of that was gone...

Stopping at the edge of a cliff, Panthalassa grabbed one of the tree branches and looked down into the abyss. He brooded on James's final words to him, and finally allowed himself to admit their truth... *'I love my father, but he's destroying the kingdom...'*

He sat down beneath an oak tree and dangled his feet over the edge of the cliff... “James!” he cried. “What should I do?” He sobbed loudly.

“The decision is too great,” he lamented. “How can I choose between dishonouring James's dying wish or betraying my father?”

He couldn't.

'My mother...' he thought... *'she knows something that I don't, and it's tearing her apart... I may have killed the only person who truly understood her...'*

He ran his hands through his hair, finding no answers. He was at his wits' end, and he could see no way out. “I'm not even nineteen yet, and I've already caused more damage than I'm worth."

He stood up. "Maybe I am just a spoiled prince, after all... and if there's any chance of real power falling into my hands, it would be better off with someone else."

Closing his eyes, he shed his final tears and prepared to throw himself off. "That's it then..." he wept...

Just as he was about to take the jump, he felt a mysterious hand grasp his shoulder, pulling him back to safety...

He looked around. "Hello?"

But his voice simply drifted into the air, vanishing beyond the dark canopy, into the endless skies above. "Who is there?" he asked.

Although nobody seemed to be around him, he felt, even if only for a passing second, as though someone was protecting him – the thought of ending his life suddenly seemed preposterous!

'So what do I do now?' he wondered.

No sooner did that thought cross his mind, that from the corner of his eyes, a gentle glow of golden energy vanished behind one of the trees... *'Well, maybe if I can't find an answer, the gods will guide me to one...'*

And so, he followed the glow.

With every step he took, he felt as though somehow, he was being guided to safety... and although the path which this mysterious spirit was taking him was filled with steep slopes, narrow squeezes between rocks, and slippery hills of well-soaked mud, Panthalassa was nonetheless filled with a certain optimism.

After an hour, he had slogged over treacherous terrain and between jagged stones, and now, most dangerous of all, the spirit was guiding him into a tunnel. *'I have to carry on,'* he thought.

Steeling himself to trudge through the watery cave, Panthalassa took a deep breath. *'Many have likely died in tunnels like these...'* his mind told him.

But as the light vanished into the depths of the enclave, he set aside his fears and took his first steps.

The cold made him shiver. Each time he brought his feet down, they splashed into the water and were submerged ankle-deep. Whenever he stood on a piece of rock that was dry, his leather boots squelched, soaked thoroughly.

His belly grumbled loudly, and he realised that he still hadn't eaten. His eyes were almost closing, at which point, he also recalled that he hadn't slept.

As he took his next step, he placed a hand on the wall of the cave to stop himself from slipping, but far from being sturdy, the stones fell away from him, and rolled down into a dark abyss, hitting the floor after a while, with a distant crack.

He lost his footing and fell flat on his face, cutting his lip in the process. Now he was awake!

'I have to be more careful!' he told himself... *'I'm lucky that I'm not falling to my death!'*

As he stood up, he resumed his stony determination and carried on walking...

'I hope I'm nearly there,' he wished.

The spirit led him through the tunnel for another half-hour. By now, he was soaked head-to toe...

For long minutes, his mind had settled into a kind of boredom. His entire body ached in fatigue. He felt as though someone had beaten him with a mallet. Yet as he turned a corner, the tunnel opened into a cave. Against the far wall, he saw the dead remains of an ancient legend...

Sitting before Panthalassa, a skeleton's empty eye sockets seemed to stare through his very soul... It wore a full suit of kenthril armour, and atop its head, stood a crown of pure gold... *'It can't be,'* he thought... *'The ancient King?'*

Edging his way closer, Panthalassa then observed four other skeletons, each one of them looking far less regal, with their suits of bronze and iron rusted beyond all recognition. As he absorbed the scene, Panthalassa realised that the postures of each corpse told the story of the king's final moments. The ancient king had died with his back to the wall, fighting off his enemies.

As he knelt before the corpse of the skeleton wearing kenthril and gold, he saw one more body laying over the king's shoulder, impaled through the chest with a golden-glowing sword.

'Take it, boy...' a voice whispered to him. *'The sword of your ancestors... my sword...'*

He wondered if he had gone mad... yet he took it all the same, inspecting the design with scrupulous attention. *'Calligian patterns...'* he realised... *'This -is- the first King!'*

As Panthalassa held the sword in his hands, he took a moment to recall his childhood stories...

In an age gone by, the Calligian Empire had been one of justice, united by their emperors in their worship of Tiius, yet over time, the nobles began to grow corrupt, bargaining away their fairness in exchange for new lands, for wealth, and power.

Already an ancient bloodline, the Lordborns had by this time separated into multiple branches, each of them owning their own estates and territories within the Empire, and one of them, the most powerful, sitting on the throne itself.

The Lordborn Dynasty which was ruling Calligia had become rotten, taxing the Empire's subjects into starvation and exhausting them through a series of endless wars – wars which often violated the moralities of Tiius.

Eventually, the last straw was drawn.

The Lordborns became divided. Some of them sided with the crown, and others, like *Antaius*, stood against it. A civil war had begun.

Lasting for three years, the war drained the Empire of all its riches and vital supplies, and although most of the royalists were being pushed back, The Lordborns' subjects in the north-western province of *Armalinua* were being defeated.

In order to save his people, *Antaius Lordborn,* who would later become known as “The First King,” had stolen the emperor’s own grand fleet, as it lay at anchor.

After commanding his people to climb aboard the ships, they set sail and eventually weighed anchor in the wild tribal woodlands of the Tan'gran'ne'se.

Legend said, as Panthalassa recalled from his childhood stories, that Antaius had been caught worshipping Odall. That he had made a desperate attempt to escape holy vengeance by throwing himself from the edge of a mountain...

'The tale's ending was a lie!' Panthalassa realised... *'Far from throwing himself from the mountain, Antaius Lordborn fought till the last! The man who must have escaped these tunnels to tell the story obviously gave him a bad name out of spite, and as a result, his history has been written by the wicked!'*

He thought on. *'Our history tells us that the kings who ruled after Antaius were just men... but here in this cave, a righteous king has been murdered... our history has been written incorrectly...'*

As Panthalassa held the ancestral sword in his hands, a flare of Duellan Magic sprang from the cross-guard and weaved its way around the blade, mingling as one with the golden glow of Tiius... “The purest form of peace is nature,” Panthalassa mumbled. The words seemed to flow from his mouth, without him thinking them.

He stared at the skeleton, imagining how he must have been in real life. "Oh how evil men must have hated you..." he said... "You never turned to Odall, but instead, you stayed true to Tiius until the day you died!"

Panthalassa closed his eyes and replayed the moment he had killed James. "I am not worthy to hold such a blade," he wept. "Even if I were, the blade itself would not be the answer."

Tears trickled down his cheeks.

"I only accept this sword, Antaius, because I am a descendant of your bloodline," he murmured. "Yet as I take it from you, I pledge to the gods a sacred vow, that from this moment onwards, I will never again shy from reality. I pledge to uphold the values of fairness and bravery, and to stand, as James did, against the looming shadow!"

As he made his way back through the tunnel, he held the sword close to him... "I will aid the druids and the Order of Tiius where I can!" he whispered...

Panthalassa, at long last had found his truth.

Glossary of Terms & Interesting Lore.

Aristinian Circle of Mountains: A ring of mountains which surround the Aristinian heartland, with the walled city of Oioidamon guarding the bottle-neck pass.

Baeres Dynasty: Emperor Celsidas's ancient family bloodline, which stretches back to the bronze age of Fulminia, when the Aristinian Empire ruled half the continent.

Caltrops: Metal weapons with four spikes, meant to be thrown onto the ground. Whichever way it lands, one spike will always face upwards. When you step on it, it goes straight through your foot/hoof.

Cangrunarkaei: A spell word, spoken in the ancient language of Calafinia, which is the name of Fulminia's first human kingdom. This spell is meant to empower holy attacks to weaken Odall's many unnatural demonic beasts.

Chronicles of Sir Vorn the Demon-slayer: The Chronicles of Sir Vorn, written a thousand years before Panthalassa's time, features the legendary Grand Paladin and his quest to destroy Odall's grip on his world. During this time, the Calligian Empire is still young and worships Tiius rather than Odall. The Calligian Empress, Lena, frequently lends him military support, and these chronicles see him travelling great distances, on both land and sea, to rid his world of Corruption Magic. After half a lifetime of fighting the Cult of Odall, Grand Paladin Vorn finally vanquishes the Cult's forces in one final battle, where he, with the help of his Order Knights, his Paladins, and the Calligian Legions, slay the demon controlling the cult, ending on a bittersweet victory, surrounded by scorched fields, burning forests and dead men. The world was saved.

Corruption magic: Odall's magic. When mortals channel Odall's magic, he whispers to them, slowly driving them insane and compelling them to commit unspeakable acts of evil. This form of magic takes control over the mortal's mind, forcing them to become addicted to its use. Odall has only one wish, which is to turn all worlds into barren, inhospitable wastelands of death. All life must die.

Deathxia: A magical, jelly-like substance which infects the living and emits spores. Odall controls it. It kills things slowly and turns them into the undead.

Holy Cathedral of Straeum: A grand building which stands opposite the Senate of Straeum. Made both for worshipping Tiius, and for enchanting weapons with Pure Magic, so that they may vanquish evil. Grand Paladins are elected in this building. There can be only one Grand Paladin.

Istarian Wars: The wars between the Kings' Union and the Kingdom of Istaria, which was forced into submission by King Xanstus Lordborn and subsequently reduced to a subject state.

Kenthril: A metal with the same colour as gold, mined directly as ore. It is twice as strong as steel, and twice as light to carry. Tiius and Duella created this metal so that whatever life form took hold of Fulminia and gained a higher level of intelligence, would stand a much better chance against Odall. Without the gods' help, this metal would not exist. Only bronze, copper and kenthril can be enchanted with Pure Magic, but only kenthril can give those who allow the metal to touch their skin temporary immunity from Deathxia.

Life-Weavers: One kind of druid in the Duellan Druidicy. They aren't quite good enough at using Nature Magic to be considered full druids, but they understand how to use the magic well enough to keep deep summer flowers alive during the harshest frosts of winter.

Nature magic: Duella's magic. She allows mortals to channel her energy to heal the world and allow life to flourish. Unlike Odall, Duella allows mortals to channel her energies at their leisure, free from becoming addicted to its use.

Nock: To place an arrow on the bowstring, ready to be fired.

Palisade: A fence of wooden stakes or iron railings fixed in the ground, forming an enclosure or defence.

Petrichor: A pleasant smell that frequently accompanies the first rain after a long period of warm, dry weather.

Pure magic: Tiius's magic. Tiius allows mortals to use his magic so that they may rise to combat Odall and enforce true Justice. Mortals who use this magic type inevitably become acutely aware of the emotions of their world. They deeply feel all the pain in their world, all the suffering, all at once… but they also feel all the joy and love. This magic type makes its users believe that the purpose of life is to make others feel happy, and it also gives them true vision, so that they may see all the unspeakable horrors forced upon the world by Odall, and how he strives to destroy all that Tiius and Duella stand for. Those who use this magic type become obsessively driven to destroy Odall and rid the world of his many evils. They also place a high value on Duella and do their best to improve the lives of those around them.

Senate of Straeum: The hall of government for the Kingdom of Straeum. Kings are not born in Straeum, they are elected. But they hold absolute power so long as they reign. The Senate of Straeum is also the building where all the leaders in Straeum's grand alliance meet to discuss how best to defend their continent from Odall and the Calligians.

Tiius's Glimmering Scepter of Justice: When the Order communicates with Tiius through Pure Magic, Tiius often speaks while holding a staff in his hand, bearing resemblance to the letter "Y". This staff can only be held by Tiius himself, and it is used to channel his immense power for the greater good of the universe, to destroy Odall. If Tiius were to step onto Fulminia personally, he could vanquish the entire Cult, along with all its Deathxia and all its demons --with a single wave of magic from his scepter. Such immense displays of his power are, however, reserved for ridding already destroyed worlds of Odall's corruption. At which point, Duella can enter the world and weave her magic so that life can begin again. So far as Tiius is concerned, Fulminia has seen his power once before, and it has been sufficient to allow mortals to channel his magic to improve the world on their own. He is hopeful that the mortal beings on Fulminia hold sufficient power of their own to use his magic and rid their own world of Odall's shadow.

About the Author.

Ben Kilgallon is a debut novelist with a keen love for medieval fantasy books, history books and MMORPGs rich with lore.

From a very early age, he found his mind drifting into a world of its own, and in his spare time, he would often find himself drawing maps of imagined worlds, alongside several characters inside them. Far from abandoning this habit, he slowly built upon this natural creativity, until one day (shortly before leaving high school), he began writing this novel, intending it to be the first of a lifelong career of follow-ups.

Printed in Great Britain
by Amazon

28233000R00123